MY GOD! IT'S A WOMAN

MY GOD!
IT'S A
WOMAN

NANCY BIRD

FOREWORD BY GABY KENNARD

ANGUS
& ROBERTSON

A division of HarperCollins*Publishers*

To women pilots everywhere whose determination, tenacity and dedication has inspired all women to reach for the stars; and to Stanley Drummond of the Far West Children's Health Scheme, who had the courage to employ the first woman pilot in Australia.

AN ANGUS & ROBERTSON BOOK

First published in Australia in 1990 by
Collins/Angus & Robertson Publishers Australia
A division of HarperCollins Publishers (Australia) Pty Limited

Collins/Angus & Robertson Publishers Australia
Unit 4, Eden Park, 31 Waterloo Road, North Ryde
NSW 2113, Australia

William Collins Publishers Ltd
31 View Road, Glenfield, Auckland 10, New Zealand

Angus & Robertson (UK)
16 Golden Square, London W1R 4BN, United Kingdom

National Library of Australia
Cataloguing-in-Publication data:

Walton, Nancy Bird, 1915-
My God! It's a Woman.
Bibliography.
ISBN 0 207 16824 5.
1. Walton, Nancy Bird, 1915-   2. Air pilots-
Australia-Biography. 3. Women air pilots-Australia-Biography.
I. Title.
629.13092

Typeset in Baskerville by Midland Typesetters, Maryborough, Vic.
Printed in Australia by Australian Print Group, Maryborough, Vic.

5 4 3 2 1
95 94 93 92 91 90

FOREWORD

Nancy Bird is one of the early aviation pioneers, for whom I have the utmost respect and admiration. They were real adventurers, and it is thanks to trail blazers such as Nancy Bird that we have our modern, safe and reliable airline systems.

I learnt to fly in the 1970s, often being the only woman in a class of fifty. I found that even at this time, there were many barriers to overcome for a woman learning to fly. Nancy Bird learnt to fly in the 1930s; it must have taken great determination and perseverance.

Nancy Bird is the patron of the Australian Women Pilots Association of which I am a member. She has always been extremely generous of spirit and was a great encouragement to me on my solo around the world flight. Nancy Bird is an extraordinary woman with the energy of a 20-year-old. She is a continual source of inspiration to all women pilots.

Gaby Kennard,

WHY THIS TITLE ?

In 1936, I was the only charter pilot in Cunnamulla, Queensland. Charles Russell, a well-known grazier, was visiting one of his properties when he was marooned by flood waters. I walked into his agent's office just as Charles was being told by phone that the aircraft was being sent to rescue him. The agent told Charles to give the pilot landing instructions, and then handed me the telephone. I took the receiver and said 'Hello.' There was a stunned silence and then a horrified voice uttered, 'My God! It's a woman.'

AUTHOR'S NOTE

Lawrence Hargrave, the man featured on the back of the Australian twenty dollar note, was an early aviation pioneer. He was lifting himself off the cliffs at Stanwell Park in the late nineteenth century and later invented the rotary engine, which was patented by the French. In 1894, Octave Chaunte, one of the greatest authorities of aviation in his day had proclaimed that if any man deserved to be the first to fly it was he—Lawrence Hargrave of Sydney, Australia. Hargrave built many model aircraft and used to send them, propelled by rubber bands, flying over people's heads as he gave lectures in aeronautics at the Royal Society in Sydney. Most of these models were housed by the Deutsche Museum in Germany because nobody else would give Hargrave any space. A few were returned to Australia and are now at the Powerhouse Museum in Sydney.

In the 1920s and 1930s, flying was mainly a sport, but it was also a challenging and romantic adventure.

We flew without any of the sophisticated, high technology gadgets that adorn the aircraft of today. Instead of expensive computers and navigational aids, we relied almost exlusively on road maps that showed the approximate locations of towns, railways, roads, tracks and little else.

Sometimes we could barely see the ground because of dust storms, low cloud or heavy rain. We navigated with a wristwatch, compass and old school ruler.

I was privileged in those days to walk in the footsteps and live in the shadows of the young airmen who returned from World War I and began establishing what is now Australia's aviation industry.

Some of those brave youngsters grew to become legends. Many became captains of the air industry, and others went on to serve their country yet again in World War II.

BARNSTORMING ROUTE, NEW SOUTH WALES 1935.

INTRODUCTION

Australians first became warbirds in 1915 when the Indian government asked our government to provide air support in the Middle East during World War I. The military flying school at Point Cooke had only two aeroplanes and one box kite. Four cavalry officers, Petre, Merz, Treloar and White, who had trained as pilots were called for duty and dispatched to Mesopotamia.

Forty-one ground crew including eighteen mechanics accompanied the pilots to Mesopotamia where they flew primitive Maurice Farman and Caudron aircraft, which had a top speed of 50 mph. These planes were totally unsuitable for the desert, and were even known to fly backwards in sand storms.

Although unreliable engines caused many forced landings, the greatest danger came from being attacked on the ground and hacked to death by hostile Arabs. One victim of such an attack was Merz, whose body was never discovered, although his machine was found chopped to matchwood.

That was in 1915, the year I was born. Kew, my birth place on the north coast of New South Wales, was a tiny hamlet whose industries were timber and dairying. Although on the main Sydney to Brisbane road, it was the sort of town you could easily pass through without noticing. My father owned the local store at the time, although soon after my birth we moved to Kendall, which was a little larger. It probably had a dozen houses. There, for the next six years, my mother brought up her ever-increasing family. Later, mother moved down to Sydney so that we could go to private schools. We lived in turn at Collaroy, Dee Why and Manly.

Years later, my mother mentioned that at the age of four, I was balancing on the back fence, arms outstretched, calling myself an 'eppy plane'. This was in 1919 when the whole of

Australia was excited by the prospect of the England–Australia Air Race.

London was full of Australian airmen, all wanting to get home after having been demobilised from the Australian Flying Corps. Bert Hinkler was among them. He had planned to fly solo to Australia as soon as he had been demobbed. However, Australian Prime Minister Billy Hughes took the wind out of his sails by announcing a £10 000 prize for the winner of the historic England–Australia Air Race. Hughes promoted the race strongly because of his friendship with another Australian pilot, Frank Briggs, who had been flying the Prime Minister back and forth to Paris to discuss the Versailles Treaty.

The job of managing the race was given to a committee from the British Royal Aero Club. They drew up rules and imposed restrictions that were hard for some contestants to meet. One rule, for example, stipulated a £100 entrance fee. This was more than many of the men could earn in a year. Race aircraft also had to have a range of 500 miles—and the winner had to complete the distance in 30 days. Ratifying these rules caused continual delays.

Hinkler, who had been the first pilot to enter the race and was ready to leave in May 1919, was very frustrated with these delays. He suspected the procrastination was deliberate to favour certain competitors. He eventually became the first competitor to withdraw. Charles Kingsford Smith failed to qualify for the race when Billy Hughes claimed he did not have enough experience. Six official crews were finally accepted.

As the planes left England and crossed Europe, international excitement mounted almost to fever pitch. Would they make it to Rome? A Frenchman, Etienne Poulet, not eligible to take part because the prize money was reserved for Australians, had already set out and was leading the field. It was not until Burma that Ross and Keith Smith, flying in the race's only long-range bomber, a Vickers Vimy, overtook him.

Queenslander Roger Douglas and Leslie Ross from Moruya, New South Wales, crashed soon after take-off in an Alliance Endeavour biplane, which was overloaded with fuel. Both were killed.

Further tragedies occurred. Rendle, Potts, Williams and Wilkins crashed in Crete. Howell and his mechanic crashed mysteriously into the sea off Corfu. The newspapers were full of the dramas.

10

As a four-year-old, I was swept up by the fervour of this great race. Almost every man, woman and child in Australia eagerly awaited news of each landing en route.

Ross and Keith Smith's Vimy soon reached Karachi and the press went wild with excitement. They flew on across the Indian cities of Allahabad and Calcutta to Burma, down the Malay Peninsula to Singapore, Timor and finally Darwin—in just 28½ days!

Nigel Love, founder of the Australian Aircraft and Engineering Company, had already chosen a bullock paddock at Mascot as an aerodrome for the competitors' homecoming. That paddock became Sydney airport. When the Vimy touched down at Mascot, it was greeted by thunderous applause.

The only other aircraft to reach Australia was piloted by Ray Parer who arrived on 2 August 1920, having left England eight months earlier. After the race, the Smith brothers had engine trouble and it took them longer to fly from Darwin to Sydney than it had to fly from England to Darwin.

All through the 1920s, exciting things were happening in both international and Australian aviation. The Englishmen Alcock and Brown had already flown the Atlantic. Seven years later Lindbergh flew the Atlantic solo. After World War I, 600 men from the Australian Flying Corps returned to Australia determined to bring aviation to this great, vast land. We had no aviation industry and secondhand aeroplanes had to be imported. Among them were Bristol fighters and other aircraft that Australian pilots had flown in England and France. Many were almost worn out and, like all military aircraft, were expensive to run.

English ex-pilots also joined the fledgling Australian industry. They emigrated to Australia for differing reasons, although few actually arrived here to begin working in the aviation industry. Tim Hervey was a typical case. He brought his bride from England in 1920 to work on a fruit growing scheme in northern Victoria. On the day of his arrival he met Harry Shaw and Lieutenant Ross walking along Collins Street in Melbourne.

All three had flown combat missions together. The two Australians had formed the Shaw-Ross Aviation Company after returning home from duty. Within a year or two, the fruit growing scheme had proved disastrous and Tim Hervey was keen to get out. At about the same time, Lieutenant Ross and two passengers were killed in a flying accident and Shaw offered Hervey the job of pilot and manager of the airline. Hervey jumped at the chance and completed the necessary tests for a commercial pilot's licence.

After joining the airline Hervey was barnstorming (joy-riding) around the Lakes Entrance area in Victoria when his engine started to overheat. Not keen to ditch into the tall gum trees over which he was flying, or the water nearby, he limped to a small island on which there was a lonely house. Too late, he realised the adjoining paddock had fence posts and barbed wire running through it. He crashed through these obstacles on landing, damaging the aircraft. He was amazed to find that the island's only occupants were Mrs Casement and her three daughters. Apparently during World War I her Irish brother-in-law, Sir Roger Casement, had been executed for being a German spy. The family was so ashamed, it had gone into self-imposed exile.

Tim spent several months on the island waiting for spare parts and, with the aid of the Casement family, repaired the aircraft and prepared a strip long enough for take-off.

Another pilot, Norman (later, Sir Norman) Brearley, risked his entire savings and took two Bristol fighters to Western Australia. After joy-riding above The Esplanade in Perth and gaining some public support (especially from the Durack family, who could see the advantage of the aeroplane for their lonely cattle stations in the Kimberleys), he began a service between Geraldton and remote Derby. He was not allowed to fly from Perth because then he would have been competing with the government-owned railway (God forbid!), so he chose this isolated part of the west coast to begin his air service.

Many servicemen returning from the war knew no other profession but flying. Kingsford Smith was fortunate to get a job with Brearley; Frank Briggs applied for the same job but went off on the first flight ever to Central Australia and was unable to take the necessary flying test in Melbourne. Only a couple of years ago I asked Sir Norman Brearley, now in his nineties, why he had not employed Briggs. He responded, 'Because he could not take the test.' When I mentioned his pioneering flight inland, Sir Norman said: 'That does not make a pilot. A pilot has it in the head and hands, not just flying off into the distance, or inland. No, I would not employ him without testing him myself.'

Aviation was beginning to spread its wings. Pilots Paul McGuiness and Hudson Fysh were given the task of surveying the route from Sydney to Darwin after missing out on competing in the England–Australia Race because their sponsor Sir Samuel McCaughey had died. As the result of their survey they decided to start up a small airline in western Queensland. They chose Longreach because there were no rail services beyond that point. Like Norman Brearley, McGuiness and Fysh started with joy-rides and charter flights before establishing a run between Longreach and Cloncurry. This was to be the beginning of the great Queensland and Northern Territory Air Services, now known throughout the world as Qantas.

Throughout the 1920s, aviation was competing with another modern invention, the motor car. Rapidly gaining acceptance, the 'horseless carriage' had become a highly desirable means of transport. Even those who could afford and were game enough to fly, wanted the convenience of a motor car, or a horse, at their journey's end as aerodromes and landing grounds were usually out of town.

In 1931, Sir Archdale Parkhill, a prominent Federal Parliamentarian, declared that aviation would never become a commercial industry. The risks and the need for landing fields would see to that! However, the oil companies did not agree. Not only did they send representatives around the country in a Gipsy Moth to promote aviation, they did what they could to help people get into flying. They financed flights, provided weather reports, offered transport from 'paddocks' to towns, and booked hotels for almost anybody who landed anywhere.

Despite the hardships and lack of financial gain, Australia's few dedicated aviators kept persisting, fuelled by sheer determination and their love of flying.

In recent years I have spoken to many service and charitable organisations throughout Australia. I have made a point of sprinkling those talks with stories from our aviation history.

It is with surprise and sadness that I realise how little is known of the contribution Australia has made to world aviation.

Because I have lived through all but a few of the years in which aviation history was being made, turning back the pages is a lot of fun. I have known many of the people who became legends. I have also known many others who were unsung heroes—the pilots who never made the headlines by breaking records or crashing aeroplanes. Records, crashes and spectacular events were the only incidents that made aviation news in the 1920s and early 1930s. In recalling the past, I am also pleased to learn that women throughout the world have achieved and contributed much to aviation history.

CHAPTER 1

In 1909, Raymonde de Laroche of France became the first woman to fly. She gained her licence in 1910, the same year as Lindia Zuereva of Russia, Hilda Hewlett of England and Belgium's Helene Dutrieu. In 1911 Melli Breese started a flying school in Berlin. America's Harriet Quimby flew the English Channel in 1912. Katherine Stinson demonstrated aerobatics in Tokyo in 1915, before returning to North America to train pilots for the Royal Flying Corp in World War I. This all took place long before Amy Johnson flew to Australia in 1930 and Amelia Earhart became a star in the American skies.

Men and women all over the world shared a deep commitment to flying. In 1921 Bert Hinkler shipped an aeroplane to Australia, took it off the wharf at Sydney, filled it with petrol and flew nonstop to Bundaberg—a distance of 850 miles. It was a magnificent feat for such a tiny aircraft. In 1928, Hinkler flew solo from England to Australia in a little Avro Avian.

As a teenager I read about these happenings in the newspapers—the crashes, successes and record-breaking attempts. Hinkler's flight in 1928 was an exciting and very emotional event. Australia went wild when he arrived at Mascot and the estimated 80 000 crowd sang:

'Hinkler, Hinkler little star,
Sixteen days and here you are.'

Bert Hinkler captured everybody's imagination. He built a glider when he was only fourteen years old. Hinkler, an exceedingly modest man, foresaw a great future for aircraft. He even said to Prime Minister Bruce in 1928: 'You know, one day people will fly by night and use the daylight for sightseeing.'

The Prime Minister was aghast. He could not believe such a thing would happen. Hinkler also predicted that the aeroplane would 'fly the ships off the sea' as far as passengers were concerned. In 1930, while in England, Hinkler designed the 'Ibis', an early amphibious aeroplane.

Like many teenagers, I was never short of ingredients to fuel my dreams. I remember the excitement I felt in 1928, when Charles Kingsford Smith and Charles Ulm flew the Pacific. Together with the American navigator Lyon and radio operator Warner, these two Australians conquered more than 7000 miles of uncharted sky in 83½ hours. The longest water hop in the world, between Honolulu and Suva, took them 34½ hours. This Pacific crossing was the greatest accomplishment in aviation to that date.

In 1928, Australia started feeling the savage effects of the depression. It was decided that I would leave Sydney and keep the books and housekeep for my father and uncle in their country store at Mt George. My mother was to remain in Sydney, while my brothers and sisters were being educated. I did not like school and was happy to leave, although I was only thirteen. My father believed in hard work and long hours and for doing the books and the housekeeping, I was paid £1 a week. That was a worthwhile sum. Days began early with a cold wash. All cooking was done on a wood stove. There were no luxuries and few amenities. My father regarded these as unnecessary. As a young man, he had quit the laboratories of his famous uncle, Washington H. Soul, to run off to work for Burns Philp in Townsville, where he learnt to be a merchant.

I soon discovered that a country storekeeper carries farmers through flood and drought, and waits patiently and sometimes indefinitely for his money. My father sent horse teams into the mountains to deliver supplies to the farming communities. These teams came back with rabbit skins and gold. Many of our customers had fled the cities to try to scrape a living out of the soil during the depression. My father gave credit to the wives of the men who cut railway sleepers; they went into the bush for weeks a time. When the bullock teams emerged and the Government inspector bought their sleepers at the railway sidings, all debts were usually paid and there was some money left over for a bottle of rum. When this was gone, and the men were rested, they would return to the bush.

My father was a workaholic and believed everyone should work sixteen hours a day. However, on Sunday afternoons I was allowed to ride around the beautiful Manning River district visiting my friends. Among them were the Somervilles at Tiri and the Duffs at Somerset. Jessie Duff, a champion equestrian, taught me to ride. I also fondly remember the Cooper, Andrews and Donkin families.

The depression days were a great eye-opener. People literally streamed out of the city. Some hid in goods trains, 'jumping the rattler' as they headed in all directions looking for work. They would come into our store asking for broken biscuits or a handout of food. Others camped up in the mountains looking for gold and living on rabbits and what they could make by selling skins.

In addition to the store, father also had the local cream contract. Several days a week we sent a truck up to the river crossing to pick up cream cans for the Wingham butter factory. This truck was our main means of transport into the 'civilisation' of Wingham, which had a population of about three thousand. Wingham had shops, hotels, a dentist, doctor, chemist, bank, local newspaper and even a golf course complete with sand greens. Once an air pageant came to town, so giving me my first chance to get airborne. My pilot was Reg Annabel, who flew a beautiful, shining Gipsy Moth—an aircraft that had revolutionised aviation. Before its arrival, aircraft had big, square water-cooled, or rotary engines, which often spewed out castor oil. They were military aircraft. The arrival of the Moth, with its streamlined nose and neat fuselage, made flying more economical and also turned aviation into a sport. Jean Batten and Amy Johnson were later to fly them from England to Australia.

I enjoyed being aloft so much that I went on a second flight and asked Reg to do some aerobatics for an extra pound. From then on, learning to fly was the ruling passion of my life.

Reg was later killed when he crashed while 'looping the loop' over the Mascot Aero Club. Little did I know that I would buy my first aeroplane from his estate in 1935.

While everyone said it was foolish to think I might indulge in anything as risky as flying, I pored over Frank Swoffer's book *Learning to Fly*.

I first discovered Swoffer when his book was recommended to me by George Campbell, a fat, shy boy who used to ride an enormous draught horse bareback over the paddocks. He did not think that learning to fly was such a crazy idea. He had learnt to fly while on holiday in Mascot and was friendly with Bill Wilson, a World War I pilot who used to drive my father's horse team. Bill, an ex-member of the Australian Flying Corps, terrified the locals as he drove that team down the mountain roads and forced it through flooded rivers. He was a friend of Kingsford Smith, and after 'Smithy's' Pacific flight, he went back into aviation only to be killed later in a motor accident. He also taught Charles Ulm to fly.

Fifty-six years later, and with decades of experience as an instructor behind him, George Campbell was still flying. Hundreds of grateful pilots passed through his capable, dedicated hands. As well as being a great instructor, he played an active part in World War II and was extremely well regarded throughout the flying world. Shortly before his death in 1987, 370 people gathered at Mudgee to honour his flying achievements.

Learning to Fly caused me many headaches. I pondered over words that meant little to me, such as lift, drag and angles of incidence. Even more foreign was the Vacuum Oil Company's brochure on combustion engines, cylinders, pistons, carburettors and crankshafts. Obviously, learning to fly from a book was not going to be easy, but I did not realise this until I gave it to my sister Joan to read. She was unnerved by the constant references to losing air speed and going into a spin. She asked, 'Doesn't an aeroplane do anything but spin?'

Although I tried hard to understand it, the magic of flying was incomprehensible at that time. But one thing I did understand completely was that I had to fly. How I saved! Every penny went into the house at the top of the hill where the two Cameron sisters had partitioned off part of their verandah as a Post Office and agency for the Commonwealth Bank. As my savings grew, so did my ambition to learn to fly. While on a visit to my mother in Manly, I took the tram to Mascot and made an appointment for a trial instructional flight. I was fifteen.

When I arrived Captain Leggett of the Aero Club at Mascot offered me a cigarette. I thought he would think I was older if I took it and smoked it, so I did. He had taught several women to fly including Millicent Bryant, who in 1927 became the first woman to obtain a pilot's licence in Australia. Captain Leggett later went to New Guinea, where, in the early 1930s, more airfreight was being carried than that being transported by the combined aircraft of the rest of the world, because there were no roads into the goldfields. Whatever Captain Leggett said encouraged me, and with high hopes, I asked him where I could buy a helmet. He directed me to a Miss Martin in the Strand Arcade. It wasn't long before I had bought a helmet, leather coat and goggles. These were to become my most precious possessions. I had everything I needed except a few more pounds and a few more years. I returned to the country to save my pennies and grow older.

In the meantime, I searched the newspapers for aviation news. In 1928 Kingsford Smith and Charles Ulm crossed the mighty Pacific Ocean from California to Australia. Then in 1929, Kingsford Smith and Ulm flew to New Zealand and back to Australia. I recall the drama of them taking off from beaches and battling through appalling storms. The papers also carried stories about barnstorming and playboy pilots. Then, I saw a small news item saying a woman had set off from London to fly to Australia in a 95 hp Gipsy Moth. No one took much notice until she reached Karachi. She was making better time than Hinkler had in 1928. Only the pilot's father and two other people had seen her off and suddenly she was world news. Her name was Amy Johnson. Having failed to win a flying scholarship from the Royal Aero Club, Amy had saved enough out of her £3 a week salary to learn to fly—and now she was on her way.

Amy knew nothing about long distance flying. Her previous longest trip had been from London to her hometown, Hull— 168 miles. She had only 100 hours solo experience and she had no experience of flying over mountains, deserts and through monsoon rains. Despite everything, she arrived in Darwin nineteen days later. Her aircraft was patched with pink sticking plaster and some shirts that had been made in Burma from war surplus aviation fabric. Amy damaged her aircraft in Rangoon and she tore up the shirts and mended the Moth's wings with 'dope' made by a local chemist. This dope, which was used for tauting the fabric, is the same product used today as nail lacquer.

Amy's flight was eventful. She crashed the Moth four times on the way out and her courage and determination were magnificent. The world applauded her.

C. W. A. Scott, an ex-Royal Air Force pilot who had joined Qantas, was sent to escort Amy across the featureless Australian outback and it was here that she met the first lack of co-operation she had experienced on her journey. Scott raced ahead of Amy to keep official appointments. He showed no consideration for the exhausted woman in his care.

While trying to land at Brisbane, Amy overshot the airfield. The aircraft turned over but she emerged unscratched. People went wild with enthusiasm, but that was the last flying she did in Australia. Amy Johnson went on to break the 'London to the Cape' record, fly to Japan and fly the Atlantic with her husband Jim Mollison. She later lost her life after running out of fuel over the Thames estuary while ferrying an Oxford aircraft during the war. She parachuted into the estuary but disappeared beneath the surface before a naval corvette could reach her.

Amy Johnson was a great inspiration to me, as was the German aviatrix Elly Beinhorn who followed her two years later. This delightful 'Flying Fraulein' landed in Australia in 1932 as part of a world tour. She had flown from Germany at a leisurely pace, not for the good of aviation, but to write a book. I went to the Grace building in Sydney where her Klemm monoplane was on display and she was speaking. Completely fascinated and inspired as I listened to Elly, my ambition intensified. I just had to fly and I wanted to be as charming and as feminine as she was. When she visited Sydney University, almost every young man fell in love with her, and she left them laughing when she referred to something in the past as 'my behind'. The students sent her a bunch of Australian wildflowers set in 800 lb of ice— and this was before the days of air transport! I still meet elderly gentlemen who vividly remember meeting Elly during that visit. I met her again in 1938 and 1951, both times in Germany, and she became one of my dearest friends.

While saving up to pay for lessons, and while waiting to be old enough to train for a licence, I applied for a flying scholarship being offered by Adastra Airways. I was duly photographed in the cockpit and the picture appeared on the front page of a Sydney paper, but I missed out on the scholarship.

Years later, Adastra's co-founder, Frank Follett, expressed disappointment that I had not enrolled at his flying school even though I had failed to win the scholarship. I explained that in 1933, Charles Kingsford Smith, the greatest airman of that time, had been barnstorming his *Southern Cross* around Australian country towns. He came to Wingham, landed on a paddock and with Pat Hall in the *Southern Cross Junior* was giving joy flights. Armed with my helmet and goggles, I went off to the field. Thirty years later, John Kingsford Smith, who was with his uncle's team, said 'We saw you coming across the field in a leather coat, carrying your helmet and goggles and said, "Where on earth does she fly!" '

When I told Kingsford Smith that I was going to learn to fly, he said he was opening a flying school in August and would be pleased to see me as a student. I was sold a flight with Pat Hall and accompanied by my friends Toots Martin and Dulcie Donkin. As we flew over Mt George, I closed the lid of Toots' cigarette tin over a handkerchief and threw it out the window so that my father would know that it was me up there! It nearly hit Pat Hall on the head and earned me a severe reprimand. Despite this, Pat soon became my chief flying instructor and it was he who sent me solo for the first time.

I was seventeen when I had saved £200 and told my father that I wanted to go back to our Manly home and start flying lessons at Mascot. He disapproved strongly, saying that I would be wasting my hard earned savings, he could not afford to keep a crippled daughter, and that it would kill my mother if anything happened to me.

Because I was one of six children, I thought my parents could well afford to take a risk with one. Despite continuing arguments, I held firm to my decision.

I had become indispensable to my father and his business. My presence enabled him to regularly visit Sydney for two days at a time. My uncle, Will Biddles, and I kept the country store going, doing the books daily, writing the cheques, paying employees and doing the housekeeping. Who was going to take my place? Ultimately my sisters all served time—doing 'my job'— at Mt George.

People still thought pilots were daredevils, adventure-seekers and 'crazies' who diced with death. Many believed the aeroplane would never become an accepted means of transport. Flying was a circus event, an aerial pageant. For those willing to pay, flying provided thrills but it was not a serious business. But, from the time I had my first flight, I dreamt about flying. I rode my horse over the hills around the Manning River, sang songs and thought of flying above the trees and the mountains. Occasionally, a lone Australian National Airways Avro 10 would pass overhead on its way to Brisbane. To me there was a magnetic attraction about those aeroplanes.

In the spring of 1933 I joined my family in Manly and began formal flying lessons. On my first day I took the Botany tram to Mascot and walked a mile to keep the appointment I had made with Charles Kingsford Smith. Of course, 'Smithy' did not remember the little redheaded girl who had enthusiastically told him that she was going to learn to fly. Hundreds of teenagers must have told him that, inspired by the chance of flying with, and talking to, the greatest airman of all time. Flush with funds from his successful barnstorming tour of New Zealand, for which the New Zealand government had generously waived his income tax, Kingsford Smith had built an enormous hangar at Mascot to house the *Southern Cross* and several other aircraft. It was here that he established his flying school.

CHAPTER 2

My first lesson was with Kingsford Smith himself. However, after the first two lessons, Smithy went off to break the England–Australia record in a 'Percival Gull', leaving me to his Chief Instructor Pat Hall. I never felt at home with Pat. He was shy with women, but he was an outstanding pilot. I saw his fantastic skill at the end of each lesson when, out of sheer frustration with the flying attempts of his pupils, he would take over the controls and whirl that Gipsy Moth around the aerodrome fence before landing in the exact spot he had chosen beside the hangar.

Pat was a friend of Dr Bobby and Ailsa Lee-Brown, who had first taken me to Mascot. Within a few months, Dr Lee-Brown was killed in the first standard Tiger Moth to come to Mascot. Years later, Ailsa married the famous flyer Scotty Allan. Ailsa was a charming, cultured woman, and an artist who found a new dimension of expression in flying.

As well as Pat Hall, I would fly with anyone who was game enough to give me instruction. Among them were Harold Durant, an ex World War I pilot turned printer; Dan Collins and 'Smithy's' engineer Tommy Pethybridge. I also took every chance I could to fly as a passenger. I learnt much from watching pilots such as Jim Broadbent, whose aerobatics were sheer artistry.

I soon realised that people climb mountains to see the same view that pilots see every time they take off. There is beauty at all altitudes. From the air, everything seems neat and tidy, yet one feels that humanity has made but a tiny and insignificant scratch upon the face of the earth. The extraordinary feeling of flying is to be able to bank and turn; to rise and fall; to have the aeroplane respond to what your hands and feet dictate. Flying really does give you the freedom of a bird. I do not think that pilots are any different from other people but they do gain an additional perspective. Once you have flown yourself, things are never quite the same again. There is something very special about voluntarily removing yourself from all earthly contact and then making a voluntary return.

Though completely unaware of it at the time, I was learning to fly at a time when history was being made. Many of the people around me were those who were achieving great breakthroughs in aviation. Sometimes their achievements were unrecorded, unheralded and unsung. Many were pioneers who have now become legends. Kingsford Smith, Ulm, Taylor and Scotty Allan stood out among them, perhaps because they were the long distance flyers. However, there were many others who flew the vast Australian continent and who now are remembered for the roles they played. Courage, determination, sheer tenacity and bravery were among the attributes these flyers shared.

Today, it seems unthinkable to some that people flew in those times. Frail fabric and wooden aeroplanes had spars stuck together with glue, which became brittle in temperatures over 40° Celsius. The wood of these aircraft would shrink. There were no aviation facilities and weather reports were based on the answer that oil company people in the mountains would give in response to a one shilling telegram, which asked if the mountains were clear. Back would come the telegram: 'The mountains are not clear.' or 'The mountains are clear.'

There were very few designated aerodromes, and landing grounds were often paddocks selected from the air or, in some cases, picked for you by the oil companies. We would receive a list of information detailing the height of the telephone wires and whether or not there were any trees or high tension wires around the paddock. Landing strips were unknown. We landed and took off into wind on whatever patch of ground was available.

The people who came out to fly at Mascot were mostly young; the well-to-do-men, and a few women, who looked on it as a sport. Most had no intention of becoming commercial pilots, although in 1934, when the extension of the airmail service was being talked about, perhaps some of them could see a future in aviation. They made the Aero Club rooms their headquarters and stayed all day, mingling with the men who formed the grass roots of Australian aviation.

24

Charles Kingsford Smith was the star of them all, together with Ulm who would sometimes lunch at the Club. They were joined by former World War I pilots such as Captain Geoffrey Hughes (father of Tom Hughes, Q.C. and Robert Hughes, author of *The Fatal Shore*). Others included Major Murray Jones, who had a fantastic war record and who represented the de Havilland Aircraft Company; Harold Durant, Frank Follett; Bunny Hammond (so named because he dug a tunnel out of a prisoner-of-war camp); Captain P. G. Taylor; Captain Edgar Johnston; Nigel Love; Joe Palmer; Pat Levy; Dick Allan; George Littlejohn; Neil Stewart; Jimmy Moir and Harold Owen, who flew out from England in 1929. Younger people joining that crowd included Mike Mather; John Larkin; Beverly Sheppard; Jack Chapman; Don MacMaster (who became Flight Superintendent of Qantas); Bob Smith (who became Route Captain of Australian National Airways and one of the four men with whom I did my commercial licence); Sid de Kanzo, who later started Cathay Pacific; Jack McLaughlin; Johnny Kerr, the Aero Club's Chief Instructor; and my father's cousin, Harold de Low.

Also among these sportsmen pilots were Tim Loneragan from Mudgee; George Falkiner from Warren; Andrew and Edward Macarthur Onslow, and their brother Denzil. In 1924, Denzil was building his own aeroplane while still at The King's School, Parramatta. He had bought a secondhand engine from a disposal sale in England after World War I. With books and magazines on how to build an aircraft and with the aid of the Macquarie Grove carpenter, he built the wings and fuselage. He bought duck fabric from the local store in Camden and his mother Sylvia stitched it to shape on her treadle sewing machine. Doping the fabric almost proved fatal when they closed the barn door and were overcome with fumes.

Denzil taught himself to fly, or so he thought, from books. Once in the air, however, he did not know how to land, so he circled and circled. His anxious mother turned the car headlights on as darkness approached and he finally got the aeroplane down. With his homebuilt aircraft, Denzil won £500 in a *Sun* newspaper competition. Much later, he was also responsible for introducing parachutes to the army. Before the war, Denzil bought a Comper Swift for himself, and imported the first high performance glider into Australia.

Always a great supporter of the Aero Club, Denzil became their President in 1950, and organised purchases of war surplus aircraft (still in boxes) from Kenya. He bought Link trainers for the Club and was Patron of the Combined Gliding Clubs. I can well remember his enthusiasm for the sport.

Among the women who flew at the Aero Club for the sheer pleasure of it were Bobbie Terry and Jean Gardiner. They were the first women to own their own aircraft. Others included Phyllis Arnott, the first women to gain a commercial licence; Meg Skelton, Ailsa Lee-Brown and Peggy McKillop. All were women of independent means. Incidentally, the first woman to be airborne in Australia was Florence Taylor in a heavier-than-air glider, which took off from Narrabeen Beach in 1909. In 1927 Millicent Bryant became the first woman to receive a flying licence in Australia. Unfortunately, she was killed in a harbour accident eight months later. She was followed by Margaret Reardon and Evelyn Follett, who later became a Director of her brother's company, Adastra Airlines.

Flying was not without its eccentrics. I recall Mr Charlton who owned a Gipsy Moth and had an assortment of sandshoes in his hangar. He insisted that his passengers wear them. This was taking Swoffer very literally, for I remember that he had suggested wearing sandshoes when learning to fly so that you got a better feel on the rudder.

The Aero Club of New South Wales was a long, squat building with a small front verandah. There was a large lawn with a half circle fence around it to give members a private viewing area for the days when large crowds came to see someone famous arrive or to view an air pageant. The front door opened into the dining room with its large oval cedar table, around which the great and not so great of aviation gathered. At one end was a small counter behind which a door opened into the kitchen. It was here that Mrs Fuller, the housekeeper, produced the most delicious baked dinners. They were two shillings each, complete with dessert. A lone poker machine stood on a table at one end of the counter, which Jim Broadbent played constantly.

At the left hand end of the dining room, a large open area was furnished with leather lounges, a few chairs, a case of trophies including the P. E. Vyner Memorial Trophy, a beautiful winged figure on a marble stand. At the far end, two doors led into separate bedrooms and a radio sat between the doors. This radio was once the cause of a confrontation between Jean Batten and some young men who were learning to fly. They insisted on playing it when she wanted to sleep. Eventually, she smashed the valves. They retaliated by locking her in her room and playing the radio (duly repaired) full blast outside her door.

The Club was always a coat and tie affair. One dared not enter in overalls or unsuitable dress. Stanley Bridgeland, the English-born Club secretary saw to that! Only seven miles from Sydney, it was a favourite place for World War I pilots to entertain their friends and 'pop out for half an hour's flying at lunch-time.' Young men brought their girlfriends on Sundays and, after a short flight, came to the Club for afternoon tea. It was quite a social club in the tradition we had inherited from Stag Lane, Hatfield, and Hendon in England.

The 1929 depression had forced the Hargrave Country Club, which was owned by the Aero Club, to close and everything was returned to Mascot. Later, the Aero Club became less exclusive. Young apprentices joined the flying schools to become engineers, and flying began again but not only as an exclusive sport. Flying schools and aero clubs welcomed anyone who had money for lessons. As we emerged from the depression, people sought many reasons to fly. The Jubilee Airmail was organised; Christmas mails were carried to and from England; and pilots rushed photos of important functions, including the Melbourne Cup and Royal visits, to newspapers. Frank Neale seemed to have a permanent job flying gold investors back and forth to Tennant Creek, but few pilots had regular jobs. Goya Henry was the most successful joy-rider at Mascot in those days, defying the Department of Aviation policy by flying right hand instead of left hand circuits, and landing on the tarmac so that he could fit in more flights. When the New South Wales police tried to arrest him, he claimed to be on Commonwealth Territory, and he was. His actions resulted in a referendum to decide if the Commonwealth should have control over flying in Australia. That referendum was probably the only one ever brought about by one man.

This was the atmosphere and environment I walked into when I first began visiting the Aero Club in 1933. Kingsford Smith's secretary Marge McGrath (known as 'Split Pin' because she was so thin) and I used to go over to the club every day for lunch, taking a 'table for two' under the window. Only a few times

27

when alone, or with the boys who were pilots, was I invited to sit at the main table—the pilots' table. The pupils of the Aero Club sat here, joined by any visitors of importance, the Club President or Secretary, World War I pilots, Smithy, P. G. Taylor, Jim Broadbent and others.

I do not think I was taken very seriously in those days. There were few enough jobs in aviation for the ex wartime pilots and the young men who learnt to fly for fun or as a sport. Women who wanted to fly provided flying schools with extra revenue, but we were not seen as potential contributors to the industry proper. Kingsford Smith told me he did not approve of women flying. It was not their place. However, this did not stop him from being kind and generous or from going out of his way to pick me up at the Manly wharf when he was in Sydney. It was a long trip to the airport. I caught a Botany tram to the Mascot Post Office and then walked a mile. A few heads would turn when Kingsford Smith met me, because he was already famous and people had read of his great exploits. However, no one took much notice when his manager, John Stannage, collected me in his jalopy.

When I made my own way to Mascot, I caught a Botany tram and walked a mile to the aerodrome. I caused quite a stir with passers-by as I was dressed in heavy trousers to ward off the low temperatures experienced in an open cockpit. In those days, women did not wear trousers. They were unknown and jodhpurs were rare. I had made a garment that looked like a cross between knickerbockers and plus fours. Wearing these, my leather coat and carrying a helmet and goggles, I was rather conspicuous.

When I rode with Charles Kingsford Smith and Marge McGrath, whom he collected from Darlinghurst, I listened to their plans, ambitions, disappointments and general aviation talk.

In 1931, following the disappearance of the *Southern Cloud* (found by chance in the Snowy Mountains 27 years later), Kingsford Smith and Ulm had gone into voluntary liquidation with Australian National Airways. Ulm had gone his own way, flying with the aeroplane called *Faith in Australia*. He was planning great things for commercial aviation, and Kingsford Smith was doing the same.

Since 1929, the Dutch had been flying to Java in the Spice Islands (now Indonesia) and wanted to extend the airmail service to Australia. In 1934, the Imperial Airways' service from England to India was extended to Singapore and the Australians insisted on flying the Singapore–Australia route. Kingsford Smith, Ulm and Brearley all applied for the contract and we all waited anxiously for the result.

Kingsford Smith was assumed to be the main contender. He had pioneered this route, had flown it three times, and had come to the rescue of the Australian government several times. One such occasion was in 1932 when the Christmas mail, flown by Scotty Allan, crashed at Alor Star in Malaya. But Kingsford Smith's application was rejected and I saw his great disappointment when the news came through. The contract was awarded to Queensland and Northern Territory Air Services, which formed a new company, Qantas Empire Airways. This company was owned 49 per cent by Qantas, 49 per cent by Imperial Airways and 2 per cent by an umpire Sir George Julius.

Qantas had chosen the right part of Australia to begin. Distances were great, roads were bad and rail connections were worse. People would fly to avoid hundreds of miles of dusty road and appalling heat. The Queensland and Northern Territory Air Services were conceived by McGuiness and Hudson Fysh on their way to survey the Australian end of the England–Australia route in 1919 and became one of the world's most successful airlines. Hudson Fysh became world head of the International Air Transport Association and was knighted. What a wealth of life and achievement since the day he headed his old car into the north-west, bound for Darwin.

When it was announced that the airmail service would be extended to New Zealand, Smithy's hopes rose and he worked hard to gain it. He had flown the route in 1929, 1933 and 1934 and was strongly supported by the New Zealand government. But the Australian government intervened, and insisted that he should use a British aircraft, even though none would be available to buy for two years. The Sikorsky company manufactured a suitable plane, but because they had back orders, declined to give Kingsford Smith any priority.

Smithy then went to see the Minister for Defence, Senator Pearce, and outlined a plan to fly the Tasman with American Martin Mariner flying boats. They were available quickly. 'But they are American,' said the Senator. 'Don't you think you are being a bit unpatriotic?' Smithy replied: 'What kind of car do you drive, Senator?' 'A Chrysler,' said Senator Pearce. 'Then don't you think you are being a bit unpatriotic?' said Smithy.

CHAPTER 3

Each day I learnt a little more about flying. It wasn't long before I was asking people if they would teach me some engineering. Tommy Pethybridge, Smithy's Chief Engineer, said to Bruce Cowan (who frequently reminded me he had to chase around finding cushions so I could see out of the cockpit and reach the pedals): 'We'll learn her to learn engineering—give her some dirty jobs to do.' And dirty jobs they were! My hands got used to petrol, steel brushes and scraping carbon off the spark plugs of the *Southern Cross*. Harold Affleck taught me how to repair the wing fabric. The wings and spars needed to be inspected periodically. This entailed cutting an 'L' piece in the fabric, sewing it up again and pasting tape over it. I learnt to become expert in herringbone stitch and those other stitches required for the trailing edge of aircraft.

I filled in my time and listened to hangar talk—the stories that pilots relate on how they got away with this and that; the one they did not get away with; crashes they survived and crashes they had heard about. Sometimes, with other pupils, I sat on the grass outside the hangar, watching people fly. We would 'talk them down' to the ground and watch them make the same mistakes again and again. Of course, we made the same errors when it was our turn to fly. During this time of learning, I would often fly over my home in Manly to the great excitement of my little brothers and their friends. One, Don Gillies, who became a marine engineer, said: 'We had nothing to wave when you flew over one day, so we ripped off our shirts, buttons and all, and waved furiously.' Another was Bruce Fawcett who became Chief Instructor on the Qantas simulator. My brother-in-law, Mervyn Garland, then a champion amateur golfer, was playing on the Manly course one day as I flew over, showing off with some aerobatics. The golfers' reaction was one of horror: 'Women should not be allowed to do such things,' they said.

Often I would take up passengers. One of my first was Jocelyn Howarth, the star of the film *The Squatter's Daughter*. The film makers had sent her out to take a flight with me and be photographed by the newly published *Australian Women's Weekly*, then in its first year. Jocelyn was a beautiful woman and was accompanied by her very handsome fiancé. However, the lure of Hollywood intervened and she took off for the States in search of fame and fortune. She found both in her marriage to George Brent, a well known actor. The marriage only lasted one night which sky-rocketed her into fame and a substantial alimony. Her name was changed to Constance Worth. It was with considerable surprise that I learnt (from Margaret Kentley's unpublished papers) that she had flown her own balloon in the American bicentenary celebration in 1976 at the age of seventy-four!

It was tremendous fun to be invited to fly with other pilots. Jim Broadbent, one of the most likeable sportsmen pilots, who owned his own Gipsy Moth, dropped in to Mascot several days a week to fly. He was an outstanding pilot and generously asked me to join him while performing stall turns and aerobatics to perfection. I felt that he could fly even if his wings fell off. Jim also broke the England–Australia record in a Percival Gull and was well on the way to breaking Jean Batten's record for the same route when something very strange happened. While flying, he saw a sandy beach and, the next thing he knew, he woke up on it, but had no recollection of the landing. Utterly exhausted, he had put down automatically! I once asked him about his record-breaking flights. He said he carried detective stories that were so thrilling he could not get back into the air quickly enough to see what was on the next page. That was his secret for not losing time on the ground. During World War II, he was piloting a Martin Mariner between Portugal and England when it disappeared without trace off Casablanca. Not even an oil slick was found.

Probably the most gracious and respected airman who dined at the Aero Club table was P. G. (Bill) Taylor who went to England in 1916 to join the Royal Flying Corps. He was one of four men in his flight who survived their full tour of duty. They pitted themselves against very superior German aircraft and engaged in dog fights without oxygen, at up to 20 000 feet. Awarded the Military Medal for bravery, he proved his courage again when he saved the *Southern Cross* by crawling out on a strut to take oil from a crippled motor and transfer it to another over the Tasman Sea in 1935. For this action, Bill was awarded the George Cross, the highest medal for bravery given to a civilian. Yet, his comment to me when I asked him why he had done it was: 'We had no alternative. Either we went into the sea or, if I was successful, we had a chance to limp back to Australia.'

In 1935, as co-pilot and navigator to Kingsford Smith, Taylor flew a single engine Lockheed Altair across the Pacific from Australia to California. This quiet, modest man also went on to conquer the Indian Ocean in 1939 and the South Pacific (from Australia to Chile) in 1951. Taylor gave the plane he flew for this crossing (the *Frigate Bird* II) to the Sydney museum where it is now on display.

It was Bill Taylor to whom I turned for navigational instruction. He once told me of a conversation he had had while ferrying aircraft for the Canadian Air Transport Auxiliary. He had been given a seat on an aircraft flying to Australia from San Diego. Not being the pilot or navigator, he was a little wary and said to the pilot, 'Have you ever flown the Pacific before?'

'Nope,' said the youthful captain, 'but I have got a book on it.'

P. G. Taylor swallowed hard.

Taylor also had a delicious sense of humour. While ferrying civilian wartime passengers, he once opened the door, turned to the cabin and said, 'Is there anyone here who has ever flown a Lockheed 14?' There was nothing but deathly silence from the passengers and Bill yelled, 'Then I suppose I had better try,' and he slammed the door and opened up the motors.

Bryan Monkton was one of Taylor's co-pilots on inter-ocean flights. He was another of the youngsters, like Kim Bonython, who had flown for fun before the war and who turned out tops when it was on.

A star from the hangar floor was Harry Purvis. He was an excellent mechanic, co-pilot and, finally, the beloved Commander of RAAF Transport Command. His career included being co-pilot to Bill Taylor on the 1951 Chilean flight; service with the Dutch airlines in Java, and work as a pilot in the inland where he wrote a book, titled *Outback Airman*. But Harry was no mere outback pilot. He was a man of international flying calibre and flew in and out of the tiniest strips in New Guinea, evacuating wounded serviceman under Japanese fire. At the end of World War II, the Americans thought so much of him as a Commandant that they gave him a DC-3.

One of the earliest pioneer pilots was Harry Hawker. If Hawker had succeeded in his flight across the North Atlantic in 1919, Australians could have claimed to have pioneered every major ocean of the world, by air. Hawker was 1000 miles out to sea when his water-cooled engine kept overheating. He made for the shipping lanes, ditched the aircraft and was plucked from the sea by a little Danish tramp steamer. Because the vessel had no radio, Harry was listed as missing, presumed lost for six days. In due course his wife received a telegram of condolence from the King. When Hawker finally turned up, he was able to read his own obituary.

Harry Hawker was a blacksmith's son from Moorabbin, Victoria. He had little education and little opportunity, yet he had a real love affair with the combustion engine. He often found work driving the cars of Melbourne's well-to-do families. In 1911 he left Australia for England where he became the Sopwith Aviation Company's designer and chief test pilot. Before he had done twenty hours solo, he had broken endurance and altitude records set by Charles Rolls of Rolls-Royce and Moore Brabazon (later to become Lord Brabazon), the great patron of aviation. Hawker de Havilland, Hawker Siddley and Hawker Hurricane are examples of how Harry's name has become immortalised in the pages of aviation history. The airport in Victoria has also been named after him.

It was also Harry Hawker who discovered how to recover from a spin. At some stage in every pilot's career, he or she is faced with getting out of a potentially deadly spin. It is a relatively simple procedure, but until Hawker courageously and skilfully discovered the solution, the spin claimed many lives.

In 1928, the first person to fly across the Arctic Ocean from Barrow, Alaska, to Spitzbergen, Norway, a distance of 2200 miles, was a little-known South Australian, Hubert Wilkins. He was accompanied by the Alaskan pilot Carl Ben Eielsen. Later in the same year, Wilkins led an Antarctic expedition during which he made the first Antarctic flight while surveying the Palmer Peninsula.

I met Hubert Wilkins at the Aero Club in Mascot in 1934 when he was visiting Charles Kingsford Smith. It was hard to believe that this unassuming man with the goatee beard was the same man who tried to take the submarine *Nautilus* under the Arctic ice in 1931.

Hubert Wilkins was born in South Australia in 1888 and was interested in balloons and airships from an early age. He learned to fly at twenty-three. Subsequently he went to England where he trained as a cine cameraman and stills photographer before going to the Balkan wars in 1912 as a war correspondent, photographer and navigator. In 1913, he joined the great Icelandic explorer Vilhjalmur Stefansson on an expedition to survey the Beaufort Sea in northern Canada. He spent three years with the Icelander and gained valuable schooling in Arctic travel and survival.

During World War 1, he was awarded the Military Cross. After the war, he joined a team of Australians to enter the England–Australia Air Race in the hope of winning the £10 000 prize provided by the Australian government. Unfortunately, Wilkins and his crew crash-landed in Crete, but luckily walked away from the wreckage.

Later, he attempted to mount a transpolar airship flight but could not raise enough money. From Point Barrow, years later, he saw the grey ghost of the airship *Norge* as it flew over the Pole. As he watched, he said: 'It matters not who does it, but that it is done.'

Wilkins' opportunity to explore the Arctic by air came when Dr Isaiah Bowman of the American Geographical Society provided substantial support for the project. Additional support also came from a Detroit newspaper and the city's business community. Indeed, even the schoolchildren of Detroit donated to his expedition. At about this time, Dutchman Anthony Fokker told Wilkins that he was building a large three-engine aeroplane that would be suitable for the expedition. Wilkins agreed to buy it, together with a single-engine back-up aircraft. The tri-motor aircraft was christened the *Detroiter* and the single-engined one the *Alaskan*. Both Fokkers were shipped to Fairbanks, but within a short time of having been assembled, both were damaged in crash landings. There is a sudden change of lift when the temperature is 50° below zero, and both experienced pilots made the same mistake of stalling their aircraft while coming in to land. The planes were rebuilt and the expedition finally got underway.

It was not an easy undertaking. Accurate maps did not exist. The Endicott Range, for example, was marked at 5000 feet. In fact it is 8500 feet high. The pilots had to navigate by dead reckoning. They followed streams and valleys, and kept a sharp eye out for landmarks. They also made their own maps while in flight. Flying above fog out over the ice-packed sea was a daily occurrence. Wilkins' knowledge of the area enabled him to read ice formations. He could tell from which direction winds had blown; and he understood pack ice and patterns on land. Each morning the oil in their aircraft had to be heated on a stove before being poured into the engine.

In spite of these awful flying conditions, pilots were flying in Alaska. Wilkins and Ben Eielsen proved that the Arctic Circle could indeed be conquered by air. On one flight, after a forced landing 100 miles from base, Eielsen and Wilkins survived a gruelling 18-day walk back to Barrow. They endured the bitter cold and faced incredible hazards while crossing ice floes. Even the Eskimos were surprised that they had survived.

To please his backers, Wilkins reluctantly agreed to make the first flight from Barrow to Spitzbergen. Before doing this, however, he returned to Seattle to sell the big aircraft. He found three young Australians who wanted to buy it, but they had little money so he sold it to them on a deposit without engines and instruments. They renamed the aircraft the *Southern Cross*, an aircraft that now has a very special place in aviation history.

Wilkins and Eielsen headed back to the polar wastes and eventually completed the crossing to Spitzbergen. The final leg was full of drama. As well as being forced down and snowed-in by arctic storms, Wilkins had the misfortune of being left behind after trying to prise the aircraft's skis loose from the frozen snow. On this occasion, and while low on fuel, Eielsen took off, thinking that Wilkins had scrambled on board after fixing the skis. However, he had been unable to get a hand hold on the moving aeroplane and was left behind. Luckily, Eielsen saw him lying in the snow, and on the third attempt, Wilkins managed to clamber aboard.

Having tackled the Arctic, Wilkins turned his attention southwards and, in the same year, made the first flight in Antarctica. Wilkins was subsequently knighted by King George V for his flight over the North Pole. He was also honoured by the Americans who appointed him their polar adviser in World War II.

As a mark of respect, after his death in 1958, the United States atomic submarine *Skate* surfaced at the North Pole and scattered his ashes to the four winds. His name became immortal in the United States but, in his own country, his passing rated only a paragraph in some daily newspapers.

Wilkins, however, will not be forgotten. Dick Smith, the Australian aviator and explorer, heard of the 'Hubert Wilkins' story and we can expect that Dick will make sure Hubert's brave contributions to aviation will not be allowed to remain hidden from future generations. The helicopter in which Dick made three fantastic flights to the north polar region already honours Hubert George Wilkins. It carries his initials as the registration.

CHAPTER 4

Many of the people who frequented the Aero Club at Mascot were characters like Guy Menzies, another of the sportsmen pilots. Once while flying around the Inverell district, he apparently saw two pretty young women riding horses across a paddock. Dashing young man that he was, he landed beside them and introduced himself. He was a debonair man with a good sense of humour. Once he told us that he was going to fly to Perth. He took off, and the next thing we heard, he was in New Zealand.

Impulse flights were common in those days. Two boys with whom I learned to fly, Rex Nicholl and a New Zealander Ray Whitehead, made a similar journey. We knew they were up to something as they huddled together talking. Oversize fuel tanks were fitted to their Puss Moth, and the next we heard, they had arrived safely in New Zealand.

They took off on 22 November 1934 from Gerringong beach, New South Wales, for the 1300-mile sea crossing. Because the Civil Aviation authorities had cancelled the Moth's registration and withdrawn its Certificate of Airworthiness, the boys waited until the authorities had left the field. Then, aided by car headlights, they prepared for their secret take-off. It was a tricky affair. Their compass was out by twenty degrees because of the metal in the extra petrol tanks. Their normal capacity of 35 gallons had been expanded by an extra 82 gallons and the extra petrol overloaded the Moth by nearly 600 pounds. Because of the extra tanks, all that remained in the seating space in the crowded cabin was one small board placed across the control box. Tied to it with string, was a cushion on which only one man could sit. His companion had to crouch between his legs. The machine's oil pipe was a length of hose into which oil was poured periodically through a tin funnel. A lump of cotton waste served as a stopper in the end of the pipe.

Rex and Ray nearly missed New Zealand completely. Fifty miles north of the country's northernmost tip, they happened to see a few rocks below them and decided that they would turn south. It was just as well they did for they found New Zealand. After landing at Doubtless Bay, they walked for ten miles and came to a river crossing. Deciding it was too dangerous to cross, they returned to the plane and slept there the night. In the morning they took off without any difficulty and flew to Auckland, only to be charged on arrival with making a flight in an unregistered aircraft, not possessing a Certificate of Airworthiness, and failing to carry the documents prescribed in the regulations.

When they appeared in the crowded court, they were liable to a maximum of six months' imprisonment or a £200 fine, or both. The magistrate, commenting that it was the first charge under the new Air Navigation Act, found the first charge proved, dismissed the other two charges and set the men free.

Perhaps New Zealand's Governor-General, Lord Bledisloe, softened the blow when he said he hoped their flight would 'stimulate the imagination and zeal of many youthful New Zealanders to emulate them.'

One of the country boys occasionally seen at the Aero Club was Tim Loneragan of Mudgee, across the mountains 170 miles from Sydney. Tim invited me to fly in his stagger wing Beechcraft so he could let me experience the power of centrifugal force in his new aeroplane. It was tremendous. As he went into a steep turn, my tummy was pressed against my backbone. Tim learnt to fly in 1927 and was a sportsman pilot. He had a holiday home at Collaroy and found flying was the quickest way to get there so he could enjoy weekends by the sea. His first plane was a Gipsy Moth, which he would fly across the mountains and land on Long Reef Golf Course. He would then fold up the wings and tow the Moth behind his car to the garage at the beach house. He did the same thing from a paddock in Mudgee. The sight of an aeroplane being towed along the road was quite sensational to the small boys of Collaroy.

Tim was buying aircraft supplies from Paul and Grey Co Ltd, a Sydney importing warehouse, when the manager showed him two Pioneer bank and turn indicators. They were the first blind flying instruments to be imported from America. Tim had read about the gyroscopic instruments and jumped at the idea of fitting one in his Gipsy Moth.

After fitting the bank and turn, plus a blind flying hood, Tim set about learning how to fly blind. Using one of his brothers as a safety pilot, he mastered several elementary manoeuvres under the hood, including how to recover from a spin.

Tim told me recently that even today, some 60 years after buying his first bank and turn, he still practices blind flying. Tim recalled another event, also reaching back almost 60 years, when he met a radio buff who said he could make a radio device that could lead a plane to any broadcasting station. Tim realised that blind flying had limitations unless the pilot could track to a location and then put down through the overcast. This radio buff, whose name was Beard, provided the answer. His device was indeed the precursor of the much more sophisticated Automatic Direction Finder of today. Beard used an ordinary wireless which, when swung in a certain direction, gave a strong signal. The point at which the signal was lost is called the 'null'. When the Beard radio set recognised the null, it registered on an instrument on the aircraft's dashboard.

Simply by keeping the needle in the centre, the aeroplane would head to the station. When it flew over the radio station, the needle fluttered and changed polarity. The pilot then knew exactly where he was.

Tim joined the RAAF in 1939 and became a flying instructor. He drilled into many young pilots the absolute necessity of 'instruments only' flying. Three of his friends, who had been members of the New South Wales Aero Club, died because they had not mastered the art, and Tim never forgot the lesson this taught him.

In 1944, Tim was sent to England to the Empire Central Flying School (ECFS) at Hulavington (Herts). It was a kind of university where pilots flew and attended lectures on all kinds of subjects associated with advanced flying. Students took the controls of British and American aircraft, from Spitfires, Hurricanes and Lancasters to American A20 Bostons. In the classroom, lectures were given on wireless, radar and radio navigation. Dovetailed with the lectures was flying by day and at night.

One of the lecturers at ECFS, Frank (later Sir Francis) Chichester, was well known to many Australians and New

Zealanders. His ability as a navigator, both in the air and on the sea is now legendary. His solo trip around the world in a little sailing ship in the 1960s was a master feat in navigation.

Tim graduated from ECFS with distinction, having gained second top position. He gained further valuable instrument flying and radio navigation experience in America. The RAAF arranged for him to attend a course at Gordon Field near Atlanta, Georgia, where an instrument flying school was run by the American Navy Airforce.

When Tim arrived back in Australia he was given the task of opening an advanced instrument flying training and radio navigation school at Point Cook. In 1945 he was awarded the Air Force Cross (AFC) for his outstanding contribution to instrument flying.

Tim did much to inspire confidence in aviation. Even at the age of 83, he still retains his flying licence endorsed with a first class instrument rating.

Tim Loneragan came from a family of flyers. All of his brothers—Bernard, Mit, Bryan and Bob—held pilot's licences. Bryan bought a Beechcraft stagger wing after the war. When he gave it a scrape down and repaint, he uncovered the Royal Standard of Norway. It had been part of the Royal Flight!

Dan Collins, a flying instructor, always came to Mascot looking immaculate in his pin-striped business suit. I flew with him on one of my cross-country training flights to Wingham. Several friends had gathered in a paddock and I invited some of them to fly with me over the town and along the Manning River. My first passenger was Dulcie Donkin who, in 1986 at her eightieth birthday party, told me she had been terrified but had not wanted to refuse. She had sidled up to Dan Collins and said, 'Is Nancy all right? Is she safe?' To which he had replied, 'I wish I had Nancy's sensitive hands.'

On another cross-country exercise, I hired a Moth VH-UOZ and again flew with Dan as my instructor to the first Canberra Air Pageant in 1933. He entered the Moth in the Aerial Derby and won a canteen of cutlery, presented to him by the Governor-General, Sir Isaac Isaacs. Fifty years later, I was invited to Canberra as the sole survivor of the first Air Pageant and was presented with an engraved vase by the Governor-General, Sir Ninian Stephens.

To gain further experience during my early days, I accepted an invitation from Charles Gatenby to fly in formation with him from Sydney to King Island in Bass Strait. I hired the *Red Rose*, an Avro Avian that had become famous because it was used by Jessie Miller and Captain Lancaster on their flight from England in 1928. Cliff Carpenter, a playboy pilot and member of a famous Sydney shipping family, offered to come as my instructor. I never knew if it was a serious offer or if he did it at the request of the aircraft's owner Joe Palmer, who may well have wanted an experienced pilot on board! Nevertheless, we set out together. We soon got lost and had to land in a wheat field near Henty to ask a farmer for directions.* We headed off again but, over Bass Strait, we ran into low cloud and became lost again. We couldn't find King Island! I knew then what it feels like to be lost at sea. We turned back to Australia, a much bigger target than King Island, and landed on the beach at Apollo Bay. After checking our fuel, we decided to go no further than Phillip Island, just off the Victorian coast.

Throughout 1934 I built up my hours and studied for my commercial licence. I found one of the best ways to remember the lectures was to write out the notes five times. There were five of us sitting for that commercial licence and I would write the lesson down and give everybody a copy of my notes. During this period, the Civil Aviation Department decided to add an hour's blind flying and half an hour's solo night flying to the Commercial examination. As the Kingsford Smith School did not have the facilities for the former, and maybe did not want to risk their aeroplanes for the latter, I went to the Aero Club for this advanced training. George Littlejohn** was the Chief

---

* Our forced landing did not go unnoticed. Recently, I met Ross McLean, an air ambulance pilot, who told me that his grandfather, Eric LeLieure, had been wanting to catch up with me since 1934. He was unharnessing his horses in a wheat field when we flew low and landed. The horses apparently broke their harness and bolted in all directions. Ross said that for years his grandfather had picked up pieces of harness in that paddock and cursed me. I wrote him an apology, even though it was half a century late!

** George Littlejohn perished with Charles Ulm on the second attempt to fly across the Pacific. Years later I learned that he had put up half the cost of that fatal flight. The two men and their navigator, Skilling, died when their aircraft went down somewhere between California and Hawaii.

Instructor then, with Johnny Kerr as his assistant. Both were excellent pilots and George did much to encourage aviation by making promotional tours into country areas. George also taught many people to fly and some of his students graduated to important positions in the industry and the Air Force.

The Aero Club was constantly struggling through the depression years and George was happy to instruct, without payment, because of the pleasure he got from flying and sharing his knowledge and joy.

George helped me polish my flying skills very quickly. Because I had flown with anybody who would instruct me, I had picked up a lot of bad habits. But times were bad and I wondered just what I was going to do with my commercial licence when I got it. Where would I work? Was my father going to be proved right when he said I would be wasting my money by taking flying lessons?

Other pilots were in the same predicament. Jobs were scarce and experience was hard to get. One of the Citizens' Air Force pilots, Bill Purton, and many others, would even pay £5 for the privilege of flying as co-pilot on the Australian National Airways Avro 10s to Brisbane. This source of experience dried up when the company—and many other airlines—went into voluntary liquidation in the early 1930s.

Bill was one of the nicest men I have ever met and I found my fervent desire to be totally committed to aviation being eroded by thoughts and feelings that I knew I must stamp on. In Brisbane, just before the Air Race to Adelaide in 1936, Bill asked me to marry him. Almost as quickly he said, 'Of course, if you still plan to go abroad and dedicate yourself to aviation, I would not stand in your way.' Bill disappeared while evacuating people from Java early in World War II. We presumed his unarmed flying boat was shot down by a Zero.

Bill's sense of humour was legendary as were some of his quotations. His reply to the Englishman who asked 'What part of the Empire do you come from, young man?' was typical: 'A far flung part of the Empire, that was not flung far enough.'

Business and professional men often arrived at Mascot for early morning flights and when we arrived about 9 am we would scan the aerodrome and its boundaries to see who was flying or who had crashed. One morning, a silver Gipsy Moth was tail high in the Chinese vegetable garden next to the aerodrome.

We rushed over to find Geoff King, owner of Kinelab Studios, quite unhurt, muttering, 'I just do not know what happened.' He had apparently spun off a gliding turn while approaching the aerodrome.

Another incident involved Sergeant Bill Brown who had rebuilt a Moth to fly in the 1934 Air Race from Mildenhall, England, to Melbourne. He experienced engine failure on take-off and went straight into the Cooks River which, in those days, was on the southern side of the airfield. His aircraft was dragged out with the bodies of the occupants still in it.

The Club attracted many people. Among them was Len Schultz who was an honorary instructor there for many years. Len was a chief engineer at a Sydney radio station and spent his weekends at the Club. Reg Swain, of Bookshop fame, was a committee member and a constant visitor to the Club. He also took many of the Club's aerial tours to various country towns. Like 'Pop' Tyler, who was a well known identity at the Club, he did much to create interest and inspire confidence in aviation.

CHAPTER 5

The years 1928 to 1936 saw a string of record-breaking flights. Kingsford Smith was to the fore with his flights from Australia to England and across the North Atlantic in the *Southern Cross*. These were followed by his flight in the *Southern Cross Junior* from England to Australia, during which he beat Hinkler's time. These men were followed by C. W. A. Scott, Jim Mollison, Arthur Butler and many others.

In 1930, Amy Johnson made her historic flight from England to Australia, showing that women could do it too! Jim Broadbent and Jim Melrose followed in 1935. Records were constantly being set and broken. It was a heady period.

We followed the achievements of these pilots every inch of the way. It takes a lot of physical endurance to start at 2 am, fly all day, and snatch only an hour or so sleep on the ground while refuelling. We knew how much concentration it took to fly blind, battle monsoons, suffer turbulent conditions and cope with intense heat and freezing cold. We admired those pilots greatly. Only someone who flew in those early days can appreciate how it felt to rely on a little motor while flying over great expanses of water, desert and jungle. Similarly, we understood the sheer exhaustion at the end of a flight and the need for a cast iron will to keep you going.

Australia's air pioneers realised that aviation would annihilate distance. With unquenchable courage, they set to work to prove it. In some cases they were spurred on by the hope of rich rewards for those who were first in the field. Some were to die in the attempt. Others were to say, as did Kingsford Smith, 'We chaps who blaze air trails have little to show for our deeds. Ill fate has marked us for its own . . .' Through all the turmoil of death, intense effort and vain hopes, came success. Today, the jets of

Australia's own world airline sweep from Sydney to London in less than 24 hours. That achievement had its foundation in the heroism displayed by Australia's aviation pioneers.

Another flight of significance to Australia during 1931, was the 15 500 mile flight around the world by the one-eyed American Wiley Post. His navigator was an Australian, Harold Gatty, who became recognised as a world leader in the field of navigation. Anne Morrow Lindbergh (wife of Charles Lindbergh, the first man to fly solo across the Atlantic) was instructed by Gatty and she believed that his system of navigation was the best in the world.

In 1934, New Zealand aviatrix Jean Batten made her first flight from England to Australia. It was her third attempt. She had previously crashed in Greece and, before that, in India where Lord Wakefield of the Castrol Oil Company came to her aid. I often spoke with Jean at Mascot and flew with her to the Cootamundra Air Pageant in 1934. I can distinctly remember the trip because when we were over Goulburn we hit an 'air pocket' and I found myself suspended in mid-air with a tin of Castrol oil in my hand. Jean always carried her own oil in appreciation of the help that Lord Wakefield had given her.

After the pageant all the little Moths started taking joy flights and I sold tickets for Jean with enthusiasm. As fast as she could take a passenger, I had another one waiting. Our enterprise came to an end when a woman put her shoe heel through the fabric of the wing. Jean was livid and, by the time it was repaired, the sun had gone down and we had to refund precious money to disappointed would-be passengers.

Speaking at the Qantas 60th anniversary in 1980, at which Jean was a guest, I recalled the incident and amazingly the man who had repaired her wing was in the audience.

One Sunday Jean and I were invited to go sailing with Johnny Mant, Peter Dawson and Beverly Sheppard. Although it rained as we picnicked in Manly Cove, Jean was full of fun and laughter and more relaxed than I have ever seen her. A romance began with Beverly Sheppard and they were often seen at Mascot together. Beverly and Bob Smith escorted Jean as far as Bourke when she flew north to try to break the record for the return flight to England. What driving force made her turn her back on romance? We knew she had gone with Beverly to the Mascot Post Office to send a telegram to her fiancé in London, breaking her engagement with him.

After she returned to England, Jean flew the Atlantic in a single-engine 200 hp Percival Gull. She was obliged to carry survival equipment over the Sahara, but at Dakar, she elected to leave it all behind, including a revolver. When asked why she did not take the gun, she replied, 'If I don't get there, I won't need it and if I do, then I'll need this evening dress,' which she had tucked into a spare corner.

In 1936 that old driving force made her tackle the England–New Zealand flight, solo. All Australia tried to stop her because the flight would take her over the stormy Tasman Sea. Even the Governor-General's wife, Lady Gowrie, appealed to her not to take the risk. Jean ignored the pleas and created a record that stood for 44 years. I met her the day she sailed back into Australia from this triumphant flight. Her mother and the Percival Gull aircraft were aboard the boat *Awatea* when it docked in Sydney Harbour. Beverly Sheppard, co-piloting the Stinson airliner from Brisbane, was coming back that evening to meet Jean—but his aircraft never arrived.

Ground parties combed the country between Brisbane and Sydney and forty aircraft covered some 65 000 square miles, during the search. Jean kept looking for the Stinson long after the official search was called off. She flew 5000 miles in 38 hours at her own expense. Nine days later, a young bushman set off alone, on a hunch, into the rugged McPherson Ranges to inspect the burning of a tree. He found the wreckage of the aeroplane and two survivors. The pilots, Rex Boyden and Beverly Sheppard, had been killed instantly. Jean was devastated and refers to it in her book *Alone in the Sky* but gives little indication of her real feelings. Mrs Batten said her daughter never recovered from this tragedy.

Jean became a recluse after Beverly's death, but emerged like a flower to help me with the Air Ambulance in 1970 only to disappear for five years in 1982. In 1987 she was traced through a death certificate to a pauper's grave in Majorca. She had been bitten by a dog and developed septicaemia. Her unclaimed body lay in the Palma morgue for two months before the magistrate ordered it buried.

In 1934, the MacRobertson International Centenary Air Race from Mildenhall, England, to Melbourne took place. First prize was

47

£10 000 and a gold cup. This event brought many international pilots to Australia, including the eventual winners C. W. A. Scott, an ex-Qantas pilot, and his co-pilot Tom Campbell-Black, who had flown in South Africa and Kenya. Tom was a great friend of Beryl Markham who later flew the Atlantic.

Other competitors were the American aces, Roscoe Turner and Clyde Pangborn; Cathcart-Jones and Ken Waller in their Comet; Wing Commander Stodart flying an Airspeed Courier, who asked me if I would return to England with him in an attempt on the record; Jim Melrose in his Puss Moth; and Geoff Hemsworth and Ray Parer, who had also competed in the 1919 Air Race. Jim Mollison and his wife Amy Johnson flew their Comet *Black Magic* only to withdraw from the race at Allahabad (where the famous Indian aviator, J. R. D. Tata, was an air marshall). Another withdrawal, but at Bucharest due to mechanical failure, was the American aviatrix Jacqueline Cochran, whom I was to meet in America several years later. There were 64 entries but only 12 completed the race.

Although very much in the back seat, I was in awe of these world famous pilots as they descended on Mascot. Jean Batten, who had just broken the England to Australia record, was gathered up by the broadcasters to commentate on the race.

The Dutch entered a DC-2 airliner in the 1934 race, piloted by Parmentier and Moll. This was a magnificent entry, and the aircraft competed with several passengers on board. Among them was Thea Rasche, the famous German aviatrix of the 1920s and 1930s. Parmentier and Moll always stepped from their aircraft looking absolutely immaculate, unlike many competitors who often looked haggard. Their only unfortunate incident was a forced landing during a severe storm at Albury. Narromine Aero Club alerted all towns en route to Melbourne that the Dutch aeroplane was in trouble. The residents of Albury immediately swung into action and using their street lights spelt the name of the town by Morse code and directed their cars to the boggy showgrounds so the headlights could light a strip. The aircraft came down safely, was bogged but continued on its way to Melbourne the next day. The Dutch later erected a monument at Amsterdam airport, Schiphol, honouring the people of Albury for their action. I am sure some of the appreciation rubbed off on me when I visited Holland. Small fry that I was, these two pilots received me in 1938 and again in 1939, and were most gracious and helpful.

The Dutch showed considerable astuteness in the air race. They proved to both Imperial and Qantas that they could fly the scheduled airline route between England and Australia considerably faster.

In 1935 I began to wonder what I could do about my future. Pilots were continually proving records could be broken, and a few women were up there with the best of the record breakers. I had used up all my money; I now had a licence to 'fly for hire and reward' but what could I do? There were no jobs for women in aviation. The idea of overnight fame and fortune through record breaking was very attractive and I began studying maps and planning a flight to Japan. It was all a daydream! I had neither the money nor the sponsorship for such an undertaking. Flying had arrived; but I hadn't. Who would want to sponsor a very unimportant 20-year-old girl?

During my training I often spoke with Mr McGillycuddy, the editor of *Country Life* newspaper who was a regular passenger on the Manly ferry. On gaining my licence, the women's editor, Hope Phelps, wrote an article about me and gave me a copy. That paper changed my life. In it was a list of forthcoming country shows and race meetings. I decided that I would go out into the country and try to attract some fare-paying passengers. Others had done it—Kingsford Smith, Arthur Butler, Nigel Love—many pilots seemed to have been barnstorming at some time. Why couldn't I? If only I had an aeroplane!

By now, my father had changed his mind and become quite enthusiastic about my flying. He offered to buy me an aircraft. So, with the kind gesture of my great-aunt Annie Thomas, who gave me £200 instead of leaving it to me in her will, and help from my father, who gave me the same amount, I was finally in the market.

Reg Annabel, the first person with whom I had flown, had recently been killed in his beautiful blue and yellow Moth. His father was tidying up the estate and had a very cheap Moth available for £400. It had been bought by Reg as a wreck and needed rebuilding. I bought it from the estate, and many years later, learned just how historic this aeroplane was.

The Qantas historian, Ron Gibson, told me that it had

originally been flown to Australia from England in 1932 by a 25-year-old Scotsman, Rab Richards. His passenger was Lady (Bee) Chaytor, the wife of Edmund Chaytor of Winton Castle in County Durham. In 1931, Rab was eating breakfast with Lady Chaytor after a very good party, when she suggested they fly to Australia. Although neither of them could fly, they made the decision there and then. Rab went out to Brooklands, learnt to fly and with 70 hours solo under his belt was soon ready to leave for Australia. Bee Chaytor also took lessons but did not achieve solo status, although she managed about 13 hours of dual instruction. She spent her time trying to find a sponsor. A company called 'Beefex' apparently put up some money because Rab called the aircraft *Miss Beefex*. Lady Chaytor's ski clothes, which would protect her from the weather in the open cockpit, made her so bulky that when Rab took off from Brooklands to fly to Lympne, he could not pull the joystick back far enough for normal landing. He very smartly removed her joystick thereby denying her any chance of taking the controls during the flight. Lady Chaytor's trip was cut short in Calcutta where she fell ill and was forced to complete the journey by ship. Without a passenger to worry about, Rab flew on and apparently crossed the Timor Sea at the same height as the flying fish.

He toured throughout Australia and had a wonderful time. He met Lady Chaytor again in Melbourne when she was displaying and promoting foundation garments. After six months in Australia, Rab felt it was time to return, so he decided to sell the aeroplane and sail home via America. Intending to sell the Moth to George Falkiner, Rab left Boonoke station for Sydney to deliver it, but became lost at Bungendore. Seeing a homestead and a suitable paddock, he decided to do a slow run over it to check the surface. Peering over the side, he suddenly looked up to see a hill in front of him. Quickly he tried to turn, but it was too late. The wing hit the ground and a dazed Rab scrambled out of his wrecked machine.

This was the aeroplane I bought, VHU-UTN, and I christened it *Vincere* meaning 'to conquer'. I was determined to carve a place for myself in aviation.

Years later, Michael Vaisey of Hemel Hempstead, England, an enthusiast of the Moth Club of England, decided to rebuild a Gipsy Moth. He advertised all over the world and picked up two original engines in Oregon, United States. One of them was from my Moth. Vaisey is rebuilding the aircraft and it is now registered under its original call sign of G-ABSD, which it carried when Rab Richards left England.

At the time I bought my pride and joy, Johnny Kerr was Chief Instructor at the Aero Club. When I told Johnny of my plans he shook his head and said: 'There is nothing in barnstorming. It has been done to death. All the cream has been taken off the cake. There is no room for women in aviation. The men are finding it a hard enough struggle.' But I had the greatest of all incentives—necessity. If I wanted to stay in aviation, I had to get out and do something.

Despite the gloomy prospect, I was determined to go on tour, but I needed a co-pilot. Luckily, Peg McKillop, who had completed her training at the same time I did, agreed to join me. During her training she had spent many hours at the Aero Club workshop learning about aircraft engines and how to mend fabric. She often said she was too dirty to come into the club for lunch.

Peg had first become fascinated by aeroplanes when living with her grandfather at 'Duntryleague' in the New South Wales country town of Orange. She would race to the tower to wave to every aeroplane that flew over. Sometimes she would ride her pony down to the paddock in which these aircraft landed, and would sit on the fence watching them for hours. In 1927, she spent the summer in Italy and went to see the Schneider Cup Races. It was here that she saw really fast aircraft in action for the first time. This experience fuelled her desire to learn to fly, despite her mother's strong opposition. When Peg turned 21 she inherited a small legacy and immediately came to Mascot, joined the Aero Club and started lessons.

Like me, she would fly with anyone who asked her just to get some extra hours and experience. Peg recalled flying with Scotty Allan in the *Faith in Australia* and told how Scotty had said, in his heavy Scottish brogue, 'Peggy, you are joost like Mr Ulm. You wander off course and I have to make allowance for variation and deviation, joost like Mr Ulm.' On one of their trips they covered the Duke of Gloucester's visit to Canberra. The *Sun* newspaper had taken photographs of His Royal Highness and chartered the *Faith* to take newspapers featuring the photos back to Canberra. However, it had rained heavily and Scotty Allan said the field was too boggy to land, so he ordered that the papers be dropped as he flew over the field. (Peg said she had to be careful that she did not go over the side *with* them!) When they returned to Goulburn the *Sun* people were angry and said they had to go back with another load and *land* them.

On the return flight Scotty told all on board to move back into the lavatory to keep the aircraft's tail down when he landed. As the *Faith* touched down and reduced speed, the tail came up threatening to put the machine over on its nose. However, to everyone's relief, the extra weight held the tail down and the aircraft sank into the bog. It stayed there for three weeks. Meanwhile, Peg and party carried newspapers across the muddy airfield—Peggy attired in a fur coat because of the cold. When the papers had been off-loaded, everybody headed for the Canberra Hotel where a shocked manager ushered them to the back door so they would not be seen by guests going to the Duke of Gloucester's ball.

Peggy was well educated, cultured, and a woman of independent means. She flew purely for fun. This was good news for me because she did not want to be paid! Because she had gone to the exclusive Rose Bay Convent from the age of six, she knew many of the country Catholic aristrocrats: the Rankins of Newcastle, the Rileys, Meaghers, Whiteheads, Fitzsimmons, Fitzgeralds, Daltons, Loneragans, Evans and a host of others. Many of these families took us into their hearts and homes, where they wined and dined us. Their gracious hospitality was overwhelming. So, unlike the men who had barnstormed before us, we often did not have to pay to stay in the 'two bob' hotels, nor buy the customary round of drinks.

At that time, hotels had a monopoly on the sale of liquor and were obliged to provide accommodation as a consequence. The bars were not allowed to sell liquor after 6 pm—resulting in what became known as the 6 o'clock swill. To avoid this 'drought', people would line up and pay for beers to consume after the bar closed. No liquor was sold on Sundays, and only travellers who came more than 50 miles could buy a drink. Drinking in one's room became a solution.

The accommodation was often very primitive with one or two bathrooms to a floor which might have ten rooms. Some of the outback hotels had tin baths and chip bath heaters into which you would feed woodchips, light them, and when the tap was turned on, hot water would flow. Lavatories were downstairs and outside, so the bath was often used to urinate in, with the result that one preferred to bathe under a running tap.

A free cup of tea with biscuits was always provided and if you left your shoes outside the door, they would be cleaned. A favourite prank was to mix the shoes or put a pair of ladies' shoes outside some shy man's door.

Peggy always claims to having been delighted when I asked her to accompany me on the barnstorming trip; she loved to be airborne. During one night flight, she carried a torch so she could see if the slots came out of the top wing. The slots extend to 'grab' the air when you have reached stall speed and she wanted to make sure they were extended! We had some wonderful experiences together and today I appreciate and admire her more than ever. She has been flying almost continuously for 57 years.

CHAPTER 6

At this time there were few aerodromes in New South Wales and so it was important to land as close as possible to the shows and race meetings to attract fare-paying passengers. Wing Commander Bell of the Shell Company helped me in this respect. Because I had chosen to use their fuel, Shell had their local representatives find a paddock and arrange for me to use it. Shell also arranged for some advance publicity, took photographs and generally were quite magnificent. I must have received the maximum possible attention for the minimum amount of fuel. My aircraft only used five gallons an hour, but oil companies had a policy of doing everything they could to further aviation. In this way they were far-sighted beyond the imagination of governments or other industries. The history of aviation could be charted by the lines of empty petrol tins scattered throughout the countryside.

I could not afford linen-backed maps for the trip, so I bought ordinary paper ones—Craig's road maps—then glued cheesecloth on the back to stop them falling apart. They were scaled at ten miles to the inch. We used to mark them off at 20-mile intervals and check landmarks such as railway sidings and road intersections as they appeared. I later flew west of the Darling River with a 40-miles-to-the-inch oil company road map. It was featureless country and, like an animal, I soon developed a sense of direction out of sheer necessity. At that time there were few 'strip' maps put out by the Civil Aviation Department. There was probably one for the Sydney, Brisbane and Melbourne routes, and one from Sydney to Bourke and up to Charleville. They only covered a strip 40 miles wide and the map that showed the area south from Cootamundra didn't even show Australia's highest mountain, Mt Kosciusko. If you wandered off course or got into bad weather, the map was a trap. Charles Kingsford Smith had many maps in the pilots' room with more detail on them and I used to spend time studying these whenever I could.

In 1935, Peg and I set out on the 'First Ladies Flying Tour' in Australia leaving from Sydney for Newcastle. For a cockpit seat, I used a large sponge rubber cushion which Kingsford Smith had discarded from his Lockheed Altair. This cushion enabled me to see out of the cockpit and reach the pedals.

That night we reached Newcastle and stayed with the Rankin family. Archie Rankin was the president of the Newcastle Aero Club. His two daughters, Sue and Margaret, had been at school with Peggy. Vera, Archie's wife, was a charming hostess and there, for the first time, I experienced the luxury, affluence and hospitality of people whose home was always open to their friends. We had not intended to take passengers from Newcastle because it was already well serviced by the Aero Club, but I did take up a few people including the Rankin girls, Phil Parbury and Franz Kohl, a German who was librarian at the local steel works. Unfortunately, Franz was still in Australia during the war and suffered severely because he was a German national.

As we flew over Tamworth, the first official stop on our itinerary, we circled the town several times to announce our arrival. I saw the local fuel agent set off to meet us at the Windmill paddock, which served as an aerodrome. A couple of cars were heading that way too, as were some youngsters on pushbikes and on foot. I suspect they were hoping to see their first crash landing!

At the time, Tamworth had an aero club but no aircraft. It also had a gliding club and one glider. I think it had crashed, but the town did have a few enthusiastic aero club members. Years later I learned how several of them had taught themselves to glide. Using an old car as a tow-vehicle, they would be towed across the paddock fifteen times back and forth to become familiar with the controls. As their confidence increased, they would increase the car's speed to about 35 mph, which enabled the glider to rise a few feet. After a few turns and touchdowns they would eventually reach a low height where they would circle around and around, just like children with model aeroplanes.

The Mayor, who had seen us circling the town, was so delighted to have two young ladies fly in that he gave us a civic reception the next day. As soon as we had finished the scones and tea, he popped us in his car and drove us up the nearest hill to see the view over Tamworth! We did not take many passengers flying, but the enthusiasm of the glider pilots was tremendous. Not only had they untied our aircraft before we arrived the next morning, they had also washed it down. We were very grateful to these young men who included Harold Joseph, Eric Carter and Reg Hannaford. I met Harold again 50 years later. He had been a flight instructor in the Royal Australian Air Force and had flown 44 different types of aircraft. I met Eric 45 years later at the 'Early Birds' (pre-war pilots) meeting. Reg is now an active owner pilot in Coffs Harbour on the north coast of New South Wales. During our stay, the glider club members pooled their funds and presented us with a small koala bear as a mascot. This bear stayed with me for many miles until we parted company while I was flying over a ship in Sydney Harbour to farewell Mr Anton Bakker of KPM Shipping Company. It was 'the done thing' in those days to fly low over a departing ship and throw flowers on to the deck as a farewell gift. My koala bear was the only thing I had in the cockpit so I threw him down. Although aircraft had to fly over Sydney at 1000 feet there were no restrictions over the harbour so we farewelled VIPs from mast level as they sailed away.

It was at Tamworth that I began earning an income from my aeroplane. I had been given £10 a week by Eric Baume, the Editor of *Sun* newspaper to signwrite the word 'Woman' under my aircraft to advertise their new magazine. I was also earning money from fare-paying passengers, and my uncle Will Biddles had sent me £5 as a present. I felt like a millionaire.

Our next stop was Inverell and we arrived on race day, the first the town had held for fourteen years because of drought. We landed in a black soil paddock beside the race course. We took up a number of passengers and I remember the enthusiasm of the children among them. They wanted desperately to fly and Gordon Munro, a well-known local grazier, came over and generously said, 'Take all the kids up. I'll pay for them.' Many young people were introduced to flying at Inverell that day. I wonder how many of them joined the Air Force five or six years later.

That night, Peg and I were invited to the Race Day Ball. The locker of a Gipsy Moth was mainly reserved for our engine covers, tools and the stakes that had to be driven into the ground to tie down the aeroplane every night. Australia had quite a history of aeroplanes being wrecked by freak wind storms. The only room left in the locker was taken up by a tiny suitcase about the size that children take to primary school. Into this case we had each packed a change of clothes, an evening outfit and a few essentials. Out came my crumpled seersucker brown skirt and little lace blouse on to which I had sewn a few bugle beads to make it look a little more feminine. Peg had a blue lace evening dress.

On arrival we were given a programme with a little pencil hanging from it and containing a whole list of names. That's what I call Super Shell service. John Gray, the Shell man, had gone around all these young men and asked them to have a dance with 'those flying girls'. All night long I had handsome young men coming up to me and saying, 'Are you Little Bird or Big Bird, because I have the next dance with Little Bird?' This was the country boys' way of identifying us—Peggy was taller than I, and her baggy flying gear made her appear larger than she was.

Fifty years later I went back to Inverell to speak at a service club and I called on the man who had started East-West Airlines, Arthur Yates. He reminded me that he had danced with me at that Inverell Ball in 1935, and that brought back a lot of memories. Arthur had been an Air Training Corps instructor. After the war he had seen an advertisement offering Avro Ansons for sale at an Air Force base at Narrandera. As a joke, he and some flying colleagues put in a tender for one at £500. To their surprise, they were successful and they made hurried arrangements to have it collected. Arthur called on Bruce Cowan and Sid Marshall to go down with him to inspect the aircraft and fly it. On arriving at the base, the Officer-in-Charge said, 'We have another one there that you could have for £500. So they bought their second Avro and thus began another Australian airline. They called it East-West Airlines and it serviced Glen Innes, Tamworth/Sydney.

Flying west from Inverell for the first time, I saw the vast great open spaces of this flat country. Huge artesian bore drains ran through the land like silver ribbons, and sheep by the thousands dotted the paddocks. From the Moth they looked like grains of rice scattered far and wide. Roly-poly grass raced before the wind, then piled high along the fence lines. Above all was the cloudless blue sky, stretching to the horizon.

Nothing had prepared me for this fabulous sight. The land seemed to stretch to eternity.

Approaching Moree, we chose a claypan on which to land, then went to the Max Hotel, which was famous for its race day parties. We were met by the ever-faithful Shell man and George Falkiner, an enthusiastic airman and possibly Australia's most eligible bachelor at that time. I also discovered that George had been appointed my escort to the Moree Ball that evening!

He had graduated in engineering at Sydney University before taking over his family sheep stud at Haddon Rig—a name synonymous with top quality wool. Like a few country people, George learned to fly and used a Moth to make regular trips to Sydney. Later, he bought one of the first American aircraft purchased in Australia—it was a Waco and the roar of its powerful 350 hp engine was impressive. These sturdy aircraft looked very advanced compared with our little Moths, and they also had a much greater fuel consumption.

George engaged Jerry Pentland, a famous World War I pilot, to fly for him. *Australian Ace* by Schaeder is a book about Jerry, his pranks and his superb aerobatic skills. Later, in New Guinea, he was to rely heavily on his fine flying qualities, before and during the war.

Following World War I, there was a Commonwealth Parade in London and some high-spirited pilots flew in it. Keeping clear of Buckingham Palace, they flew up and down the Thames at no feet nothing and just a few feet above the heads of the parade. One daredevil, however, dived so low over Australia House he terrified the VIPs who were guests of the High Commissioner. A Court Martial and punishment was demanded, but the culprit was safely on a boat on his way back to Australia before any action could be taken. Rumour suggested it was Jerry.

George Falkiner was one of the first people to have the name of his property painted in large letters on the woolshed roof. During floods, aircraft dropping supplies and feed for the sheep would see the name and know exactly where they were. Names on homestead roofs are now an accepted part of the outback.

CHAPTER 7

We continued on our barnstorming tour, flying south to a property called Malaraway, near Bellata. Unfortunately, the perished tyres of my rattletrap Gipsy Moth burst while landing on the black soil plains. We telephoned the Aero Club for replacements and Beverly Sheppard and Bob Smith flew up with a pair of newly designed 'do-nut' tyres—the first to be seen in the West. They cost £5, which meant that it took ten flights to pay for them. We stayed on Malaraway with one of the graziers, Colin Kelman, who had learnt to fly, and his manager. In 1935, it was risking your reputation for two spinsters to stay on a station overnight with two bachelors, but we had no option. When speaking at a function some 50 years later, I met somebody about my age who said, 'Oh yes, we heard about that,' the tone of his voice suggesting that the locals had wondered, and talked about our stay.

Peg eventually married Colin Kelman in England, and in 1936, they established a record when they flew a Monospar aircraft from England to Australia. Peg laughingly says, 'I was the first "expectant" pilot to make this flight.'

After replacing our burst tyres we flew to Burren Junction and stayed at Burren Station with the Fishers who were wonderful hosts. Burren Junction had only a dozen buildings but it sported magnificent, first grade tennis courts. We took up some of the Davis Cup team members who were there for a big tennis match and various other VIPs and enthusiasts including Jim Russell, the sports writer. There was, however, one jack..roo who refused to fly with us because he was not interested in flying. Five years later, he had entered the Air Force and, before the end of the war, had survived a severe Spitfire crash to become one of Australia's most decorated airmen. His name was Bobby Gibbes.

Later, he started an airline in New Guinea, which was called Gibbes Sepik Airways.

Flying was a lot of fun in the early 1930s but because the machines and the facilities were less than perfect, you needed to be able to see the humorous side of things, especially if you earned your living by flying. There are many amusing anecdotes about the experiences of our early bush pilots. I had my fair share while flying 'by the seat of my pants' and these remain in my memory.

I remember well the many instances where people went out of their way to help those of us who had taken to the skies. I recall arriving at Walgett in 1935, for example, where the local Show was already in progress. I was surprised and delighted to see that the black soil plain had been graded. This was very uncommon. It turned out that the Shire Engineer, William Thomas, had graded it especially for us so we could land close to the Show and attract paying customers. At the time I did not know of his gesture and it was not until I was speaking at the Kuring-gai senior citizens' annual meeting in 1986 that his daughter, Mrs Bickerton, told me that her father had gone to the trouble of getting the grader out because he had been anxious to help us.

I also heard that Mrs Ryan, who lived next door to the showgrounds, was very cross about an aeroplane landing so close to her home and had locked the gate to stop the aeroplane landing!

The first charter job that I flew came from the Nevertire district of New South Wales. Wrenford Matthews of Wahroonga station wanted me to fly him north-east to Carinda, which is between the Macquarie and Castlereagh rivers. He wanted to look at some sheep he had on agistment. Peg and I checked over the engine the afternoon before our flight and we didn't finish until after dark. I then organised the necessary maps, ready for my early morning start. When I started the engine in the morning, I noticed the oil pressure took a long time to come up. Choosing to ignore this, I took off and circled Gobabla homestead on my way to pick up Wrenford Matthews. As I was about to straighten up and head for Wahroonga station, the engine coughed and fluttered, and I felt gusts of compression coming back at me. I thought I was on fire! I pulled the throttle back and put down in a steep side-slip on the only available bare ground, an area beside the house, dotted with prickly bushes and foraging chooks.

Fortunately for me, I was not on fire. While working in the dark the night before, we had failed to tighten one of the spark plugs and it had blown out while I was circling above the house.

We fitted a replacement and cleared enough space to take off by dragging out bushes and moving logs. As the space was short and the Moth did not have brakes, I asked two men to hold the wings while I raised enough revs to give me power for a quick take-off. At my signal they let go and soon I was flying off to meet Wrenford. It was my first forced landing and I was a little shaken by the experience, but I did not tell my passenger what had happened when I arrived a little late.

At Carinda I landed in a paddock beside the school. In the early days of aeroplanes it was usual for country district schools to declare a half-holiday when an aircraft was in town, so the children could inspect it. When it was time to go, it was impossible to take off from the paddock in which I had landed because the wind had changed direction. One of the locals, Wal Henderson, offered to tow me with his truck on to the main street, which was a long, dusty, straight road. To get to it, however, we had to negotiate a culvert and, with a man on either side, lift the wings over the white culvert posts.

Not all our intending passengers actually got into the air. One such hopeful was Frank Clune whom we met at the hotel in Nyngan. He used to travel through the country doing people's income tax returns and he was most anxious to fly with us when we went out to the clay pan early one morning. After swinging the propeller for three hours, I still had not been able to start the engine so Frank and his friend finally set off for Bourke in his car. Meanwhile, the local garage mechanic Ray Donahoe took off the magneto to try to find the trouble. Late that afternoon, after repairs were completed, I swung the propeller and, to my great delight, the engine started.

I dared not stop it as we were already due at Pep-O'-Day station. We took off to follow the road but became hopelessly lost, so we landed on a claypan near a homestead to ask the way. Years later, Pat Glenny told me that her brother had seen the aeroplane coming into land and said, 'I'll fix those people. It's probably a jolly salesman landing on OUR claypan to sell me something.' He raced off and drove down to the aeroplane and was flabbergasted when out jumped 'a little girl' almost in tears saying, 'Please, can you show me the way to Pep-O'-Day station, we have to be there before the sun goes down?' He gave us directions and immediately we were in the air again, landing at the station with the aid of car headlights.

At Narromine, south of Nyngan, we discovered one of the best aerodromes in Australia. The railway line leads right in to the airport, which is never boggy even after exceptional rains. We were met there by the President of the Aero Club, Tom Perry, who drove out to greet us. He immediately chartered the aeroplane so that his son Dick could inspect a landing ground he had bought at Dubbo. Peg went off with Dick while I sat and talked with Tom Perry who suggested I should buy an aeroplane with a cabin that would take two passengers and try for charter work. In the meantime, he offered me a job with Western and Southern Airlines at Dubbo.

I was to learn a lot about Tom Perry over the years. He had owned what was the Narromine aerodrome where Ross and Keith Smith had landed. Actually, it was a large paddock on which he ran sheep. They were no trouble to muster with a flight or two over the top! An air pageant had been held there in 1926, and during World War II, it had been a large Air Force base with more than 2000 trainees constantly under instruction. No one paid a penny in rent or landing fees at Narromine aerodrome. It was one of Tom Perry's contributions to the war effort.

Next to the aerodrome he had given, on peppercorn rent, a large area to create the town's golf course. He personally watered every tree on that course by hand.

The golf course and aerodrome are monuments to a fine old gentleman who had the foresight to give his area a landing strip within walking distance of the town. It is still an active airfield and now one of the world's top gliding centres. A former Australian Flying Corps pilot, Bruce Irving, and observer Bowden Fletcher, invited everybody to land at Narromine. Everyone who was anyone landed there—with two famous exceptions—Bert Hinkler and Amy Johnson.

Tom Perry was the main sponsor behind Western and Southern Airlines in an attempt to give the 'west' an airline long before it was ready for such a service. He also financed hard working engineer and Queenslander pilot May Bradford into a Klemm Eagle aircraft and took out a policy on her life.

Tragically, May collided with an aircraft on take-off from Mascot while joy-riding one weekend.

Her undercarriage caught the wing of Peter Hoskin's De Souter aircraft, which was taxiing across her path. She flipped over and burst into flames. All three women on board were incinerated. She was to have been buried as a pauper until Tom Perry stepped in and made sure she had a decent funeral.

By the time we were ready to leave Narromine, Tom had sown the seed as to how I could buy a new aeroplane. However, it was one thing to go barnstorming on a shoestring, using the day's takings to pay for the next day's petrol; now I had to decide whether I dared undertake a big debt when I was not sure about my ability to pay it off. Would people trust a 19-year-old-girl pilot, not just on joy-flights but on the long cross-country hops which were my only chance of making a living out of charter work? Would I be able to talk people who had not flown before into flying with me instead of exhausting themselves on those rough and long drives over bad country roads? Would I be able to stand the worry of knowing that when there were no passengers and no charter work, or when bad weather washed out flying for days on end, I was running more heavily into debt with every wasted day?

A few days later the Moth put on another starting tantrum, which made us more than two hours later than our advertised time of arrival at a country show. I knew then that I had not a hope of staying in the air unless I could get a more reliable aeroplane with a larger passenger capacity. At that time, however, Peg and I were making plans for our second barnstorming tour in the same aircraft.

Between the barnstorming trips, I went to Dubbo at Tom Perry's request. As mentioned earlier, he was the major financier behind Western and Southern Provincial Airlines, which flew a Monospar, the Codock and Gannet aircraft built by Lawrence Wackett. The airlines started a service from Sydney to Dubbo, Narromine, Nyngan and points west. There was no aerodrome at Dubbo, which is why he bought several acres of land almost opposite the present one and had it licensed as an aerodrome. I helped him paint the tops of the fence posts white, and erect a wind sock. Mr Perry then asked me to station myself at Dubbo to sell shares in the company and fly up and down the town daily, over important race meetings, football matches and livestock sales to try to make Dubbo air-minded. I also spoke to the audience at the Roxy Theatre and the local people including the Mayor Mr Duffy who after a month, said to me, 'Little Miss Bird, you are wasting your time. Dubbo does not need an aerodrome. You will never compete with the overnight train journey to Sydney.' Today it is one of the busiest airports in Australia.

Recently, I was speaking to a group at the hospital in Bowral and recounted this story. Afterwards, Charles Krinkel, while moving a vote of thanks, said that he had been a carpenter in Dubbo at the end of the depression and one day the team was told to get out and move some stones off a sheep paddock, because some 'Sheila' (me) was going to land there!

CHAPTER 8

While staying at Bells Hotel in Dubbo, I met Reverend Stanley Drummond and his wife Lucy. He had founded the Far West Children's Health Scheme in 1924 and each year its services were extended. Stanley Drummond had a driving desire to help people, particularly the children who lived outback beyond the reach of medical help.

He had been appalled by the number of youngsters suffering from trachoma, a disease brought on by glare and dust, which gradually destroys sight. Stanley Drummond liaised with Macquarie Street specialists and organised a workable scheme whereby most cases could be brought to Sydney for treatment. While in Sydney they would stay with Mrs E. E. Hill (who later became matron of the Far West Children's Health Scheme).

Stanley Drummond then began to campaign for holdiays for these outback children, most of whom had never been away from the tiny towns in which they had been born, and none of whom had ever seen the sea. The New South Wales' Department of Education agreed to let him have the use of the Manly public school buildings for three weeks during the Christmas vacation and, every year, a group of 11- to 14-year-olds enjoyed a seaside holiday.

When I first met him, the baby health clinics were being established and developed all over New South Wales and Stanley Drummond had organised the use of railway carriages that he converted into mobile clinics, which would be shunted off at the remote sidings. Wherever the railway went, so too did the new baby health techniques and information. Beyond the railheads though, many miles from the nearest doctor or nurse, mothers were rearing their babies alone. The Far West Children's Health Scheme would send sisters out by car to give these families free medical attention and advise them about feeding and caring for their infants. This proved to be very expensive in time and money, as it was common to spend two or three days travelling between stopovers. During summer, the temperature was often over 45°C, and after a storm, cars became bogged and often delayed for days.

As a trial, Stanley Drummond wanted me to take my aeroplane to Bourke and fly the nursing sister on her visits to the tiny settlements and homesteads beyond the rail terminus, many miles to the west. By now Peg had joined me in Dubbo. After hastily reorganising our schedule to allow us to be in Bourke to meet Sister Webb, we began our second barnstorming tour.

There was not a lot of difference between the tours. We were still treated very well in every town we visited. We were shown the sights and invited to all the festivities; and we were still dependent on the Shell man for information on landing grounds. In our determination to choose paddocks close to the showgrounds, we would sometimes abandon suitable fields in favour of paddocks that called for skilful flying, sideslipping in and using the maximum length of the area for take-off.

Everywhere we were greeted by hordes of inquisitive boys who appeared from nowhere after they heard us flying overhead. They were always keen to touch the machine and talk about it, eager to be allowed to help, and if possible, fly in it. Often, when landing in rough paddocks, the slipstream threw up dust, straw and mud like a threshing machine. I remember being at Urana, the Whitehead's beautiful property, and how their boys helped us with the everlasting job of washing the dust off the aircraft to restore her to gleaming silver again.

Here and there we would come across World War I veterans and spend hours sitting on the ground, in the shade of the aircraft's wings, listening to their nostalgic reminiscences of the early flying days. They seemed so old to us then, but now I realise they must have only been in their thirties!

Kingsford Smith barnstorming around the country with the *Southern Cross* certainly inspired a few of the country men to fly. One was Hillston grazier Frank Thomas who, by 1933, had his own Gipsy Moth. Always on the lookout for a means of using it, Frank obtained a job with the Mackay Expedition to Central Australia in 1935, only to have it wrested from him by Beverly Sheppard, who said he would do it for nothing. Such was the competition for experience in those days. Frank Thomas later joined Qantas, flying as co-pilot and then captain. After the war he disappeared while crossing the Indian Ocean in a Lancastrian on a regular passenger flight.

Between country shows in the south, we would fly back to Arthur Butler's hangars at Cootamundra for maintenance. His two reliable engineers, Williams and Weatherall, were always willing to help us and this was a great comfort when we were touring. There were only a couple of incidents during our barnstorming days when people were uncooperative. One was at Barmedman when the Governor of New South Wales was due to arrive. The oilman had been chosen for the honour of driving the viceregal party and did not want to take our petrol out to the flying field. He simply dumped it by the fence and drove off. Everybody else in the town was lined up waiting to see the Governor so, without helpers, Peg and I had to heave the four-gallon tins up on top of the aircraft ourselves. As we were pouring it some of the petrol splashed on to Peggy's arm. There was no water available for her to wash it off and in the searing sun her skin became painfully blistered and burnt.

The other incident was the theft of our fuel. Owing to the Gipsy Moth's temperamental engine we would often be late arriving at a destination. On one particular Saturday afternoon the Shell representative, Ray Highett, left petrol in four-gallon tins at Giralambone, a tiny settlement north-west of Dubbo. By the time we arrived, somebody had pinched it! However, these incidents were certainly overshadowed by the kindness and generosity shown by almost all the people who lived in the country at that time.

In Wagga we flew the most passengers we had ever flown in one day—101 joy-flights! As there was a long queue for most of the day, we took off, flew around the showground, over the town and down again. Nobody ever got their money's worth when we were busy. However, many people were terrified at just being in an aeroplane. They did not know whether it was a flight of five minutes or an eternity! One thing was certain, they were your friends for life once you got them back on the ground again.

We rarely took days off, but one day Peg and I decided we would go to the picnic races at Hay. Before we set out I received an urgent telegram requesting me to pick up Dr Lethbridge from

67

Narrandera and fly him to the hospital in Hay to attend a seriously ill heart patient. Two return trips were required, so it was almost five hours' flying. Approaching Narrandera, I could see the expanse of water, which was the flooding areas in the Riverina. It was a controversial topic at the time. Many people predicted a disastrous future, but it is now the great rice field of Australia.

A month before we were due at Bourke to meet Sister Webb, we arranged to go to the air pageant in Narromine and enter the Moth in the Derby. Recapturing the atmosphere of these pageants is difficult. They were tremendous fun, incredibly exciting and everybody who was deeply committed to flying seemed to be there. Narromine had been a base for flyers since the early days of aviation and, as early as 1926, could boast that it had 3000 people and 1000 cars at its first pageant. In 1935 many different types of aircraft were entered in the events. Among the now museum pieces were a Demon, Wapiti, DH89, Dragon, Airspeed Courier, Monospar, Curtiss Robin, a De Soutter with a Gipsy engine and another with a Hermes engine, a BAM Swallow, Westland Widgeon, several Avians and a Genairco.

I entered my machine in the closed circuit aerial derby, which was one of the funniest races in which I have ever competed. Each contestant was required to state his aircraft's cruising speed and a time was allocated by the handicappers. It appeared that most entrants understated their cruising speed and the air was full of aircraft throttled back almost to danger point. Squadron Leader D. E. Stodart, RAF, flying an Airspeed Courier monoplane, won the event and Peggy and I came second. Peggy was in the front cockpit with a stop-watch begging me to throttle back further!

I was delighted with our success, although an examination of the results would indicate that I told the second smallest 'lie'.* I brought my aircraft across that finishing line throttled back almost to stalling point in my efforts not to finish before the allotted time. It was both fun and a serious attempt to run a genuine air race. At many other pageants the winner's name was drawn out of a hat before the race started and the other contestants were honour-bound to fly around in circles, if necessary, to avoid crossing the finishing line before the already

---

* We had all exceeded our speeds, but George Falkiner, the winner, had exceeded his the most.

elected winner. This was to avoid the danger of aircraft overtaking one another.

Peggy and I were presented with a silver cup as our trophy and the general view was that it should be filled with champagne at the Narromine Hotel the next day. Tom Perry, President of the Club, vetoed the suggestion claiming that Sunday was an unsuitable day for such a celebration.

While we were at Narromine, Tom Perry took me to see the manager at the Bank of Australasia to arrange finance for my badly needed new aircraft. I did not understand guarantees, or even finance for that matter, but realised that Tom Perry was going to be my guarantor. He drew up an 'agreement' in his own handwriting, and although I remember only parts of it, it stated that he could use the aircraft with me as his pilot if he should wish to do so (which he never did). He later took out an insurance policy on my life, which would have covered his guarantee if I killed myself in an air crash.

Years later, after I had sold my aeroplane and paid off the debt, I still wrote to Tom Perry. I never flew over Narromine without calling in to see him. He was a dear man and nobody will ever know how many people he helped. Our friendship was to last until his death in 1954.

Three days before my twentieth birthday Peggy and I set out for Bourke on a flight I will never forget. Flying from Hillston, a distance of 240 miles, the last 130 miles was country over which we had not flown before. I had heard a lot about the great plains west of the Bogan River and east of the Darling River, but I was not prepared for the sea of timber which I had to cross first. It stretched as far as the eye could see in every direction. There were no landmarks to guide us and not even a hint of a landing field if an emergency arose. I thought of the last instruction on the 'Regulations for Operations of Aircraft, commencing January 1920'* which read: 'If an emergency occurs while flying, land as soon as possible.' But where?

---

* These regulations included a list of twenty-five 'do's' and 'don'ts' for pilots. Many of them are still relevant today. Modern aviators would be amused at two of them: 'Don't take the machine into the air unless you are satisfied it will fly' and 'Pilots will not wear spurs while flying'!

As our flight progressed, the trees moved below us like a dark sea. No roads broke the mantle of green. As we flew northwards we crossed a railway line running east/west, so somewhere to starboard lay civilisation. A few tracks crossed our path as we looked down from that lonely sky. Perhaps we'd see Cobar in an hour before heading into the vastness again. What a relief it was to suddenly be out of the timber and over the black soil country that heralded the approach of the Darling River. For years the Darling can be nothing but a sluggish stream between high banks; then the rains come, and almost overnight, parts of the river will be very wide. It is also a frontier between what people who live out there call the 'inside' and the 'outside'. To the city dweller, Bourke may seem the absolute back of beyond, but to the many who live hundreds of miles beyond it to the west, Bourke is practically synonymous with city life, although it is 487 miles north-west of Sydney. The locals speak with a faintly pitying air of some neighbour who has moved to Bourke, Nyngan or Nevertire, as having 'gone inside'.

There was something very soft and welcoming about those black soil plains after hours spent above the dense timber. As we flew in over the tall gum trees that fringe the river's main channel, the sun was going down in a brilliant blaze across the town.

The next morning, leaving Peggy in Bourke, I took off with Sister Webb on my first Far West Children's Health Scheme flight. Sister Webb had been an Australian Army Nurse during World War I, and had worked in the far west for many years. I shall never forget how brave she was that day. She loathed flying and certainly had no desire to go by air. I packed her into the Moth's front cockpit with baby scales at her feet and clinic equipment stacked all round her. We took off from Bourke and headed south-west, flying low above the meandering Darling River to Louth.

I had been told that Louth had a good aerodrome close to the town where I could land, but it turned out to be a small paddock, thickly dotted with paddymelons and rabbit holes. I looked for the wind sock so that I could gauge the wind direction and saw it hanging listlessly in the still air. As I came into land, however, it stood on its end in a swirl of red dust, caught by a willy-willy, and all I could do was to skirt the field and wait for the wind to pass.

Sister Webb and I were met by the local policeman and escorted to the hotel where we unpacked her clinic equipment and set up in the sitting room beneath the pictures of highland cattle, flamingos and the proprietor's family portraits. While she weighed the babies and counselled their mothers, I distributed books and comics to the older children. The schoolteacher had declared a half-day holiday so that everybody could inspect our aeroplane.

We left for Urisino in the late afternoon. Our destination was 70 minutes flying time away. As we took off towards the west, I realised that this was the loneliest stretch of country across which I had ever flown. Flying into the 'never never', it was imperative to intercept the Bourke-Wanaaring road. The road was an important landmark, the lifeline that would lead us to Urisino.

Spiralling willy-willies were abundant in the sky and the turbulence from the thermals threw our Gipsy Moth about like a paper toy. For a moment I thought of the dramatic event in 1930 when Hitchcock and Anderson, trying to find Kingsford Smith who was lost in the north-west, had landed in country like this and died of thirst. It never occurred to me to carry water, and yet that is what had cost them their lives. There were no roads or tracks if you had to force-land in this country. It would be like looking for a needle in a haystack, and even if you were found in time, it would not be worth salvaging the aircraft from the scrub.

I listened to the purr of the engine and banished such thoughts from my mind. 'Keep your eyes out for that road,' I said to Sister Webb, 'it should come up on our right.' If I missed it, what would be the next landmark? The Broken Hill/Tibooburra Road. Would I have enough fuel to reach it? No, I must edge north and pick up that road then follow it out to Urisino station.

Navigating with only my compass and watch, I waited anxiously for the road to appear. I knew this was the country where Mrs Ernie Jackson had died. She contracted pneumonia after the birth of her fifth child. They put her on a mattress in the back of a truck and started out for Bourke, 144 miles away over incredibly bad roads. At Wanaaring, still 100 miles west of Bourke, her condition had deteriorated so much that she died. Mrs Jacksons's death was one of the reasons why Stanley Drummond wanted me to station myself in that part of the country. He knew an aircraft could have brought her to hospital in an hour.

71

This was also the country that had deceived several contestants in the 1934 Air Race and later the American pilots during the war, throwing them miles and precious hours off course. It was a hazard to all pilots, without radio or navigational aids, who were not familiar with the area. I was getting anxious after the first 30 minutes, when with great relief I spotted the road. I followed it over Wanaaring, and on to Urisino station.

This station was the most surprising place in the west. After landing the Moth we walked along the bare track to the homestead, which is surrounded by a 9-foot high corrugated-iron fence. When you open the gate, however, you feel that you have walked straight into the Garden of Eden. The fence had been built to keep out the drifting sand. Inside were smooth green lawns, clipped hedges, fruit trees, flower beds and vegetables, which had been watered every day by thousands of gallons of water pumped up from artesian bores.

Urisino had been taken up by Edward Killen in 1884 when the only way of travelling into Bourke was by horse-team with a change of horses sent in advance with a station hand to wait at Tinapagee and Kerribee. I thought of the courage of women like Killen's wife Annie, who had left a comfortable home in Melbourne to raise a family three days' difficult travelling away from doctors, hospitals, post offices and stores. In the days when I used to land there, Urisino was a million and a quarter acres. The property was managed by a charming, but shy, bachelor, George Henderson. Today it has been divided into dozens of smaller properties, but the home station remains practically unchanged. A fine all-weather landing strip has replaced the rough paddock where I first landed.

On my next visit George Henderson told me: 'Never land on this property without water.' On the day we landed, Urisino station was deserted. Everyone was out searching for a missing Aboriginal tracker. When found, he was 'swimming' in the sand, delirious with thirst in a temperature well over 40° Celsius. Like many who have died in a desert, he had imagined the sand was water. George gave me a large unbreakable flask and from then on, I never flew without it filled with water. In winter, I also carried emergency rations of raisins, barley sugar and chocolate.

From Urisino, Sister Webb and I set out by car on a 180-mile round trip to visit 40 children on lonely homesteads. She made this trip every six weeks in a car provided by Urisino station.

I was amazed by my first sight of these outlying settlements, and by the primitiveness of the living conditions. We saw families in their corrugated-iron shacks on stony ridges, without a bush or tree to break the monotony. The landscape was a little better around the sub-artesian bores where the bore-keepers' families lived. At some bores, 100 000 gallons of water were drawn up each day. There would be a few trees here and the birds would gather close to the water. The galahs were not in pairs or dozens, but in hundreds. We would see a grey cloud of them ahead of us, clustered around the water. As we approached, they would fly off, and the grey cloud would turn to pink as the birds wheeled and banked.

The heroism of some of the outback women was inspirational. Their courage was sustained year after year in terrible conditions. They had no help, conveniences, proper diet or holidays. Many of them took great pride in their homes, trying to keep them spotlessly clean despite the eternal, blowing sand. One woman on whom we called said she had swept the house three times since breakfast and asked us to excuse the state of it! 'You know how it is,' she said, 'the whole country's been blowing through it since early morning.' She was proud of her little house and the 'white rosewood' furniture, which she and her husband had made out of the wood from kerosene cases.

After we completed our round trip by car, we flew from Urisino to Hungerford, a township that straddles the border between New South Wales and Queensland. Here I realised the difficulty the sisters had in counteracting the prejudices of the older people in the outback who had brought their children up on bread and salt meat and were proud of it. They could not see much sense in the new ideas the clinic sisters were trying to introduce. 'I never had nothing of those things,' they would say, 'but look at my Johnny and my Sam—they're fine men.' And they were fine men—tough, resilient and hard-working, but their stamina may have been greater and they might have had some of their own teeth beyond their twentieth birthday if they had had good fruit, vegetables and regular medical and dental attention. All that the clinic sisters could do was to try to influence the younger people. By encouragement and understanding over the years, the health of these isolated children gradually improved.

At Hungerford I made the mistake many pilots make once in a lifetime—I left the throttle of the machine open when I went round to swing the propeller. I do not know why I was not chopped down before I could get out of the way; but I know I must have done a fast sprint as I raced after the aircraft, jumped in and closed that throttle. The Moth would not have been worth salvaging if she had crashed into the trees beside the landing ground, 135 miles beyond Bourke. To have taken her, rattling back to civilisation on a truck, would have finished what remained of her.

From Hungerford we flew south-east to Yantabulla, my first experience of trying to follow a disappearing road. Prevailing winds cover much of the country with drifts of sand and, from the air, it is impossible to see some of the roads. Just outside Yantabulla there were swamps filled with mosquitoes that bred prolifically after the rainy season. Their constant biting often killed young goats and horses.

The policeman's wife at Yantabulla made us a cup of tea when we landed that day in a temperature of 45° Celsius. 'You know,' she said, 'it's absolutely wicked to send people with young children out here. We can only get fresh meat if one of the properties around will supply it because the town is too small to support a butcher's shop.' She and her family were also denied fresh fruit and vegetables. They were available in Bourke and Dubbo more than 200 miles away, but the freight costs were prohibitive. She brought her children up on bread, milkless tea and salt meat. Those with properties could kill their own fresh meat and grow vegetables, but it was a different proposition for the public service people there.

That day we were able to do something to help. The aeroplane was full of beautiful fruit, which the Urisino people had given us to take back to Bourke. We emptied it out for the Yantabulla policeman's little children and their friends, together with the emergency iced-water ration from the vacuum flask. That was a wonderful treat: ice was something quite unknown in Yantabulla. Because there was no electricity, there was no refrigeration except for the very Australian canvas water-bag, which hung on the verandah in the hot wind.

About 10 miles out of Bourke, I saw my first wild camel. It was lying beside a fence and I went down low to have a good look. The animal did not seem worried by the aircraft, it just turned and looked at me mournfully. Back at Bourke I told Peg about the camel, whereupon she leapt into the aircraft, took off to see the creature and flew over it at such a low level that it was driven to stand up and make protesting faces. Even today camels live wild in inland Australia, descendants of those brought by Afghans in the 1860s and later years, to carry goods in outback areas.

With the completion of that tour for the Health Scheme, our second barnstorming tour also ended. Peggy and I now headed south-east for home.

My last flight in the Moth was when I took a jackeroo, Dal Mein, over a polo field in Sydney, but the engine packed up and we had to force-land at Mascot. I felt sad putting her down. She was up for sale now because my new aircraft was almost ready for me to take delivery. The Moth would have to find a new home. In many ways she had been a brute and there had been times when I almost thought I would have to light a fire under her to warm her up on some icy mornings when she would not start. But Peggy and I had made two successful tours in her. We had had an enormous amount of fun and we had learnt about flying the hard way—and perhaps the best way of all.

CHAPTER 9

I was in Sydney for a month awaiting delivery of my new aircraft and finalising my arrangements with the Far West Children's Health Scheme. Although Reverend Stanley Drummond and other organisers were impressed with the success of our first aerial clinic tour, they could not afford to buy and maintain an aeroplane. The plan was that I should station myself at Bourke and they would pay me a retainer of £200 per year and guarantee me work of another £200 to have my aircraft available to carry out their clinics in the more remote areas. It would start as a six month trial, and because the Far West Children's Health Scheme was paid an annual subsidy by the Commonwealth government, no-one would be out of pocket if the trial was unsuccessful.

My operation as an air ambulance and clinic service was to take precedence over everything else. However, to make ends meet, I also had to take on whatever charter work I could find. It was obvious that I could not take an aircraft that cost £1700 out there and maintain, fuel, hangar and fly it on a total annual income of £400. As I had come to know the people, conditions and country on my two barnstorming trips, I was hopeful that I could pick up enough work to keep myself going.

Aviation jobs were very hard to come by and at least this job would keep me in the air. In making this decision I became the first woman to operate an aircraft commercially in Australia. I do not feel it was a great achievement, I just had to do it. The other women who had taken out commercial licences had no need to make a living. Also, having seen the conditions under which the outback women were rearing families, I was deeply in sympathy with what Stanley Drummond and his people were trying to achieve.

The ship carrying my Leopard Moth eventually arrived from England, and there is only one word to describe the way she looked—magnificent. She was a high-winged monoplane with a French-grey fuselage, silver wings and scarlet stripe, struts and undercarriage. There were two passenger seats, side by side in the back of the cabin, and a bucket-type seat up front for the pilot. They were upholstered in high-grade grey leather, which had a wonderful smell. The cabin was carpeted in the same colour. The Leopard had a generous luggage locker, an extraordinary luxury compared with the tiny one in the Moth. There was also a cabin-heating system and air-chutes for ventilation. After months of flying the Moth in helmet and goggles, with my head and shoulders out in the burning sun or the freezing wind, I could see that the comfort of the Leopard was going to be heavenly. Her cruising speed was 120 miles per hour compared with the Moth's 80 miles per hour.

I only had a few days to learn to fly her. Major Murray-Jones of the de Havilland Aircraft Company, which had built the Leopard, gave me a few circuits and much valuable advice about how her performance might vary in the heat and rarefied air out west. I later learned that the de Havilland company was very concerned about me taking the Leopard up to Bourke during summer. Two things worried them. They knew I was not very experienced and they knew that the aircraft's performance would fall off in hot weather.

In those last days just before I left Sydney for my second trip to the west, the appalling news came through that Sir Charles Kingsford Smith and Tommy Pethybridge were missing in the *Lady Southern Cross* somewhere over Rangoon. They had left Lympne Airport, London, for Australia on 6 November 1935, determined to make the attempt despite the fact that Kingsford Smith had bad influenza. They knew that if they postponed the flight they would be running into the monsoon season. They took off from Allahabad on 7 November, and Jimmy Melrose, who was also flying to Australia, reported seeing what he thought were the lights of Kingsford Smith's Lockheed Altair about 150 miles south-east of Rangoon at 1:30 am the following day.

If Jimmy Melrose saw the aircraft, and he was sure he did, then he was the last person to do so. Months later a barnacle-encrusted undercarriage structure, axle and tyre were found washed up on Aye, a 700-foot island jutting straight up from

77

the water in the midst of a low-lying archipelago. They were taken to Rangoon and then to America where they were positively identified as having come from the *Lady Southern Cross*.

Jack Kingsford Smith, who was only twelve years younger than his famous uncle, told me that after extensive enquiries they discovered Smithy had been following airline strip maps that did not show the islands in the Bay of Bengal. Presuming Smithy came down to follow the coastline because of bad weather; he would not have known the island of Aye was in his path.

Months after his disappearance, Jack Hodder, manager of a Malayan tin mine, climbed to the top of the island and found evidence of blue paint where he presumed the Altair cut through the trees and plunged into the sea.

None of this was known of course, when the news was first heard in Sydney. We only knew that Charles and Tommy Pethybridge were overdue. As the days passed, any hope that they might be found alive dwindled away.

People have often asked me what Smithy was like. He was a jovial man and liked playing jokes on people. He enjoyed a drink with the boys and strumming his ukulele. Women threw themselves at his feet as they do to most famous men including stars and politicians. Working in the hangar with him for eighteen months, I learned to admire and respect him.

Kingsford Smith was outgoing and very generous. He was philosophical and showed no signs of bitterness when he lost the Singapore–Australia mail route and failed to secure the Tasman contract. He had flown that ocean six times, circumnavigated the world, saved the airmail several times, including the rescue at Alor Star and Timor, and broken every record in Australia with his Altair. Smithy crossed the Pacific from California to Australia, as well as crossing it a second time from west to east in that single-engine aircraft.

Kingsford Smith was a great aviator and part of the breed of young, courageous and high-spirited fighter pilots who returned from World War I, determined to fly for a living. They became 'daredevils' of the air—Kingsford Smith even performed wing walking! These Australian Flying Corps (AFC) pilots were concerned with building solid, reliable, safe aviation. Kingsford Smith could see the potential in aviation. The vastness of Australia could only be likened to the situation in America, yet we had neither the rail nor road services of that country;

Kingsford Smith saw that aviation was the logical solution to our distances.

It was with a heavy heart that I packed my clothes and maps into the Leopard and headed west once again.

Before taking off it was necessary to add ballast to keep the tail down. The machine had been designed for a heavier weight than my 100 pounds. I can remember feeling very lonely as I climbed to cross the Blue Mountains at 6000 feet and looked back to see nothing but the tail of the Leopard Moth following me. I had done only two hours flying time in my new machine when I set out from Sydney. She was soon to become my companion though, and whenever I felt lonely or had nothing to do I would walk to the aerodrome and clean her. The Leopard must have been the most spotless aeroplane in the skies.

My first worry as soon as I landed at Bourke was to find some sort of shelter for my precious aeroplane. I could not bear to leave my aircraft out in all that awful Bourke weather, remembering how three Air Force machines, tied down there on the airfield, had been wrecked by a windstorm. Sudden gusts and freak winds of high velocity were common.

By early afternoon I had found a man who agreed to put up a hangar within four days. Unfortunately for me, though not for the graziers, it started to rain the next day and work on my hangar was held up. Several times during that time, when I saw the windstorms approaching, I went out to the aircraft and sat in her until they had passed, just to keep her firmly on the ground. As though my weight would have made the slightest difference!

By the time the hangar was finished, the poor little Leopard Moth had spent several days in a scorching sun that made her wings and fuselage so hot you could not touch them. This started the shrinking of her wooden frame, which was the fate of all wood and fabric aeroplanes in those high temperatures. Years later, the Civil Aviation Department put rigid restrictions on wooden aircraft in these climates.

After arranging accommodation for my aircraft, I found a room at Fitzgerald's Hotel in the town. I shall always be grateful to Mrs Fitzgerald, because when she heard what I was doing she offered me full board for only £2 a week. That meant a great deal to me, especially as I had no charter work lined up, and in a few days, would have to pay £70 for my hangar. The room was very small and looked out to the east over a fine vista of corrugated-iron roofs. That tiny room was to be my home for more than nine months.

In 1935 it was unusual for young girls to live on their own at country hotels. Hope Phelps, a *Country Life* reporter, told me that a grazier's wife who had heard that I was living at the hotel turned to her one day and said, 'But is she respectable?' The way I dressed must have added to her suspicion that I was not altogether respectable. I only had a few clothes and had to look after them because I knew I would not be able to afford new ones for several years. So, when doing engine checks and washing the dust and insects off the Leopard Moth, I wore shorts in summer and overalls in winter. The sight of me walking in shorts from the hotel to the flying field apparently shocked some of the more staid citizens.

I also used to wear a topee because I found it by far the most practical headwear in that heat. I remember the standing joke of the manager of Hale's stores, next door to the hotel. He would be doing his chores early each morning as I walked past on my way to the aerodrome and his greeting was always the same: 'Good morning, Hat. Where are you taking that little girl?'

In the country, people's keen interest in their neighbours makes them kind, warm and hospitable. I do not suppose there is anywhere in the world where people are friendlier, or make you feel more welcome, than in the outback. They make friends easily and do not forget them. Many times I landed on a property perhaps only to ask my way, stayed half an hour and made friendships that have lasted a lifetime.

It may sound strange that a pilot should land at an isolated homestead to ask the way. However, it was often necessary in those days. There were no aviation charts, only road maps showing bush tracks. The overland telegraph line was one of the few landmarks out there. The line was cleared on either side so it could be seen from the air, and this line saved many lives. If you were lost you looked for it; if you were out of fuel you would come down beside it, scale up a post or throw a rope over the iron post and cut the wire. This usually brought a linesman out within a day or two to find you and the break.

Maybe I took a lot of chances in those days flying over vast, waterless, seemingly uninhabited areas, often without anyone in the world having any idea where I was or where I was heading.

Today the movements of aircraft are controlled by regulation, and pilots are not allowed to take off into the blue without saying where they are going and what time they will be at their appointed destination.

Poor Sister Webb! When we set off on the clinic round—Bourke, Louth, Urisino, Hungerford, Yantabulla, Ford's Bridge—I tried to assure her that flying in the Leopard would be so much more comfortable than in the Gipsy Moth that she was bound to enjoy it. However, the weather was usually hot and the air was as turbulent as a bucking horse. Once, when we landed back at Bourke, she said to me, 'I can tell you one thing, if ever I go home to England, I will go by ship!'

That first Christmas in the west was memorable. By the end of the year I had seen enough of the country to know that children brought up in such great heat, discomfort and isolation were missing many of the simple treats and pleasures that other, more fortunate children, took for granted. Sister Webb and I discussed how many of these children had never seen Father Christmas or even received Christmas presents. It seemed sad that they should be deprived of traditional Christmas excitement.

I decided to do something about it and approached people in Bourke who gave me a few shillings towards some gifts. I also told George Henderson, the manager at Urisino station, and together with his station hands and jackaroos we raised five pounds. Armed with a list of the children and their ages I triumphantly headed for Bourke to buy whatever toys were available from Mr Rodda's tiny store. Christmas stockings had been a thrill of my own childhood, so I wrote to Nestlés asking for a donation of 40 stockings. I was overjoyed when they promptly arrived in the post.

Another change was now to be made in the clinic arrangements for the Far West Children's Health Scheme. With my aircraft stationed at Bourke, it had been decided not to send the clinic train there any longer, but to open a clinic in Bourke run by Sister Silver who would do the regular aerial clinic tour with me in the Leopard.

I asked Margot Silver if she would like to come on the special Christmas trip and she gladly agreed. We were to fly to Urisino, pack all the Christmas presents into a car which the station would lend us, and make a tour of more than 100 miles to distribute them. It was a boiling hot day with the temperature at 45°C when we packed the Leopard with the presents, not forgetting the Father Christmas costume I had borrowed from one of the Bourke stores. I never weighed anything I put into this aircraft and I have no doubt the designers would have been shocked to know how often she was overloaded. As long as I could close the door it was fine with me. I did not realise until years later how foolish this was and how overworked my guardian angel had been.

I think we had three punctures on the part of the trip we did by car and there was a blinding dust storm all the way. Sister Silver deserved a medal for the time she spent in that hot Father Christmas costume at each homestead, but the reactions of the children made it all worthwhile.

Vera Hamilton, a writer for the *Sydney Morning Herald* social pages, had heard about our Christmas tour and wired me requesting exclusive coverage. She was expecting me to write the article, but because she did not make contact with me again, I did not do anything more about it. In those days it was fashionable for women to read the social news and then pass the gossip on to the men in the evenings. But I had little understanding of the value of publicity in 1935.

When Margot Silver and I returned to Urisino that night, we dined with the manager and his staff. She did not know that she would marry the man sitting opposite, Charles Weiss, and become mistress of two famous cattle stations, Mount Margaret and Brunette Downs. Here, Margot hostessed many distinguished guests. They dressed for dinner every night and, as one employee said, 'We would have worn tiaras if we had them!'

In emergencies I acted as an aerial ambulance, which made a lot of difference to the people in remote areas. Before my flights, sick and injured people were driven hundreds of miles. One accident, which occurred before the aerial ambulance was available, involved a 15-month-old boy. He was in a sulky with his mother when something startled the horse and it bolted, overturning the sulky and dragging it behind. The child was thrown out and hit by a flying hoof, suffering a deep gash to his head. The boy's father had to saddle a horse and ride 32 miles to Urisino to borrow a car to take him to a doctor. But the rains had started. The roads were flooded and for a week the car could not get through. This child's life was saved—but others were less fortunate.

The emergency trips made it worthwhile being stationed at Bourke. I took patients requiring urgent attention to their nearest hospital; others needed to get to Dubbo so they could catch the overnight train to Sydney where they would receive specialist attention. My passengers also included people who urgently needed to get to the city to see relatives who were seriously ill or dying.

Jim Russell, a grazier, claimed I saved his life when I flew him to Wilcannia Hospital when he was seriously ill with pneumonia. He was stranded for several days before a boundary rider happened to ride by and found Jim's wife and children nursing him. She could not drive the car and the children were too young to ride for help.

I also remember a call coming in one Sunday afternoon for me to fly out to Springdale station, beyond Wilcannia, and pick up an urgent haemorrhage case and fly her to hospital. With one hand, the officer on duty at the telephone exchange was putting through calls to get me more information about how to get there and where the available landing ground was, and with the other he was ringing private numbers all over Bourke trying to find the Shell man to tell him that I needed fuel immediately for my flight.

That patient, Gladys Linnet, approached me many years later and said, 'I would not be here, nor would these three children if it hadn't been for you and your aeroplane.' My eyes filled with tears as I remembered the case: I had raced the daylight to Wilcannia to pick up the patient and doctor. I can remember my anxiety at the size of the paddock that I had to land in and the stockyard fence that the men removed in minutes so that I could have a longer run for take-off. As it all came back to me I realised afresh what a worthwhile job Stanley Drummond had given me to do.*

In these emergencies I was given every help by the local telephone exchange. The operators were wonderful; they relayed

---

* In 1985, when speaking to a group of retired people at Mowell Village, Castle Hill, a gentleman in the audience stood up and said, 'I was the padre who helped Dr Cole lift Gladys Linnet out of your aeroplane at Wilcannia fifty years ago.' His name was Rev. Laurence Lambert and until then I had not known it.

messages and when they struck difficulties, in very wet weather for instance, they would try every possible way of getting through. To contact a place only a couple of hundred miles away it was sometimes necessary to go around as much as 1500 miles of communications via Sydney, Melbourne, Adelaide, Broken Hill and Wilcannia.

As the months went by those western plains which at first had looked dead level, featureless and difficult to navigate in, were to become so familiar that the inadequacy of my little oil company maps no longer mattered.

Charter work is inconsistent. You can go for days with hardly any work and then everyone wants you at once. On busy days it was nothing for me to fly out from Bourke early in the morning with a passenger, have breakfast at Brewarrina, fly to Cunnamulla for morning tea and be back in Bourke again by lunch. That was a round trip of about 380 miles and involved 3½ hours flying time. There was every chance that I would be doing about the same distance again in the afternoon. I became familiar with the landing grounds—the ones where you had to watch for sheep and cattle, others where you had to come in low over the trees, the natural clay pans, and Yantabulla where I landed among squashing and popping paddymelons.

I was continually breaking new ground too. I once had to land beside a homestead in a paddock where nothing larger than a cockatoo had landed before. In the outback you not only had to be your own engineer, booking clerk, weather prophet and luggage porter, you needed to be a psychologist as well, able to judge during a long distance telephone call whether the person you were talking to was a cautious, pessimistic or a wildly optimistic type. What appears to one person to be a large, obstacle-free landing area with a smooth surface can turn out to be a sloping piece of ground, pockmarked with rabbit holes and carved out of tall timber.

Whenever I had to land at a homestead I had never visited before, I would ask that the worst holes and stumps be marked with cloth or paper and, when I was overhead, that someone would run their car over the intended strip at 40 miles per hour so that I could see how much the vehicle bounced and swerved. This told me what the surface was like and gave me a stump-free track on which to land. Sometimes I would ask them to lay a bed sheet on the ground to mark the spot. I now think of all those sheets the poor women had to wash! I would also ask that when they saw the aeroplane, they light a small smoky fire to give me wind direction. Unfortunately, they would normally light it when they heard the aircraft, and by the time I arrived the fire had gone out.

One of my worst experiences was the day I flew Eric Bartlett out to inspect stock on a property beyond Hungerford on the New South Wales/Queensland border. Maps were inadequate and the advice I had been given by telephone was to intercept and fly along the 600-mile dog-proof border fence for 30 miles west, turn and then fly five miles north. This, I was told, would bring us over the small homestead we were looking for among the mulga trees. Apparently I overestimated my speed and flew over a house where people were waving energetically. So I looked for the marker indicating where they thought I could land.

I forgot my flying instructor's words: 'When in doubt, don't . . .' and, in desperation, picked a clearing between trees that my approach showed only too clearly had stumps everywhere. I went around again, said a quick prayer and put the Leopard down with my hand-brake partly on before my wheels touched the ground. As soon as they touched I locked the wheels and then eased the brakes for a split second as one wheel went over a mound of earth, which should have overturned us. I jammed on the brakes again and pulled up 8 yards from a big gidgee tree—and came very near to having a wing lopped off. It was a crazy place to land and I should have had more sense.

I had come down five miles short of my goal! The people had not been signalling for us to come in at all, they were simply waving out of sheer pleasure at seeing us up there. They had never seen an aeroplane out that way before. It did not occur to them, even when they saw us circling, that we were going to try to land.

We all agreed on one thing, some clearing would have to be done before we could take off again. As the day cooled down all hands turned out to chop down small trees, level mounds of dirt and clear away sticks, stones and stumps. By nightfall we had a short run—all too short—but there were tall trees at the end of the runway and we could not do anything about those. I lay awake all that night and if I took that aeroplane off once, lying there in the dark, I took it off fifty times.

I listened to the wind. Was it changing? Was it rising? Would there be a stiff breeze by morning to help us off the ground and over the trees? Or would it be a light breeze, of no use at all? Would I dump my petrol, my passenger or the heavy saddle he had brought with him!

Daylight was just beginning to show through the trees when we set out for the Moth. Using a garden hose I began to siphon off all the fuel except the bare minimum we would need to get us back to Bourke. My only objective was to get rid of it to lighten the load, but when it began to run into the ground the men were appalled at the waste and ran for tins. Petrol was expensive out there and deliveries were infrequent, so my aviation fuel was a treasure to them.

By the time we were ready for take-off, the wind had changed and our carefully prepared strip was useless. Out came the axes and shovels again and we started clearing a runway at right-angles to the one we had made before. By late morning we had made a second take-off ground. I liked this one better than the first because the end was blocked only by low mulga scrub. Our thanks and goodbyes were brief because we were afraid the wind might swing round again before we could take off.

With the brakes hard on, I pushed the throttle open to full power, creating a minor dust storm behind me. As the engine roared and the machine trembled, I let go the brakes and raced forward. I lifted the aircraft off the ground and over the trees. My passenger and I had time only to turn and give one another a congratulatory smile when I began to feel something was wrong with my engine.

I climbed as quickly as I could, clutching for every inch I could get above the dense timber. But the engine was missing: I had not imagined the vibration and now it was increasing all the time. I had to act quickly. Should I land in the scrub, smash up the aircraft and perhaps ourselves as well? Or take a chance by turning and trying to find the landing ground again? It was the only landing ground I knew of within 30 miles, so I decided to turn and limp back. The vibration was getting worse every minute and I had some of the most anxious moments of my life finding that poor little ground, which seemed to have disappeared among the trees. Not until I was dead in line with it could I see it plainly, and I was so relieved that it looked positively magnificent.

Once down it took me about an hour to locate the trouble. Two plugs had badly oiled up and were not firing. How dreadfully inadequate I felt at times like this, with my elementary engineering knowledge. While I could do the general maintenance work, it was when something went wrong that I felt desperate. With fingers crossed, I took off again and headed southeast for Bourke. My passenger seemed quite unmoved by all this and slept like a log until we were safely on the ground.

CHAPTER 10

It is fun to be a survivor and to go back to places of my early flying days and meet people who were children (now grandparents) when I landed on their claypan. They recall all sorts of incidents. Some even produce diaries which told what they thought of 'that flying girl'. Lorna Gibbons remembered me putting down in the scrub. Many years later she showed me her diary, which noted it was noon on 11 January 1936. In her schoolgirl hand she had written a full page, but here are two extracts:

> . . . we were wild with excitement not knowing an aeroplane was coming. The plane was swooping down over tree tops looking for vacant ground. At last Miss Bird brought her little Leopard Moth safely to earth with a sudden but perfect landing . . .

> . . . Miss Bird had engine trouble and had to return to landing ground to overhaul it. A little touching up to engine and everything was OK, the plane was once more in the air and this time for good . . .

That afternoon Bourke's best automobile engineer and I checked out every section of the Leopard's engine. By the time we had finished it was running beautifully, and at 6 am the next day, I took off for Dunlop station to pick up my passenger Mr Wood. He was the manager of the station and I was to bring him back to Bourke in time to catch the nine o'clock train. It was a lovely morning as I came in over Dunlop singing to myself, enjoying the sun and the morning air as I closed the throttle and started to glide in. Then the motor died and I landed with a dead engine. I could not believe it for a moment, so I started her up again to make a check. Sure enough, there was something wrong. At less than 1200 revolutions the motor would not idle; above this it was fine. What on earth could it be?

It was pretty clear that whatever it was an experienced aircraft engineer would be needed to put it right. What it would have meant to me in those days if there had been an aircraft engineer in Bourke! There seemed to be two courses open to me: because the machine seemed to be all right at high revs, I could take off and pray that she would keep going until I reached Bourke. I could then get in touch with an engineer at Cootamundra or Sydney and beg him to come up by the first train or plane. Alternatively, I could ring from Dunlop and get a Sydney engineer to come to Bourke and then travel down the river 70 miles to the station. However, as the roads were impassable after heavy rain, he would not have been able to get through for several days.

I plucked up enough courage to trust my engine to get me over the trees and up to a reasonable height. This was good country and once I had adequate height I knew I could pick a spot and glide in to land if necessary. Naturally enough, I would not take a passenger on that sort of flight. So I said goodbye to the Woods, and as I opened the throttle and began to roll forward, I listened to the motor and wondered if it would keep going. Then, as I gathered speed, the trees came towards me. I had passed the point of no return. I was committed to take-off. Would the motor hold? Would I clear those trees? Slowly I gained enough height to turn back to the claypan if necessary. I began to breathe more freely.

As soon as I started to glide in to Bourke aerodrome the motor cut and I landed once more with a dead engine. I rang de Havilland's in Sydney and they sent Harry Wicke on that night's train. It did not take him long to find the trouble, but only a skilled engineer could have done so. Shrinkage in the diaphrams of the petrol pumps was allowing air to be sucked into the fuel lines. I had another kind of engine trouble too—air locks caused by the high outside temperature boiled the petrol in the feed lines. Arthur Butler also experienced this trouble and was able to have special air chutes made in the cowling of the Dragon aircraft used by his pilots on the airmail run from Cootamundra to Charleville.

Someone who has not lived in drought-stricken country cannot know just how outback people feel about rain. To me it became the most wonderful God-given gift to man. It sounded like music, especially on a tin roof; the smell of it was intoxicating and the feel of it was soft and refreshing. After returning to the city I was shocked to hear people complain of the rain. Often I remembered a line from Shakespeare I had learned at school, 'It droppeth as the gentle rain from heaven.' Whether it is a tropical downpour or light misty rain, to me it is always beautiful.

It was extraordinary how quickly the rain transformed the countryside. Almost overnight a green mist of tiny plants would appear on the bare soil and within a few weeks there were thick pastures, fat sheep and cattle, myriads of birds and flocks of fat-lamb buyers from Sydney, Melbourne and Brisbane. It was a joy to fly over the country at these times, though not quite such a pleasure to come down on waterlogged landing grounds or to land beside flooded roads to rescue motorists from cars hopelessly bogged in the gluey red mud. After rain, the rare black cockatoos with tangerine feathers on their tails used to appear, and kangaroos, emus and galahs were plentiful. So were the mosquitoes. West of Bourke they have bigger, more fierce and persistent mosquitoes than anywhere else in the world.

On one visit to Bourke, the Ridge family was weather-bound. Like most station people, their three young boys were enthusiastic race horse followers. They talked about the Easter Show and the big race meeting to be held on Easter Saturday in Sydney, a high priority in the country. One of the boys asked his mother what Easter was all about. Mrs Ridge said she tried to explain the religious significance to them—how Christ was crucified on Good Friday and three days later rose from the dead. The youngest son, listening intently, chipped in and said, 'Gee, he had tough luck. He missed the Sydney Cup!'

In times of wet weather, nearly everybody wanted to fly and things looked rosy to a charter pilot. I had calls from Charleville, Quilpie, Thargomindah, Thurlogoonah, Brewarrina,

Tibooburra, Cobar, Wanaaring, Wilcannia—from every direction and every sort of client. (Medical calls always took precedence of course and my charter work had to wait.) Stock buyers from Bourke were my main clients when the drought had broken. Once the grass starts growing they want to replenish their stock, and there was fierce competition between the stock and station agents to obtain my services to fly their clients to various places to buy sheep.

Allan Moxham, the stock and station agent at Bourke, used to say, the minute it started raining, he would book me up, but often his client had never flown before and was petrified at the thought of flying with a 20-year-old girl. However, Allan had a very good system. He would take them to the Fitzgerald Hotel, introduce them to me, say how safe I was and then offer them a whisky. He might even give them another whisky and finally he would break down their resistance. Usually the clients were married with children and had big insurance policies, but in the 1930s the insurance companies did not cover people who flew. After a couple of whiskies, however, they normally showed enough Dutch courage to fly with me.

On one of these flights to Cunnamulla, Allan Moxham and Vince Barrett were my passengers. Vince had never flown before and did not want to begin now. The clouds were down almost to tree-top level when we took off and we were flying through shifting grey curtains of mist and rain. The only way I could see where I was going was to fly low over the telegraph line and the road, with the cabin windows wide open so that I could look down. There was nothing to be seen through the front windscreen! It is good to know the country is dead flat and that you are not going to suddenly run into a mountain. It is also rather thrilling to fly under such conditions with your eyes glued to that line which can disappear so quickly, or along the road making sharp turns every time it turns, to keep it in sight.

I asked Allan to watch the line of trees that marked the Warrego River and Vince to watch the telegraph line. This kept them occupied. If I had taken them up into a clear blue sky to 3000 feet, they would have been terrified because there is no sensation of speed at that height and they would have time to think of all the things that could happen. (I have since learned that passengers love dangerous flying!)

When we landed at Karmoo, the Youngs' property near Cunnamulla, I explained to Vince that flying was not always

91

as eventful as our journey had been. To my surprise he said, 'I loved every moment of it' and immediately booked me up for several trips he wanted to make in the near future. In fact, the journey had converted him so much that he wanted to know how to go about learning to fly.

On some journeys, I would have to land at the nearest tiny town to get local instructions to find a property. One old man told me over the telephone to follow a track that led out by the windmill and woolshed. 'You'll come to a gate about six miles along the track,' he added. 'And you'll know it's the right gate, 'cause I had a mob of sheep through there this morning and you'll see the fresh droppings.'

On another occasion, Jim Broadbent, who flew the airmail to Charleville, told me that there was a marvellous landmark three miles north of the border fence. 'There is a dead horse and you can smell it at a thousand feet,' he said. He was right. We were able to use it as a checkpoint while the aroma lasted!

Another time I received a call to go to Thargomindah, an old mining town then inhabited by only a handful of people. It was 120 miles west of Cunnamulla and it used to be (it was later almost deserted) the central township of the eastern part of Australia, being almost an equal distance from Sydney, Melbourne, Brisbane and Adelaide. I was to pick up two passengers and fly them to Cunnamulla to catch the train for Brisbane. On enquiring about a landing ground, I was cheerfully told there was one, but it was covered with stones about an inch-and-a-half in diameter and that the only two aircraft that had landed there previously were both damaged. Not so good, I thought, so I checked with the Shell man who said emphatically, 'No darned good.' However, there were several claypans not far outside the town and he went off to the telephone to urge Thargomindah to look for one that was smooth and dry enough for me to land the Leopard.

When I arrived, I found that they had lit a smoky fire from an old tyre to give me my wind direction and the whole township had assembled on the edge of the claypan to watch me land. I soon discovered that I was to have three passengers, not two. A Mr Hughes had ridden 75 miles across the Grey Range to be included in the flight to catch the train. I explained that I had room for only two passengers in the Leopard and he said,

'Alright then, I'll buy the jolly aeroplane.' He meant it. In the end, we worked out that I could make the trip twice before dark and the departure of the train. That was a good afternoon for me—nearly 500 miles at a shilling a mile.

There was an amusing sequel to this trip. Thargomindah had been flood-bound by the sudden rising of the Bulloo, one of those waterless rivers that become miles wider after rain, and I had been asked to bring with me butter and other foods that were in short supply there. One of those affected by the shortage happened to be the local postmaster, who was also the correspondent for the Brisbane *Courier-Mail*. Imagine my surprise when, weeks later, someone sent me a cutting with the not-so-small headline: 'Nancy Bird Flies Food to Starving Flood Bound.'

Stanley Drummond was displeased with the news item because no credit was given to the Far West Children's Health Scheme and he reprimanded me . . . but the first I knew about it was when I saw the cutting. Looking back I can see what good publicity he could have made out of some of my trips. However, it never entered my head that it was news or that I should report it even to the Far West Children's Health Scheme.

Many of the people in Bourke were under the impression that I was a wealthy woman who flew an aeroplane and stayed in the west just for the fun of it—and I did not do anything to correct this impression. When you are young you are sensitive about admitting that the only new clothes you get are your sister's cast-offs and that you cannot afford even a newspaper. My ambition was to see the overdraft on my aircraft get smaller every month.

I do not think money has ever mattered a great deal to me, which was certainly a fortunate thing in those days. It has never been the key that opened doors for me. The good things I have had in life, and the wonderful opportunities, have come through friendship, not through my bank account. I have known what it is like to be poor and I do not think I would ever be afraid of it. Naturally enough I appreciate the things money can buy. I like to be able to buy good clothes when I want to and send flowers to my friends on occasions while they are alive and not wreaths when they are dead. I feel quite strongly that many people, women especially, fall into the habit of thinking security is the most important thing in the world and that they miss out on much more valuable things as a result.

My first flight to Adelaide was in May 1936 with two passengers, Mrs A. M. Davis who owned the Cunnamulla Hotel and Mr Richardson. We flew from Cunnamulla over the bare, eroded red hills and the dusty mullock heaps to the parks and trees of Broken Hill. I was advised there to take the long way round because the shortest Broken Hill–Adelaide route would take me over some very nasty country. Over Peterborough I discovered my petrol tanks had not been filled sufficiently and I decided that I hadn't the necessary safety margin. I circled for a while looking for a decent landing field. I put the Leopard down on a slightly sloping paddock that was thickly covered with stones and, within a few minutes, half a dozen cars and the Shell lorry had dashed out from the town just in case I needed fuel or assistance. Quickly my tanks were filled and the youngsters, having recovered from their astonishment at seeing an aeroplane flown by a woman, took great delight in clearing a track for the aircraft so that I could take off again.

Ten miles out of Parafield aerodrome, a Moth (the first aeroplane we had seen on the journey) passed on my left, but it was not until I landed that I discovered it was my old Moth, now owned by the South Australian Aero Club and piloted by the South Australian woman pilot Brownie Lunn. Brownie was the first woman in that State to hold both a navigator's and engineer's licence. Churchill Smith of the Aero Club took me under his wing and I met Harry Plumridge, Jim Melrose, Roy Gropler, who flew a Klemm Swallow from England to Australia in 1936, and other flying people in quick succession. Jimmy Melrose was the blonde, youthful-looking South Australian who flew in the 1934 Air Race and broke the England to Australia record. After the race he shared his emergency rations with me and talked about his experiences in the race. In his company, my heart missed a beat.

Jim called his aeroplane *My Hildegarde* after his mother and was often photographed with her, which endeared him to everybody's mother.

When we took off on the return journey to Cunnamulla we had company for the first 120 miles. Jimmy was flying alongside me, carrying the South Australian Premier and a parliamentary party to Dawson. However, we struck bad weather and he disappeared into cloud,* so I decided to put down in a field of stubble near Hallett.

After landing along the furrows at Hallett, we left the aircraft, crossed a creek and climbed through a couple of fences to a farmhouse to ask if we could use the telephone to report our forced landing to Broken Hill. The farmer and his wife gave us a magnificent morning tea with freshly baked scones and thick cream. We spent a comfortable four hours with them before the weather cleared sufficiently for us to take off again. Weeks later I read an account of this incident in a women's magazine. The farmer's wife expressed her feelings at the sight of the aeroplane descending from the fog and her excitement at the thought of the two women dropping from the clouds to have morning tea with her.

When I got back to my home base at Bourke after that trip, it was raining heavily and a passenger was waiting anxiously for me to fly him to Nyngan to pick up the night train for Sydney. I knew I could not land at Nyngan because the claypan there was under water, but I offered to take him to Narromine, 79 miles further on, with its good all-weather aerodrome. Thick sleety rain was falling and Bourke aerodrome was so wet that if you got off the loose metal runways, the plane bogged down at once. I could not see beyond the boundaries of the field but I knew there were no mountains on my 210-mile route and a good straight railway line to follow most of the way. So we took off and flew down the line at practically tree-top level under the low clouds, my one prayer being that I would not meet another aircraft coming up in the opposite direction and hugging that railway line too.

I was surprised when reading notes I had made in an exercise book at the time of my constant references to dust and thunder storms. There was a particular reference to that trip where I admit to being forced down so low on the railway line that I was just above the tree tops. I go on to say I would have turned back many times except that I was afraid of losing the line. I am convinced I have a guardian angel, because if I had turned back, I probably would have been caught in fog and low clouds

---

* A few weeks later Jim was dead. His Heston Phoenix aircraft broke up above the clouds, presumably due to structural failure in a severe storm. I heard the news of his death in Brewarrina and flew back to Bourke, crying most of the way.

through which I was ill-equipped to fly. In that country, it could have been fatal.

At Narromine the next morning I had a phone call telling me that a stiff breeze had started to dry out the landing ground at Nyngan and there were two passengers, Sid Coleman and Dick Pearson, waiting for me there to go to Brewarrina. They were both ex-pilots, with experience in flying in the west, and I knew that if they considered the Nyngan claypan safe to land on, then I would too. As I was gathering speed for take-off, I hit a bump I had not seen on the roadway that crosses the aerodrome. I was airborne without sufficient speed, so the Leopard sank to the ground again. I had two choices, either to close the throttle and land, perhaps in a bog that lay ahead, or try to get the Moth into the air. In a split second I decided on the latter course and pulled the aeroplane off the ground before she was quite ready. The Leopard wallowed under the strain. Quickly I aimed her down, the wheels touched the ground and I lifted her just a few inches, then held her down gaining every ounce of speed I could before pulling her up steeply over the telephone lines at the end of the field.

I do not know who received the biggest fright, me or my passengers. They knew what a close shave we had experienced and Sid Coleman laughed once we were in the air and said, 'If you had gone in then, you would have wiped out aviation in the west in one sweep.' We were the only three pilots in the area.

Though he did not show his feelings, it must have been a bad moment for the other passenger, Dick Pearson. Some years earlier he had lost a leg when he crashed in his own aircraft while taking off from that same aerodrome. I think this was the first time he had been up with me, but he accompanied me quite often afterwards. Some of the happiest days I spent out west were when I stayed with Dick, his wife Lorne and their delightful children at Quantambone station. This property was one of the largest west of the mountains, the first grant of land made in the western division when that part of the country was opened up in 1863. Major Druitt was the first holder and he built a magnificent 13-room homestead there. Dick had turned the garden into a paradise for birds, with trees and hedges growing inside the enclosures in which he kept his pheasants, finches, love-birds, curlews, Chinese ducks and fowl. His wife used to have the jackaroos in for coffee every night and treated them almost like sons. In those lonely far flung places, encouraging the 'boys' to shower and tidy up each night was important. Lorne became one of my dearest friends and staunchest supporters.

While I was at Bourke, John Kingsford Smith, who sat for his commercial licence at the same time I did, arrived to make a film of the Aerial Clinic's work for Cinesound. It was called *Angel of the Outback* and later it was a success overseas. Sister Silver and I were in a flying scene, rushing off on an errand of mercy! I have seen this film several times since and realise how little the town of Bourke has changed, whereas there has been a huge change in film technique. Making that film was a novel experience for John Kingsford Smith in more ways than one. When we landed again he told me that he had never flown with a woman pilot before and felt very brave. He was!

CHAPTER 11

In December 1936, the South Australian government held an air race from Brisbane to Adelaide via Sydney and Melbourne to publicise its sesqui-centenary celebrations.

Aviation maps were not good at this time and none of us had radio, which would have been useless anyway because there were no ground facilities either. Before the race, however, I had flown to Adelaide with my younger sister Joan to have a look at the route. On our way we found Nhill, a tiny little country town, tucked under a group of trees beside a slight rise in the ground. On this journey I was a little taken aback when my sister asked me how many times the aircraft was supposed to bounce after landing!

One of the competitors in the race was a little-known garage proprietor from Hamilton, Victoria, who had imported an American Porterfield aircraft for the event. Rumour had it that he did not have enough money to get it out of bond. Somebody must have come to his aid, however, because not only was he in the race, he won it! His name was Reg Ansett. He became the greatest airline operator in Australia, but not without waging a war with amazing tenacity for the right to be independent. To this day his name is carried on Australia's major domestic airline service.

The air race was magnificent fun and I enjoyed every moment of it. After all those months of being a lone pilot in the west I was back with people who flew and who spoke my language. There were 31 starters including Mrs Harry (Dolores) Bonney (as she preferred to be known) in her Klemm KL32; Freda Thompson in a Gipsy Moth; Ivy Pearce with Jason Hassard, an airline pilot whom she later married, in a twin-engined Monospar; and May Bradford in a Klemm Eagle. With my

Leopard Moth, this made five female entries in all. I was one of the few flying solo in the race.

There was a fine variety of machines in the race: Jimmy Broadbent piloted a Tiger Moth; 'Skipper' Moody a Stinson Reliant; Brian Monkton and Scott Maddocks had entered the oldest aircraft, a DH9 which rumour said had once set out to bomb Berlin during World War I but had turned back because it could not make the distance. Ernest Collibee had entered the only Australian machine, a twin-engined Gannet.

I had stayed the night with Scotty Allan and his wife Ailsa, and as we drove to the aerodrome, Scotty's parting advice to me was, 'Now remember Nancy, air races are won by not hurrying.' It was a glorious sunny morning as we started out, amid all the excitement that goes with the beginning of an air race. I was the 26th to leave, taking off immediately after another Leopard Moth piloted by J. Robins and just before Ernest Collibee's twin-engined Gannet. I felt like a sparrow in front of an eagle. The first stop was Coffs Harbour, 200 miles away, where we had tea and sandwiches while our aircraft were being refuelled, signed dozens of autographs and fought off small boys who wanted to climb all over the aircraft.

As we were allowed up to two hours on the ground at Coffs Harbour, it was amusing to see how those of us who knew that part of the coast hung back. We were aware that a north-easterly springs up almost every afternoon and we wanted the advantage of that nice tail wind, which is strongest at about 3000 feet. It was pretty bumpy flying down to Sydney at that height, but it was worth it. I averaged 140 mph all the way.

Jean Batten came out to meet me at Mascot together with Mrs James Melrose and members of my family. On the next morning of the race, weather reports threatened mist and low fog over Bowral, although for a while I thought they would not be bothering me. While checking the Leopard, oil flowed out of the oil tank and I thought I would be grounded with an oil leak. But the engineer quickly diagnosed the trouble: I had filled the oil tank when the engine was hot and as it cooled the oil flowed back to the tank and overflowed.

We took off at two-minute intervals from Mascot and the day's minor disasters began at once. The DH9 blew a tyre on take-off and Monkton and Maddocks had to ground-loop to avoid hitting the aerodrome fence. They were able to take off an hour-

and-a-half later with a slightly oversize wheel borrowed from a DH50.

On this hop we refuelled at Cootamundra (where Captain P. G. Taylor worked out for me that I had averaged 150 mph) and then set off on the 300-mile journey to Melbourne. Again, my knowledge of the country was a tremendous advantage. Misty rain was falling like an opaque white curtain dead ahead. To the east it was becoming darker and more threatening every minute.

As I neared Wangaratta I could see the worst weather was ahead, with the clouds coming down quickly to the hills. Now was the time to make up my mind whether to stay on my compass course and chance going over those 4000-foot hills blind, or to veer off to the lower, flatter country in the west, adding about 30 miles to my distance but giving me the railway line as a guide. I thought about the value of my aircraft and my own neck and chose the long way round.

Flying low so I could keep the railway line in sight, I was suddenly amazed to see three large Air Force Wapitis immediately below me, their geared propellers slowly and majestically powering them through the air. Away to my right I saw another machine flying my course but at a higher level. Clearly the misty, foggy air was getting too full of aeroplanes for comfort. In front heavy rain was lying across my path, so I took the Leopard down even lower where I would have more chance of keeping the railway line in sight and headed into the storm.

The farther I flew, the more I wished I hadn't! I had both windows open as wide as I could, my face was streaming with water and my hair was hanging down in rats' tails. Then I realised I was not much above the trees and that if the line suddenly turned around a hill on my blind side, I might hit it. How I wished I had found a nice flat paddock to land in before I headed into this murk! I thought of turning back but feared having a head-on collision with another aeroplane. Then, just as suddenly as I had come into it, I was out of the cloud and Seymour was below me. Looking decidedly damp, I put the nose down and I dived over the finishing line at Essendon in fine style.

Four aircraft were still unaccounted for when I landed. People hung around worrying, wondering, and waiting for news. I prayed that nothing had happened to anyone. What a relief when we knew where they all were! Mrs Harry Bonney and A. G. Bond had a forced landing at Seymour; Harry Plumridge, flying the South Australian Aero Club Miles Hawk, had been forced down at Euroa; and Pat Moore-MacMahon was forced down at Benalla.

Freda Thompson and I discussed the conditions on the way to the aerodrome the next morning and we thought it very unlikely that we would be allowed off the ground. There was a burst of laugher as the weather report was read to us: 'Morning mists, fog on the hills, light rain changing to thunderstorms, low clouds, *otherwise* fine.'

There seemed to be aeroplanes to the right, left and all around as we took off at one-minute intervals. I was flying a compass course to Nhill, allowing five degrees of drift and keeping low to avoid the clouds. I found myself so low I began to think I might hit a sheep in a paddock, so I climbed a bit, wondering where I was. Soon I saw Roy Gropler's blue Klemm making for a gap in the hills. Since he was a South Australian I reasoned that his machine should know its way home from Melbourne even without the pilot, so I followed through the gap and waved to him as I passed in my faster aircraft.

When I was over Nhill, I commenced a dive over the aerodrome and had to do a most uncomfortable zigzag climb to avoid a Klemm Eagle, which was coming in to land. Next I found I was in the way of a Stinson. Every time I approached I had to clear off again to get out of the way of somebody who was trying to dive over the line. When I finally got down, I joined in the fun of watching the other machines come in from every point of the compass. It was amazing how many had got lost within 20 miles of Nhill. My survey of the route had paid off! Two of the pilots in fast machines had been following each other around and around in circles, each waiting for the other to lead him in. Then one landed in a ploughed field to ask directions from a farmer, while the other circled, hoping to profit by his enquiries.

For the last leg of the race the take-off order was altered. Aeroplanes were to take off according to the speeds they had averaged. I was amazed when I learnt that my little Leopard was to be held back with the three fastest machines. I was immediately branded a dark horse. Ahead of us were 90 miles of sandy desert covered with low mallee scrub. The sensible thing to do would have been to fly around it, but this would have added too much to our time, so we flew at only a few hundred feet above some of the most unpleasant-looking country in

Australia. Over the Mount Lofty Ranges a vertical current of air carried me up to 3000 feet in spite of the fact that I had the engine throttled back.

Then Parafield was in sight—journey's end. I put the nose down and dived towards the line, determined to get the last ounce of advantage out of the Leopard as I crossed. I had won the Ladies' Trophy by one minute, plus the prize for fastest time overall between Melbourne and Adelaide. The Ladies' Trophy was a gold brooch, which had been designed on the Royal Naval Air Force badge owned by Jim Melrose. His uncle, who had flown in World War I with this service, had given it to him.

The fastest time for the complete race was recorded by 'Skipper' Moody, the pioneer pilot of western Queensland whose name and reputation as a flyer were legendary when Qantas was a struggling airline.

I left for the far west again and a change of plans. The Federal Government had withdrawn the £200 subsidy it had been paying the Far West Children's Health Scheme for using the emergency strips they built between Nyngan and Bourke, Louth and Fords Bridge for the airmail service. The Far West Children's Health Scheme was then forced to remove the retainer fee that they allotted me.

In those days there were only two medical services operating in Australia: the Australian Inland Mission service based at Cloncurry, the Bush Church Aid Society's Moth operating from Ceduna in South Australia in 1936 and my Leopard working from Bourke as a Baby Clinic and Aerial Ambulance. Incidentally, Arthur Affleck, later Regional Director of Civil Aviation in Papua New Guinea, was the first flying doctor pilot in Australia. He was a bank clerk when he decided he wanted to learn to fly. He did the first civil aviation course in Australia and was one of three chosen for training by the RAAF as pilots at Point Cook. After being trained, he flew the first airmail service between Melbourne and Hay. Arthur's mechanic was Arthur Butler, destined to become one of Australia's leading airline operators. Arthur Affleck began flying the Cloncurry Flying Doctor Service as early as 1928, but even by 1937 there were only two new bases.

The Flying Doctor Service had established a base at Broken Hill during 1937, but this did not affect me because Broken Hill was 330 miles from Bourke. I would not have dared fly cross country because there was nothing by which to navigate. In any case, the Flying Doctor Service was a medical service for people in remote areas where there were no doctors. At Charleville there were several medicos and it is interesting to note that when Doctor Dorothy Herbert established herself there after World War II, people said no-one would go to a woman doctor. Dorothy flew her own aeroplane and was an exceedingly popular doctor. Women preferred her. Patients arrived with chickens, cakes and all sorts of gifts, to show their appreciation for a woman doctor to whom they felt they could pour forth their innermost souls.

In 1936 I decided to move to Charleville because the airmail landed there en route to and from Singapore and there was a skilled engineer, George Harriman, who was employed by Qantas. Although nobody could detect anything unusual in my engine, I could hear a new sound, which was a constant worry to me. (I discovered that a garage mechanic had used copper wire instead of a split pin, which vibration had sheared through. The grating of the metal was the sound I could hear.) The flying was pleasant over good country until I was close to Charleville; but the main pleasure for me was being with other flying people and I knew I would always see some of the Qantas pilots—Bill Crowther, Scotty Allan, Russell Tapp, Lew Ambrose, Frank Thomas, and Bill Purton. Seeing Bill quite made my day. Romances were very mild affairs in the 1930s. A greeting and a few words in passing meant so very much.

It was also great fun to be at Harry Corones' Hotel. Harry, a Greek, was a real character. He would do anything for flying people, such as driving us to and from the aerodrome. Late arrivals would always receive just as warm a welcome. Early departers would find a meal prepared for them before take-off. Harry had the contract to feed Qantas passengers and crew when they touched down in Charleville for lunch, en route from Brisbane to Singapore. There were thirteen stops between Brisbane and Darwin and another six before Singapore. The flight took the Qantas de Havilland 86 the best part of three-and-a-half days.

Lunch in Charleville was one of the highlights of the trip. Harry erected trestle tables on the earth floor of a hangar and served hot steaks. Some dignitaries, like Lady Mountbatten, had lunch with their feet literally 'on the ground'. However, the turbulence was often so great in the summertime, that many passengers didn't feel like eating. One Captain remarked to me, 'We went up to 8000 feet and couldn't get out of it.' Back in Brisbane he was heard to say, 'How that girl sticks it out west I don't know, the turbulence is terrific'.

Wherever pilots gathered you would hear stories of Harry Corones. One involved a Sydney judge who left his rifle at Harry's hotel after a day's shooting. Harry telephoned the judge and said in his strong Greek accent, 'You left your gun behind.' It was a bad line and he had to repeat himself. 'Gun, gun,' he said. 'G for Jesus, U for onions and N for pneumonia'!

In 1936, Charleville had a population of 3000, and during my first few weeks there, I had a large number of joy-riding passengers. The novelty of having an aeroplane in the town wore off after a while when fewer and fewer people wanted to go up. Now that a licensed ground engineer was available I felt obliged to conform with the regulations and submit to a weekly engine inspection. I had to have a certificate of safety, which was issued each week, and this added to my operating costs. I did not want this expense—I really only wanted an engineer when I was in trouble.

Altogether Charleville did not work out very well for me, because my expenses were too high. Though the petrol was cheaper in Charleville than anywhere else, it did not offset the other costs such as the hotel bill, hangar rental, and engineering costs. I suggested to the Queensland government that I start in Charleville the same service I had operated at Bourke, as they too had a Queensland Bush Children's Health Scheme. My sister Joan was also training as a baby clinic nurse so she could join me. My proposal was turned down flat, I presume for financial reasons.

So I moved to Cunnamulla where there was a large claypan close to the town. Mrs Davis had invited me to be her guest at the Cunnamulla Hotel. It was an attractive proposition, which I gratefully accepted. Already a great deal of my charter work came from the Cunnamulla district and I loved the town. I also came to love Mrs Davis, who treated me like a daughter. She ran her hotel like a big country club, where town and country people met. It was the social centre of the district. Each morning and afternoon a large traymobile loaded with cups, tea and bread-

and-butter was wheeled into the lounge-room. Visitors to the town, local business and professional people all knew they were welcome to join the daily gatherings, for which Mrs Davis made no charge.

I found that there was another advantage for me in operating from Cunnamulla. The Shire Engineer, Wally Shiewe, loved aeroplane engines and whenever I had any trouble with the Leopard, the Shire Council allowed him the time to put the problem right. In 1980 as I left an 'Early Birds' dinner in Sydney, I shared a cab with John Shaw who was on his way to Queensland. John mentioned that he was in charge of the State's aviation during my stay at Cunnamulla.

I had never been bothered by the Department, yet I could not have complied with any of the regulations. I never had more than one safety certification and yet I was supposed to have one every week. I was over 100 miles from the nearest ground engineer and had a garage mechanic and the Shire Engineer work on my aeroplane. I asked Mr Shaw why they were so lenient towards me. He replied, 'We had our spies.' I was so shocked I could have fallen out of the taxi. He said, 'We had people who went out there and saw how the aeroplane was kept and that it was under cover. When the Shire Council allowed Wally Shiewe to work on your engine, he would telephone me and tell me what he had done. At other times I would phone and ask him how things were going. We could not supply a service, so we either had to stop you flying or keep a check on you while appearing to turn a blind eye.'

Not all were so lucky. Dr Clyde Fenton, who flew out of Darwin, was constantly in trouble with the Department. He was the original flying doctor and flew himself; nowadays the flying doctors have pilots to fly them to provide medical services. I never met this magnificent man of whom I heard so much and who was regularly in the news because of his confrontations with the Department.

Dr Fenton believed the aeroplane was merely his means of transport to the sick and injured, so he refused to bow to the bureaucracy that insisted he had to have a piece of paper authorising him or his aircraft to do certain tasks. He said he was there to save lives. Despite the Department cancelling his licence he kept flying. Consequentially, when he did pass the required flying tests for its renewal, the Department refused to sign his licence. He defied the Department and continued to operate as a flying doctor. He was subjected to court appearances, which finally resulted in a £5 fine and costs awarded against the Department.

When he crashed his aeroplane beyond repair, the appreciative locals gave him a replacement aircraft.

Clyde Fenton was the first flying doctor. His dedication and determination were exemplary. However, others who cannot be overlooked include Reverend Keith Langford Smith, who flew a Gipsy Moth in Arnhem Land in 1931, Reverend Leonard Daniels of Wilcannia and members of the Bush Church Aid Society in Ceduna, South Australia.

Years later Dr Geoffrey Young was to write another page in medical aviation. He was offered £4000 a year to station himself at Forbes and regularly visit remote areas that had not seen a doctor in years. He used to fly a DH Hornet Moth, with the patient's head beside him where the side-by-side seat had been. He would administer to the patient while in flight.

CHAPTER 12

It was early summer when I moved to Cunnamulla. The hot nights took an awful toll of my strength, especially as I always started long charter flights soon after dawn to avoid the worst turbulence caused by the heat of the day. Often I lay awake till two in the morning because of the heat, with my alarm set for 4 am. In the worst of the weather I learnt the local trick of dunking my pyjamas in water and wringing them out before putting them on. There was no air conditioning and for one reason or another fans did not seem to have moved south from Singapore. Waiting on the claypan for the first light, I often thought of Kipling's words, 'The dawn comes up like thunder.'

Although I had moved over the border and into Queensland, I was still doing the same kind of work as before, and more often than not, flying the same people. I remember old Mr Crouch and his daughters Irene and Sybil with whom I became friendly. One evening they were to meet me at my hotel and we planned to go to the local ball together. I was wondering why they were an hour late, when finally they rushed in saying, 'Sorry we are late. We were about to leave when we discovered the dogs had no meat and we had to go out and shoot a kangaroo.' I visualised them throwing an oilskin over their evening frocks, jumping into the ute and rushing off to bag a kangaroo before going to the ball. I wondered how their city sisters would react to that story!

In June 1937 while out west I heard that an American woman pilot was attempting a flight around the world at its widest girth on the equator. She was flying the highest powered, most expensive aircraft to be privately owned at that time. It was a Lockheed Electra.

I thought it would be a welcoming gesture to fly to Darwin to see her, but when I looked at the mileage from Cunnamulla,

I realised that the cost of fuel was beyond my means. So I did not go to Darwin to meet Amelia Earhart.

Her next stop was Lae, New Guinea, where Sid Marshall worked on her aircraft while another Australian repaired her radio. Amelia took off from Lae with her first class Pan Am navigator Fred Noonan while Sid filmed her with his cine camera. Her plane was so overloaded that after becoming airborne, she held it down and it disappeared off the end of the runway, over the sea, before gaining height. Sid stopped filming, so sure that she had crashed. He could not see any sense in wasting film on an empty sky!

Little did Sid know his film would be the final glimpse of Amelia Earhart before she disappeared into the Pacific on her way to Howland Island. The United States Navy had stationed a small ship *Itasca* to receive and send radio messages and a landing strip had been prepared for her on the tiny island. One of the last messages they received from her was, 'I should be on you, but I cannot see you.' Years later I flew over the island on a Qantas flight and realised how difficult it would be to see beneath scattered cloud or against the rising sun, which was when Amelia had been due to arrive there.

Others have disappeared in the great oceans of the world, but none has created such speculation and controversy as Amelia Earhart. Her disappearance has intrigued the world. There have been many books written on her life and her fatal record attempt. Like Kingsford Smith, it seems that she has taken the knowledge of her final hours with her.

It is great to be a survivor, picking up snippets years later. On one occasion at Strathfield, Nell Sandinfords introduced me to a View Club meeting, saying she knew the back country in which I had flown because her uncle, Jim Davey, lived at Fords Bridge, 40 miles north of Bourke. Nell went on to relate a story of me flying ice cream, which was a rare treat, to a picnic given by her uncle long before the days of refrigeration. So impressed was he that Jim decided as soon as his boys were old enough, they too would learn to fly. One son, Bill, became a popular charter pilot and founded an airline at Dubbo. Lord Howe was another one of the routes he flew and he employed Aminta

Hennessy, who became the first woman captain of a regular over water passenger service to fly this route. On several occasions, when travellers discovered to their horror that there was a woman pilot in command and they voiced their alarm, Aminta would cheerfully retort, 'Well the choice is yours. You have the option of a lovely holiday on Lord Howe island, or there is just time for you to get out before we take off!'

Again, when I was speaking at a function many years later, a woman came up to me and said, 'Do you remember me? You landed at Goodooga and I made you a cup of tea.' Of all the thousands of cups of tea I have drunk in my life, that is one I do remember. When I poured it out there was a flea in it. I can distinctly remember wondering what to do—embarrass my hostess or remember I was in the back country. I flipped the flea out and drank the tea. However, I did not have the courage to tell her that story, even though so many years had passed.

Miss Robin Burton also approached me at a function. She told me her father had been manager of Albilbah station while I was out west and she was brought up there. At that time the station was owned by Wally Macanash and his wife, who was Banjo Paterson's sister. 'Albilbah' is Aboriginal for 'big waterhole', and Isisford was the nearest town, 25 miles away. It was known for its girls, goats and glass bottles. (Girls because they were great, goats because like many outback places they were running wild, and glass bottles because there were no bottle collectors out there and the bottles were discarded everywhere!) Miss Burton told me that when Amy Johnson landed at Charleville, after her successful England–Australia flight in 1930, all the family went more than 150 miles to meet her.

She also told me how she broke her arm while cranking her car. It was necessary to travel 150 miles to the doctor on horseback and the horses had to be changed twice before they were met by a car on the other side of the flooded Barcoo River. This type of accident and the distances involved were so typical of what happened out west in the early 1930s before medical assistance was available.

Even today the hospitality and generosity of these people is magnificent. Recently, when I asked Judith Barton, a member of the Queensland branch of the Australian Women Pilots' Association, if she would be able to find somebody who could give me a bed for the night if I could not get accommodation at Longreach, she immediately replied, 'You must stay with us. We are only 40 miles out of town!'

Later I attended the opening of the Stockman's Hall of Fame at Longreach and again Judith asked our party to stay. 'But there are six of us in the aircraft,' I protested. Judith simply said, 'You can all stay with us and if we run out of beds, the shearing sheds all have facilities and are very comfortable. I've had 28 people in the house at once!'

This marvellous woman raised her own turkeys and snow peas in temperatures that reach more than 45°C and in the words of Kipling, '. . . meets with triumph and disaster and treats those two imposters just the same'.

The Stockman's Hall of Fame was built to recognise the achievements of those outback people whose determined efforts contributed to the pioneering of the nation.

The Australian Women Pilots' Association became involved when Jean Gardiner donated $20 000 to be used as a memorial to the early women pilots of Mascot. The intention was to put up a plaque in the building at the international terminal in Sydney, but the request was turned down by the Regional Director of Aviation. It was felt the Association would not be able to separate those who actually contributed to aviation, from those who flew for pleasure.

At the time, Queensland's Premier Sir Joh Bjelke-Petersen was trying to start an Air and Space Museum in Queensland and Jean, through AWPA, offered the donation to that state. Sir Joh grabbed it with both hands. His intention had been to buy the contents of the Albury aviation museum and transfer it to Queensland and build it up from there. However, the Victorian government decided not to allow this museum to leave the state, with the result that Queensland was unable to get the museum constructed.

Jean then became interested in the Stockman's Hall of Fame because she wanted to see the results of her donation. She had witnessed her parents donating money to various causes, but they had not been alive to see them come to fruition.

The first requirement was that the women pilots who were to be featured had to have made a significant contribution to the inland. I was a pioneer in that field and was therefore included. Originally, there was difficulty in defining criteria for selecting other women aviators, none of whom had served the inland.

Finally it was agreed by the organisers that each should be a pioneer in her field.

Women mentioned in the Hall of Fame include: Millicent Maude Bryant*, who became Australia's first licensed aviatrix in 1927; Evelyn Follett, who gained her licence in the same year and flew in many sports events before becoming a director of her brother's flying school at Mascot Aerodrome; Meg Skelton of Inverell, who was also licensed in 1927 and set about helping and encouraging other women who wanted to learn to fly; Freda Deaton, another who earned her licence in the same year; and Megan Reardon, who won the inaugural Oakes Ladies Air Race in 1928.

In 1929 Bobbie Terry became the first woman to own her own aircraft, a De Soutter, which she used on the family property in the New South Wales district of Quirindi. In the same year, Phyllis Arnott became the first woman in Australia to be granted a commercial licence, but Phyllis chose only to fly for pleasure.

In 1930 these women flew with their instructors from Mascot airport to welcome Amy Johnson at the end of her historic solo flight from England. Not knowing that the courageous aviatrix was being flown from Brisbane in another aeroplane, these enthusiastic young aviators unwittingly tried to 'escort' the wrong aircraft. On landing they discovered their error, and immediately took off again to complete their mission.

In 1928, Dorothy Reis became the first woman to obtain a licence in Queensland and ferried her father, an insurance assessor, around the vast state on his many trips. In 1930, Nancy Lyle of Melbourne bought a Gipsy Moth to fly members of her family more than 500 miles to their property in north-west New South Wales. She was the first woman to fly from Melbourne to Adelaide, and later, from Melbourne to Tasmania. Her 1937 publication *Simple Flying for Simple People* was the first text book on cross-country flying for non-commercial and non-government pilots.

In 1929, Dr Kit Bloomfield returned from Harvard University and was the first Victorian woman to obtain a pilot's licence, although Mrs Paddy Bell, who came to Australia in 1928, had an English licence and was the first woman engineer. She

---

* Eight months after becoming a pilot, Millicent was killed in the *Greycliffe* ferry disaster on Sydney Harbour.

converted her British licence to an Australian one. Lady Sommers, wife of the Victorian Governor, learnt to fly in 1929 and had her own machine. This was a great boost to sports flying and the Victorian Aero Club.

In 1931, Jean Gardiner, who used her aircraft on the family's grazing property at Baradine, New South Wales, was probably the first woman to cross the state by air when she flew from Adelaide to Broken Hill, then to Sydney and back to Adelaide for the servicing of her aircraft by the distinguished pioneering aviator, Horrie Miller. In the same year, May Bradford became the first aviatrix to be employed as an engineer. She flew at Mascot, giving joy-rides until she was killed in an aircraft accident. Irene Dean Williams of Western Australia flew a Gipsy Moth solo from Perth to Sydney and back in 1932, sponsored by Berlei, the undergarments company.

The first woman in the British Empire to gain an instructor's licence was Freda Thompson, OBE. In 1934 she also became the first Australian woman to fly solo from England to Australia, and in 1948, became the Victorian Aero Club's first woman president.

In 1935, Esther Mather (L'Estrange) became the first woman captain of the Queensland Aerobatic Team, which won the 1938 Sesquicentennial Australian Championships. Esther jokingly claims she flew for the Fuhrer. Before World War II, she flew a Dutchman, as she thought, all along the Queensland coast. She later learned he was a German spy!

In 1936 Barbara Hitchens made her flight from Australia to New Guinea. After successfully negotiating the water hop, she became lost in the treacherous Jimi Valley. She was finally rescued, putting an end to the grave concern the authorities held for her safety. In the same year licenced pilot Connie Jordan became a ground engineer with Qantas. In Charleville and Brisbane, Connie was the only engineer licensed to sign out all types of engines. Later, in Sydney, she maintained flying boats, the only woman to do so at that time.

It was Mrs Harry Bonney, however, who regularly made the headlines with her outstanding contribution to Australia's aviation history. Dolores is a cultivated, educated woman who had attended finishing school in Germany. She considered herself a 'golf widow' soon after her marriage when she had moved to Brisbane. Unable to drive a car, but inspired by Amy Johnson and her husband's cousin Bert Hinkler, she decided secretly to learn to fly. It solved her golf problems! When her husband found out, he promptly bought her an aeroplane.

In 1931 Dolores spent Christmas Day with her husband in Brisbane. However, on Boxing Day, the strong pull of her European background, which required her to be with her family at that time of the year, prompted her to fly from Brisbane to Wangaratta—1000 miles in a day. It was a hot turbulent day when she left Archerfield and arrived at sunset for the family gathering. Dolores was met by the local press, who told her that she had created a long distance record for a woman and was therefore headline news.

No longer was she a 'golf widow' but Mrs Harry Bonney a distinguished aviatrix who had flown into history. She insisted on using her husband's full name, as she had no children. This meant his name would carry on through her achievements.

The following year she flew around Australia in just over 95 hours, and in April 1933, set off for England.

During a storm over Malaya she landed on a beach, damaged her aeroplane and was not rescued for several days. During this time she hauled the engine from the sea and single-handedly cleaned it all down to prevent it from rusting. Finally, she continued her journey and landed in England in late June after 157 flying hours.

She capped her career with her fourth record-breaking flight in 1937 when she flew solo in a Klemm 32 from Australia via Singapore, India and Egypt down through Africa, reaching Pretoria after 211 flying hours. It was an outstanding flight and her record still stands today; no-one else has attempted it.* On this flight, she was at Karthoum the same day as Amelia Earhart who was on her fatal record attempt. However, Dolores did not wait to see her.

When I went into the outback in 1935, I had intended staying for six months but loved it so much that three years soon passed. In this country the sky could be pitch black at night. The stars

---

* Apparently the authorities made Dolores agree to put up the money for a search if she was lost in the Sahara. They regarded this courageous woman as a jolly nuisance.

looked like silver and the only sound would be the whisper of the wind. When flying, the great arc of the sky increased the higher you went and the sunsets were beautiful beyond description. The silence was something you could almost hold in your hand and the people were as big as the distances.

I loved the country and the people but isolation from the flying world meant that I was developing rigid flying habits. I was constantly flying the aeroplane instead of letting it fly itself. I do not consider that I was a good pilot, but I was a safe pilot—perhaps sometimes too cautious. I was always aware that if I cracked my plane up out there, it would probably be beyond salvage. My passengers and the patients I carried were placing their lives in my hands cheerfully enough, not knowing that I carried no insurance. I was very conscious of their trust. It was a big responsibility. I have been fortunate all through my flying career because I have never had a flying accident of any sort, have never injured myself or my passengers, or damaged an aircraft.

If a skilled aircraft engineer had been available to me at the time, instead of having to wait until something went wrong, or if I had had another pilot, a partner, with whom I could have shared these worries and problems, I think I might have been able to take advantage of the openings I had made for myself out in the west. As it was, I was to throw them all away.

I had been unable to convince the Queensland government that an aerial clinic should be established. However, within a few years the west suddenly became air-conscious, largely because many men entered the Air Force during the war years and aviation itself developed rapidly during and after World War II. The first Flying Surgeon Service, for example, was considered essential to the well-being of remote Queenslanders and was government funded.

In 1938, John Flynn (commonly known as 'Flynn of the Inland') and his party were passing through on their way to Birdsville and stayed overnight in Cunnamulla. He begged me to give up flying in the west. He was convinced that it was killing me. 'Nancy, my dear child,' he said in his fatherly, kindly way, 'you've got to give this up. You must realise that you are a woman and this is too tough for you. You are carrying too much responsibility and you are too isolated.'

I knew John Flynn and his wife Jean well. When there was only one Flying Doctor base in Australia, I used to talk with them at the Canberra Hotel, Brisbane, about their plans for the future. Those plans called for a mantle of safety, which John hoped to throw over the whole of Australia. He would point out the places on a map that was kept under the plate-glass top of his dressing table. His wonderful vision was to result in the Royal Flying Doctor Service, which now has bases throughout Australia. Together with the Bush Church Aid Society at Ceduna in South Australia, the Flying Doctor has brought thousands of isolated families within reach of emergency medical attention. Combined with the radio link, which began as a pedal-operated radio because its power was generated by the use of bicycle pedals, the Service has broken down the inland's barriers of isolation and loneliness.

Could John Flynn see that the isolation and lack of facilities for a 22-year-old girl were beginning to tell on her; or maybe because I was a woman, not even he was taking me seriously? Shortly afterwards, huge developments were made in aviation and it was only five years later, in 1943, that it was considered imperative to have both the Flying Doctor and Public Health Service operating in the far west.

On 1 March 1938 a call came asking me to fly from Cunnamulla to Goodooga. I had to pick up a passenger and fly him 520 miles to Sydney. Two days later he was ready to fly back again and we took off from Mascot in the early morning light. As we neared the mountains I could see there was not much room between them and the clouds. Everything inside me revolted against those clouds and those mountains. It was almost as though the Leopard wanted to stand on its tail rather than go into them. So I turned back and landed again at Mascot. I felt frustrated and defeated, but the pilots there supported what I had done. They said, 'Only a fool pushes through when there is fog on the mountains.' But in my heart I felt that I could have got through if I had wanted.

I was recoiling from going back to the isolation, the turbulence, the heat on the claypans, the constant worrying about paying off an aircraft and having engine trouble. I never wanted to fly again—not even in a Link trainer, which never leaves the ground.

When I recently read Arthur Butler's unpublished autobiography, I learned that there had been a contract out for taking the airmail from Bourke to Adelaide. Had I known of it, even to fly the mail from Bourke to the railhead at Broken Hill could have completely changed my financial situation during 1935.

At this stage in my life the words of Defence Minister H.V.C. Thorby seemed to sit heavily upon my shoulders. Thorby believed flying was not biologically suitable for women, although he said there were some exceptions like Jean Batten and Amy Johnson. Generally, he felt flying was not consistent with a woman's role in life.

I did not return to the outback until many, many years later and then under different circumstances, but I know I left a bit of my heart out there. It is some of the grandest country in the world and I came to know the magnificent qualities of the country people.

CHAPTER 13

I had made the decision not to fly any more, but what was I to do? I could see that aviation was growing in Australia, although I could not see a place for a woman as an airline pilot. I thought perhaps my future could be in the administration and catering areas. While flying in the west I had been invited by KPM, the Dutch shipping company, to be their guest on the inaugural flight of the Australia to Java extension of the KNILM (Royal Netherlands Indies' Airways) service. Maybe I could visit other countries and see what was happening in aviation outside Australia?

In the meantime, the Secretary of the National Council of Women wrote to the Australian Government to try to restore the subsidy for the Far West Children's Scheme so I could continue my work out there. I also went to see the Prime Minister, the Rt. Hon. J. A. Lyons, to discuss reversing the subsidy decision. The Secretary of the National Council of Women, Ivy Marsden, wrote to many people trying to ensure I stayed in Australia. Many women had taken an interest in my activities. They were the leaders of emancipation and because I had broken into a traditionally masculine field, they saw me as an example. There was even a poster that read, 'Will Australia lose Nancy Bird?' All very flattering, but I had real concern at that time about my future in aviation. The subsidy was not continued and I accepted the Dutch airline's invitation. I would go to England, study civil aviation development and bring my knowledge back to Australia. At that time I had no idea how I would use it.

I put the Leopard and my hangar at Cunnamulla up for sale and, by the time I was ready to leave Australia, both had been sold. After paying off my debts I was left with about £400. This was the same sum with which I had started in the business of aviation. Before I left for England, my Leopard crashed, killing the pilot, Gordon Young, and seriously injuring his cousin. It was never rebuilt although the engine later turned up at the South Australian Aero Club. I believe the aircraft mechanics were intrigued by the old-fashioned crankshaft. Later, when browsing through the log book, they were amazed at the accounts pasted in by me, mostly from local garage mechanics who serviced what have become today's vintage cars! Though they did not have any aircraft engine experience they did a wonderful job—another example of the ingenuity and resourcefulness of the outback Australian.

I can laugh at myself now. However, prior to leaving the industry I made a press statement which in part stated: 'There is no future in the air for women as pilots; I have sold my machine and given up my career as a pilot to concentrate on commercial ground organisation.' The article in the *Sydney Morning Herald* continued, 'Miss Bird, who has flown more than 70 000 miles in Australia without mishap, will leave by the KNILM plane next Sunday for Java en route to Europe.' I continued a defence of my rationale:

To my mind, the only opportunities left to women as pilots are stunt or long-distance flights; publicity flights—trying to beat the altitude record or endurance tests for the benefit of somebody's soap; or in private charter work. I think that private charter will soon be almost non-existent, because with the development of airways and the enlargement of the network, people would much rather travel in one of the luxurious passenger planes, than in a small private machine. I suppose that there will always be emergency work, particularly outback, but the tendency is for private charter to diminish rather than increase.

Fifty years later this proved to be entirely incorrect. Charter flying has flourished and if people get together they can fly very cheaply.

I also went on to say, 'On my coming tour of Europe and America I will concentrate on the study of commercial ground organisation from the passengers' viewpoint. If possible I want to obtain a job at some of the airports in Holland, England and America, to learn first-hand everything I can—about traffic and passenger management in civil aviation.'

As it happened I was not a passenger on the Dutch airline's inaugural flight because all seats were needed for VIPs and journalists. In July 1938 I left on the third flight to Batavia (now Jakarta) in a Lockheed 14 Super Electra, the fastest commercial all-metal aeroplane on the market. The route on to Holland in a DC2 was across Burma, India and up the Persian Gulf. I felt I knew all the refuelling places so well, having been at Mascot through every hour of the great record breaking flights of the early 1930s, which had taken the same route out from England. Amy Johnson, Jean Batten, Jim Melrose, C.W.A. Scott, Kingsford Smith, Jim Broadbent and a dozen others had all landed at these places, which included Singapore, Allahabad, Jask and Baghdad. I slept in the same rest-houses and hotels in which they had stayed overnight because, at that time, airline aircraft did not fly at night.

In my luggage I had letters of introduction from Edgar Johnston, Director-General of Civil Aviation, to important aviation people in Europe and America. Edgar had volunteered for the Air Force to get out of the mud in France during 1916. There were 230 hopefuls lined up for interviews and, as they answered questions, they were told to either step forward or backward. A couple of weeks later, he was advised that he had been selected for training, and after 23 hours solo, was sent back to France to take part in aerial combat. During my training at Mascot, I had met Edgar at the Aero Club.

His kindness to me was remarkable. Due to Edgar's help I met many interesting people who showed an enthusiasm for aviation and others who were just interested in a young woman from a distant country. I remember meeting the Controller of Civil Aviation in Finland; at dinner his wife expressed her surprise to find I was 'so pale'. Apparently she had expected me to be black.

Our first night was spent at Darwin and the following morning we refuelled at Koepang. We were given a second breakfast there, as we were winding the clock back by flying west. To see a Dutch breakfast of ham and cheese prepared in the rest-house was my first taste of the world outside. We then flew on to Bali, where the bare-breasted women were a shock to my puritan upbringing!

Batavia, capital of that beautiful emerald green island where east and west mixed, was our next stop. I spent a few days there and was lavishly entertained by the Dutch people and the Australian Consul while awaiting a seat to Europe on a KLM DC2 flight.

I spoke to several of the pilots operating out of the area and none of us could know that soon so many would be evacuated to Australia. Others would lose their lives, shot down in unarmed aeroplanes or strafed on the lonely beaches of north-west Australia.

One KLM captain with whom I flew in Holland was the big Russian Dutchman, Ivan Smirnoff. His story of landing his burning aeroplane in the sea, then wading ashore with his passengers as Zeros strafed them on the beach, is a tragic and dramatic tale.

Smirnoff was in Java with a plane load of evacuees, anxiously anticipating an air raid at any moment. He was finally given the clearance to take off at 1 am. Just as he was closing the door, an official rushed up to the DC3 and thrust a small package into his hands, with instructions to take it to Australia where someone would collect it. The captain tossed the parcel into a safe box and concentrated on taking off. It was pitch black, as not even torches were allowed and he could hear the Bandoeng ack-ack guns in the distance. Java was conquered within three days by the Japanese.

There were 11 people on board the aircraft including the pilot and crew. As it approached the Australian coast, the aeroplane was attacked by Zeros, and Smirnoff ordered everybody to the floor. The only exceptions were a mother nursing her baby, and the captain. The Zeros riddled the unarmed machine with bullets, hitting passengers and crew. One engine caught fire. Smirnoff, who collected four bullets in his arms and thigh, anticipated an explosion. He headed for a strip of sand on the coastline, pancaked the aircraft minus one wheel and ploughed it into the surf to extinguish the fire. He then told everybody to wait for pauses in the strafing and then get out of the aircraft and hide under it for protection. Only one crew member was injured following these instructions and when the Zeros ran out of ammunition, they flew off. Smirnoff then helped the injured to shore and tended to their wounds. The mother died that night.

Smirnoff sent one of the men back into the aircraft to salvage everything of value, including the small package. Hit by a wave

(*Top*). The 'Gatsby' days of flying at the Aero Club. From left Pat Levy, Jim Broadbent, Phyllis Arnott, Jack McKechnie, Freda Deaton, Dick Allen, unknown, Frank Follett, unknown, Bunny Hammond, Harold de Low (my cousin), George Littlejohn, Mr and Mrs Wedwood. Photographed on the 1931 Melbourne tour.

(*Above*). The flying Loneragans, Mit, Tim and Bernard, photographed about 1932. They were sportsmen pilots who contributed much to aviation.

(*Above*). Mrs Harry (Dolores) Bonney on her arrival at Wangaratta in Victoria on a hot summer's day in 1932 after her record flight from Brisbane, through 640 miles of turbulent air.

(*Top*). I put up my hand to hush the mechanics who were teasing me as the photographer took this picture beside Charles Kingsford Smith's Percival Gull. In 1933 he broke the England-Australia record in this aircraft.

(*Above*). A small crowd would soon gather whenever Peggy and I landed in a paddock; people were fascinated by an aeroplane.

(*Top*). Some of our patients came to say goodbye to Sister Silver and myself at Hungerford's rough aerodrome.

(*Above*). This photograph was taken with Mrs Muriel McKeig and Pat Pearson at Dungalear Station, Walgett, during my first barnstorming tour. From left to right the jackaroos are Gordon Simpson, Scotty Graham, Bill Stevens and Teddy Capper.

(*Top*). Occasionally someone else would swing the propeller. This saved me walking through the slipstream, which was disastrous for my hair.

(*Top*). George Falkiner (left) of 'Haddon Rig' leaning on his Waco aircraft with World War I ace, mischievous Jerry Pentland.

(*Above*). Dressed in their Sunday best, mothers and children meet the baby clinic at Byrock in 1935.

(*Top*). An advertisement for a sheep lick painted on the tail of the Leopard Moth helped me to pay for petrol.

(*Above*). 'Spots' was my mascot in the Leopard Moth, as I awaited take-off time in the Brisbane-Adelaide Air Race in 1936.

(*Top*). Dr Cole and Reverend Roberts lifted patient Gladys Linnett out of the Moth when we arrived at Wilcannia, on one of my flights as an air ambulance. Reverend Lionel Lambert took the picture.

(*Above*). The Reverend John Flynn, founder of the Flying Doctor Service, and I stand beside a Qantas De Havilland 86 airliner in Charleville in 1936. This was the northbound lunch stop, one of 13 between Brisbane and Darwin for the twice-weekly service.

(*Above*). Hanna Reitsch flying the first autogiro, forerunner of the helicopter, in the Berlin Deutschlandhalle in 1938. Every evening for three weeks Hanna flew the helicopter at the Motor Show.

(*Top*). Trading in the open cockpit of the Gipsy Moth for the comfort and luxury of the cabined Leopard Moth was no hardship.
(*Above*). Desperation — I had engine trouble and the nearest ground engineer was more than 200 miles away. I would have married the first one to come my way.

(*Above*). In a secondhand fur coat, I rugged up against the cold of Berlin in December 1938.

(*Above*). Kurt Björkvall survived ditching in the sea on his 1937 attempt to fly from America to Sweden. The writer Baroness Blixen had intended to accompany him, but was lucky to miss the flight. I flew with him to the north of Sweden the following year.

(*Top*). I went to Mascot to lend my maps to Jean Batten as she set out to search for the missing Stinson airliner, in which her friend Beverly Sheppard was killed when it crashed on the Lamington Plateau.

(*Above*). The American-German Society hosted by Louis P. Lochner (4th from the left), head of United America Press, gave a luncheon in 1938 to honour Hanna Reitsch (3rd from the left) on her acceptance into the Luftwaffe. Elly Beinhorn is sitting next to Lochner.

(*Top*). The women who flew to meet Amy Johnson in Sydney in 1930. From left, Evelyn Follett, Bobby Terry, Meg Skelton, Amy Johnson, Alice Upfold, Freda Deaton, Phyllis Arnott and Margaret Reardon Davis.

(*Above left*). A studio photograph taken while I was in London. The Red Cross made this photograph into a button to help raise funds for the war effort.

(*Above right*). Unpacking the models of aeroplanes we had never seen in Australia, which I brought back for the *Wings the World Over* exhibition in 1939.

(*Top*). I was already in love with Charles Walton when we reached Fiji.
My shipboard romance has lasted more than 50 years.

(*Above*). A ferry pilot during the war years, Iris Critchell has run her own Flight
Academy in California for 30 years. I was lucky to have her as my co-pilot during
the 1958 Powder Puff Derby. She also gave great support to Gaby Kennard after
her dramatic Pacific crossing in 1990.

(*Above*). Myself as Commandant of the Women's Air Training Corps with Margaret Reardon, better known as Mrs A.M. Davis of the Red Cross and the Flower Club, and the second woman in Australia to gain a flying licence.

(*Above*). Gwen Caldwell ('Starkie') of the WAAAF with Wing Commander Keith Bolitho at Rathmines Flying Boat base near Newcastle in February 1945.

(*Top*). Betty Hyler Gillies, co-pilot to Nancy Love, in the Flying Fortress they were to deliver across the Atlantic during the war. Already on the runway at Goose Bay for take-off, the flight was cancelled. No reason was ever given.

(*Above*). As the first foreigner in the 1958 Powder Puff Derby, I was proud of my kangaroo on the fuselage. Iris Critchell and I were placed 5th in the field of sixty-one.

(*Above*). The German aviatrix Elly Beinhorn was my greatest inspiration. Her first job in aviation was in Portuguese Africa in 1931 with a scientific expedition. I met her in Australia the following year.

(*Above*). Robin Miller, dubbed the 'Sugar Bird Lady', packing her oral vaccine and sugar lumps to give Aboriginal children in the Kimberleys during the polio scare. She was a heroine of the Flying Doctor Service and of women pilots everywhere.

(*Top*). I thought the face was familiar as I taxied up beside Danny Kaye at Van Nuys airfield in California. Loretta Foy and I had been practising for the Powder Puff Derby in 1961.

(*Above*). Jerrie Cobb was the first woman to qualify for space flight in 1960, but it was not until 1981 that Sally Ride went into space. Jerrie went on to medical mission work in the Amazon.

(*Top*). One of Australia's most famous airmen, P.G. Taylor (later Sir Gordon), with my children, Tweed, his godchild and John, now a charter pilot in Narromine.

(*Above*). Brigadier-General Hans Ulrich Flade, chief of Air Staff of the Luftwaffe until 1986, with Baron Koenig-Warthausen, who flew a 20hp Klemm around the world in 1928.

(*Top*). June Scobie, widow of Challenger's commander, came to Bundaberg to return a little piece of Hinkler's glider recovered with the wreckage of the shuttle found floating in the Atlantic. Tom Quinn shows us a replica of the glider.

(*Above*). Sherelle Quinn was one of the first women pilots employed by Qantas. Now a first officer, she saved for her flying lessons by picking strawberries, working in a factory and doing nightshifts. She used to hide her flying manuals under the bed, so her parents would not worry.

(*Top*). Australian women pilots gathered at Canberra Air Force base to present mementoes to the first two women accepted as pilots in the RAAF. From left, Glenda Philpott, Joy Caldwell, Robyn Williams, Nancy Bird, Debbie Hicks and Joan Bracken.

(*Above*). Captain Van Messel and I, two old early birds, meet in Holland. A former captain of KNILM (after the war, chief pilot of KLM), Captain Van Messel was a valuable asset to the RAAF Transport Command during the war years.

as he was clambering out, the man dropped everything, tried to retrieve the packet but could not find it. It seemed of little consequence at the time. Everybody was fighting for survival and he and Smirnoff agreed to look for it later.

Stranded on an uninhabited desolate beach with little food and almost no water, Smirnoff rationed out their meagre supplies. He erected parachutes for protection from the blazing sun and then reset them to gather water when a storm passed. Realising they would perish without sufficient water, he invented a makeshift distilling plant using a kerosene tin, blow torch and piping from the aircraft. Everybody had to take turns in keeping this operation working and, apart from turning very small quantitites of sea water into drinking water, it kept the survivors occupied. As the merciless sun beat down on them, their lips cracked and they all suffered terrible dehydration.

The crew had trouble getting the radio to work because the battery was flat. Finally, their SOS signal was received, but by the Japanese. They came and bombed the stricken aircraft and then flew away.

On the third day Smirnoff sent a party of the fittest men to look for fresh water. The first evening they returned exhausted and unsuccessful. The next day, the Dutchman said, 'Go. Don't come back. If you keep going maybe you will be found. Then you can send help to us. If you come back here you die—we die too.'

On the sixth day, when nearly all hope was gone, the RAAF found them and dropped food and water supplies to get them through until a search party arrived. Five lives, including the baby, had been lost. The next day the search party arrived and in their weakened condition all the survivors had to walk 20 miles to the nearest mission. Fortunately they did not know this when they started out and their later enquiries were met with, 'just a little bit further'.

After this incredible ordeal Smirnoff eventually reached Melbourne where he was met by a bank officer and a detective who asked him the whereabouts of the small package. He told them what had happened and that he did not even know what was in the parcel. He was told that it was just £250 000 worth of diamonds. Some time later, there was a court case in Perth to find out what happened to these diamonds. A beachcomber had found some precious stones lying on the beach and was acquitted of stealing them; an Aboriginal woman had given directions to the police to find a buried petrol can, in which there were diamonds; and a Chinese merchant said he had been given some of the diamonds in lieu of money, when a group of Aborigines had bought shirts and shorts from him. That little lot was worth £10 000.

Another of the pilots who evacuated from Java was G. van Messel who later became Chief Pilot with KLM. When he reached Australia van Messel joined the Australian Transport Command and was greatly valued by the Command's leader Harry Purvis, who was an outstanding engineer and aviator. Harry was P. G. Taylor's co-pilot on the flight from Australia to Chile. It was Purvis who told his medical officers, including Dr Ion Morrison, that Japanese Zero pilots always shot the pilots of enemy aircraft. In case that happened to him, Purvis drew lines on the windscreen to indicate how the aircraft should be positioned at different altitudes so the medical officers could land safely.

Van Messel was also one of the last people to see Amelia Earhart. She had visited him at his home at Bandoeng to show him over the aircraft during her record bid.

My next stop on the KLM flight to England was Singapore, where I met Jessie (Chubbie) Miller, the Australian woman who started out from England with Captain Bill Lancaster in 1927 in an Avro Avian named *Red Rose*. After continual engine trouble and bad luck they finally arrived in Australia in 1928. I was flying the *Red Rose* when I was almost lost at sea in Bass Strait during my training.

Chubbie was not a pilot when she started out on the flight, but undoubtedly she learnt on the way. Flying with someone else's husband was a scandal in the 1920s. When it was revealed the couple had fallen in love, the scandal escalated.

In 1929 Chubbie became a licensed pilot in America and flew an experimental and unstable aircraft called the *Alexandria Bullet*. It had been grounded when a test pilot refused to fly it. Another test pilot survived 26 turns of a spin before regaining control. Chubbie put in a new engine and broke American Laura Ingall's coast-to-coast across the United States and return record. Chubbie also courageously flew a charter flight from the States to Havana but became lost at sea and was missing for six days on the return journey. Lancaster found her on a sandy beach on a lonely island well out in the Atlantic. Their romance continued despite Lancaster's wife refusing to grant him a divorce.

When the depression hit, Lancaster took up flying in El Paso, leaving Chubbie with her ghost writer Hayden Clarke. When Lancaster returned, Hayden Clarke, whom Chubbie had agreed to marry, was found shot dead. Lancaster was charged with his murder. Ultimately, the court found that Clarke had committed suicide. Shortly afterwards, Lancaster tried to redeem his public image by attempting the England to the Cape record in an Avro Avian. Twenty-nine years later his mummified body was found beside the aeroplane in the Sahara Desert where he had forced-landed and died of thirst. He had kept a diary that told of his daily hopes of being rescued. In the sand lay his wallet with his last letter to Chubbie Miller tucked beside her photograph. His love for her had never faltered.

In 1938 when I met Chubbie in Singapore she was married to an airline captain, Flight Lieutenant John Pugh. In recent years she has been the subject of a television mini-series, *The Lancaster–Miller Story*. A film about her life has also been proposed.

After Singapore, we spent each night on the ground and there was often time for sightseeing. At Jodhpur I accompanied a large Dutchman, who spoke English with a Scottish accent, to see the fort. Just as well I had this man for protection, because I was wearing shorts. Even today, women in India do not show their legs, but I was completely unaware of the disapproving glances and my faux pas.

Arriving in Holland, KLM was a most gracious host. I stayed near The Hague in a seaside hotel at Scheveningen and was horrified to learn you had to pay to go on the beach! To an Australian whose country has thousands of miles of beaches, this was incredible. I was later to find the same situation at Cannes in France. During their occupation of Holland in World War II, the Germans used the word Scheveningen to test an unidentified person. If he could not pronounce 'Scheveningen' he was not Dutch, and therefore either a foreign enemy, an escapee or a spy!

The Dutch recognised that I was a curiosity in the world of aviation. They understood the value of marketing and promotion and saw in this rather naive and quite unsophisticated young Australian an opportunity to expand the public's awareness and acceptance of air travel.

123

My first ever press conference was arranged by KLM in Holland. I did not understand what was happening before being ushered into a room where several journalists were sitting around a large table presided over by KLM's Executive Director Hans Martin. Hans had flown with Wilbur Wright and been invited to join KLM as a Director by its founder Albert Plesman in 1912. He retired from the board after World War II. Princen Geelings, a very sceptical publicity manager towered behind me. He later revealed that he thought I was one of those girls who had 'convinced' a director I was worthy of a free trip to Europe. Hans Martin introduced me and I answered the questions they fired at me.

I must have answered some of them adequately because Princen Geeling was completely won over and KLM decided to help me. In return they would use me for all the publicity I could give them. All the articles I sent back to my friend Constance Robertson of the *Sydney Morning Herald* were printed and the Dutch were delighted. I was unique in Europe where 23-year-old girls were usually heavily chaperoned and protected. Here I was virtually on my own!

I believe the Dutch still felt a warmth towards Australia as a result of the epic landing in Albury of the KLM DC2 during the 1934 England–Australia Air Race; Parmentier and Moll's obviously kindly disposition towards Australians; and Kingsford Smith who gave world fame to Dutchman Anthony Fokker's aeroplane, the *Southern Cross*.

Like many of us in Australia, the Dutch were very enthusiastic for further use of air transport. Under the leadership of Albert Plesman, they took great pride in their national airline, which had begun as a service from Amsterdam to London in 1920. As a young Flight Lieutenant in the Dutch Air Force, Plesman had envisaged a world united by the air. He said, 'The birds have no nationality.'

Plesman even set up an inexpensive restaurant at Schipol airport to encourage people to watch the aeroplanes fly, while enjoying their meal. He developed pride for the Dutch national airline. In the first years of the airline service it took a determined type of person to be a passenger. They had to be equipped with helmets, goggles and hot water bags! In 1921, Anthony Fokker built enclosed cabin aircraft, which KLM brought into service.

As I sat with Albert Plesman at a pavement coffee shop in The Hague, I had no idea of his greatness. After this brief meeting, he contacted KLM offices in Europe, and instructed them to help me if I called on them. This enthusiasm and friendliness resulted in Lufthansa and ABA (later Scandinavian Airlines) treating me as a VIP. Together with KLM, these airlines were world leaders in the industry thanks to their efficiency and forward thinking.

CHAPTER 14

In 1938 KLM was opening a service direct from Amsterdam to Manchester and asked me if I would fly to this destination instead of London. When I arrived at Ringway, Manchester, I was taken back to see a large photograph of myself in the airport building, advertising their new direct service. I joined in the celebrations of the airline's opening there with Lord Trent, owner of Boots Pharmaceuticals, the Dutch officials, Amy Johnson's sister and brother-in-law, then Manchester's Deputy Mayor. Later I was to meet Amy again, this time in London when she was semi-retired. I was to learn that when she flew the Atlantic with her husband Jim Mollison in 1933, Amy had wanted to divert to pick up some more fuel towards the end of the flight. Jim refused, however, and they ran out and had to crash land in a bay off the United States coast. Jim resented the fuss made of Amy and went back to England. It was Amelia Earhart who stepped in and invited Amy to stay with her while she recuperated.

From the time I stepped off the DC2 in 1939 I was caught up in a whirlwind of meeting exciting people and enjoying wonderful experiences. I was also invited as a guest of the BBC programme 'In Town Tonight', produced by Mike Meehan. Alex Henshaw, who had recently broken the Cape record in a Mew Gull, was featured on the same show. Jim Broadbent had previously introduced us and we soon found lots in common. Alex invited me to visit Arthur Clouston whose England–South Africa record Alex had broken.

Clouston was ill in bed, but what an evening I had listening to these two magnificent record breakers recount their flights hour by hour. Clouston stated: 'Henshaw's flight to the Cape and back is probably the most outstanding solo flight ever made.'

Alex had won the 1938 Kings Cup Air Race in his Mew Gull, designed and built by Edgar Percival. His designs were revolutionary and enabled world records to be set by pilots including Kingsford Smith, Jean Batten and Beryl Markham.

In the war years Alex was Chief Test Pilot at Castle Bromwich, a leading Spitfire factory where 11 694 Spitfires were produced and 37 023 test flights made. He and his team survived 127 crashes. He almost lost his life when, on one occasion as he was parachuting from an aircraft that was breaking up, his boot fell off and disappeared into a cloud. Alex grabbed his harness release and unconsciously tried to throw off his parachute to chase his favourite flying boot! Henshaw's book *Sigh for a Merlin* is a must for all those who flew Spitfires.

Alex obviously loved adventure and excitement, but he also showed great sensitivity. He refused to join the Air Force and remained a thorn in the side of the top brass and bureaucracy because he always said precisely what he thought. As a civilian, he was able to maintain both his authority and freedom of thought. He never had a strike or a moment's sabotage on his station and tolerated nothing but 'all out' for the war effort. Once, he demonstrated the Spitfire flying upside down at 300 feet for Winston Churchill. Alex's book *The Flight of the Mew Gull* is an exciting account of his London–Cape Town record.

Another major Spitfire testing base was at Worthy Down and was led by Supermarine's Chief Test Pilot Jeffrey Quill. When I met him after World War II, I was completely enchanted by his sensitivity and incredible skill. If one named the world's greatest test pilots, Jeffrey would have to be in the top class. It was his responsibility to take Spitfires into the sky, put them through maximum strains and stresses, all the time being prepared to jump if they exploded in his hands or the wings came off. That required a rare degree of courage.

Jeffrey's book, *Spitfire—A Test Pilot's Story* puts to rest any suggestion that pilots are bus drivers. He glosses over the fantastic development of the Spitfire—the trials and his striving for perfection, even though the bureaucrats, as late as the 1930s, did not favour an Air Force and some disarmament lobbyists in 1936 were keen on cutting it back!

In his book, Jeffrey writes that towards the end of the war almost every Spitfire picked up at the factory for delivery was flown by a woman pilot. He expressed great admiration for the job they were doing.

A most distinguished Luftwaffe fighter pilot, Colonel Wolfgang Falck told me they lost more aircraft in delivery flights by inexperienced young pilots than they lost in certain periods of combat. Some of course would have been lost through mechanical failure and bad weather but such conditions existed all over the northern war zone.

Mike Meehan helped me make several BBC broadcasts and kindly organised for me to be invited to several business functions and shows. At one I met Charles Laughton and his wife Elsa Lancaster. The Australian media were present at this performance and made an exaggerated statement saying I had stolen the show. What nonsense is written in the interests of parochialism.

I met many distinguished people during this exciting time. I had already met Lord Semphill at Mascot when he flew a Puss Moth to Australia in 1934 and I was to see him again at one of the functions I attended. I also met Group Captain McNamara, who won a Victoria Cross in World War I for his daring landing in the desert to rescue a fellow pilot. He introduced me to Sir Francis Shelmerdine, Comptroller-General of Civil Aviation, who promised me every assistance in my research work.

When I think back now, I must have made many faux pas. I remember during a dinner at a Berkeley Square mansion that I was the only woman who put her grapes in the finger bowl!

These were the true 'Great Gatsby' days of flying—people who flew for sport and fun. Aero Clubs flourished and the safety and excitement of aviation were promoted by enthusiasts landing in paddocks for picnics, and pageants being held at grassy aerodromes. Unknowingly, a pool of pilots was being formed who were later to be the instructors of a rapidly and hurriedly expanding Air Force.

Among this group were Denzil and Andrew Macarthur Onslow of Camden with whom I renewed my friendship in England. The brothers had intended flying back to Australia in a de Havilland Dragon they had bought. I was invited to accompany them as navigator. I did go to Croydon with them to fly the Dragon, but decided I would see more European aviation while I had the opportunity. I had only been in England three months and as I was politically naive, still intended going to Germany despite the Munich crisis.

Camden, their home aerodrome, became a war-time Air Force base, but to this day is an active airfield, retaining its country atmosphere and 'touch of class'.

It was suggested by the Secretary that I join the Royal Aeronautical Society in London so they could help with publicity and typing letters. That is how I came to know Florence Barwood, Under-Secretary to the Secretary, and the real back-bone of the society.

I found the society most helpful on this visit. However, on returning to England in 1986, I was disappointed to find that it had become quite insular. I did not get any further than the assistant librarian who condescended to get off his Mr Pickwick's stool to tell me that belonging to the Australian branch of the Royal Aeronautical Society 'was not the same thing'. The Royal Society is a worldwide organisation but perhaps with Australians buying British newspapers, beer, real estate and now their banks, their attitude to us has changed somewhat!

While in London in 1938, I wrote a few articles for newspapers and this helped me pay my £2 per week rent. When one of the articles appeared calling a willy-willy a 'dust devil', I nearly died of embarrassment. They dramatised my story and made me look like a little heroine being chased by these dust devils in the Australian outback sky. I prayed that no Australian would see the articles.

The weekend before I left England to return to Holland a Women's Air Rally took place. The rally had been organised by Gabrielle Patterson, who later became an ATA pilot. I was delighted to catch up with Elly Beinhorn who gave an excellent display flying a Messerschmitt 108 with a retractable undercarriage. We had never seen a woman fly such a powerful aircraft before. Another woman pilot was Pauline Gower who was probably the best known in England at that time, with the exception of Amy Johnson.

Unlike the Dutch and Australians who wanted to promote aviation, the British seemed disinterested. I found I could learn little from Civil Aviation in England. I wanted to experience flying to Scotland, but Scottish Airways could never guarantee its service, because the weather was so bad. The *Flying Scotsman* train, however, got through no matter what. There was little incentive to fly and you had to be really keen to travel by air.

Naturally I was determined to fly whenever I could and I used the air service to go to Scotland. That flight stays vividly in my memory—it was the only air fare I was required to pay in 13 months overseas. The cost was three pounds.

One Scottish family who did persist with aviation were the Hamiltons whom I later came to know. Lord Clydesdale, the eldest son, made an historic flight over Mount Everest and his brother, Lord Douglas, with whom I went to Farnborough, crashed in Africa. He and his son were returning from a flight across the Atlantic when they became lost and flew into the mountains at Cameroon.

Australians are now sought by all the world's leading airlines but in 1938, there were only a handful employed by such companies. Jim McCann, son of the South Australian Agent-General in London, was working for KLM at the time. He knew of my desire to return to Holland and I received a letter from Mr Kaufman inviting me to fly back to Amsterdam whenever a seat was available. I was to learn a lot about KLM, which was undoubtedly running the best airline in the world at that time. I discovered they were keen users of the Link Trainer and they were also most generous in sharing their knowledge and experience.

Back in Amsterdam I visited KLM to thank them for their kindness. I was flabbergasted to hear that I was welcome to a ticket anywhere and everywhere in Europe.

In 13 months from July 1938 I travelled 45 000 miles and visited 25 countries. Good luck followed me wherever I went. With only a single exception, I was the guest of KLM, Lufthansa, ABA (forerunner to Swedish Airlines) and others. Of course, there were difficult times and I frequently went without a meal to save a few shillings as I only had a couple of hundred pounds for expenses. It was an enthralling experience though at times, tinged with loneliness.

I did not have an itinerary before I left Australia but many people kindly gave me contact names. Eventually my main route covered Holland, England, Germany, a white Christmas in Sweden, then on to the USSR and America.

The Dutch treated me like a VIP. I was invited to many prestige functions and included in a reception in Paris during the famous air show in 1938. I was also fortunate to meet Anthony Fokker's Sales Manager, Mr Schmidt. The original Australian National

Airways aeroplanes were Fokkers as well, but because Australia was only allowed to buy British aircraft, they had to be built in England under licence, and were called Avro 10s.

I took German lessons in my room at the Museum pension in Amsterdam and visited the many museums, keen to improve my education. To see the originals of world famous paintings and look into a canvas that you had heard so much about at school, was an extraordinary sensation. I learnt who Rembrandt was while living next door to his museum where many of his fine paintings are displayed. I was even flattered by the attentions of a young blond German baron, who was probably a forerunner of the Fifth Column!

Equipped with a few German words I arrived in Berlin in 1938 as the Germans marched into Czechoslovakia.

My first night in Berlin was spent at the prestigious Bristol Hotel where a bunch of red roses from Elly Beinhorn awaited my arrival. Elly had married Bernd Rosemeyer, Germany's most famous racing car driver, winner of the 1937 Grand Prix of the United States and a local hero. Bernd had died in an accident less than a year before my visit. Mother of a baby son, Elly bravely continued her flying and was already one of the world's most famous aviatrices.

Within a couple of days of my arrival, Elly invited me to lunch at the German Aero Club. I was amazed to find it was located in the Haus der Flieger (house of the flyers) in Prince Albrecht Strasse. It was a large, substantial building of impressive appearance. At one time it had been home to Germany's Upper House of Parliament. There were two beautifully furnished lounge rooms, one larger than the other. On the end wall of the main lounge was a life-size oil painting of Adolf Hitler. Facing it from the opposite wall, was a similar painting of Hermann Goering. In the centre of the long-sided wall was a large, striking oil painting of what appeared to be Richthofen's famous 'Flying Circus' of small tri-plane fighters. There were many other rooms including the ballroom, which could accommodate 1200 people.

Military and civilian flying men, their friends and approved visitors were the only people admitted, although the Club apparently had a million nominal members who paid membership subscriptions without being entitled to use the facilities.

In November 1938, Germany was in the 'guns before butter' days. You certainly had to produce your passport to obtain butter! I was obviously not thought to be a security risk because I was invited to inspect the Junkers factory. Lufthansa and the Shell representative, Heinz Nitsche, who became personal pilot to General Christians in the war years, organised this visit. Through them, I also flew to Frankfurt on the maiden flight of the Junkers JU88 and to Vienna on the Focke Wulf Condor. I did not know then that they would become troop carriers.

During this time Germany was giving aviation high priority and I met many leading pilots, including Ernst Udet, who was second only to the 'Red Baron' as the outstanding air ace of World War I. At the outbreak of war in 1939 he became the Luftwaffe's Quarter-Master General. Flying was his vocation, but time and circumstances forced him into a desk job. Unable to accept his position or agree with policy, he committed suicide in 1941.

Another was Baron Frederick Karl Koenig-Warthausen who had flown a 20 hp Klemm around the world in 1928. During the circumnavigation he shipped this tiny aircraft across the Pacific and Atlantic. It is a fascinating story. He originally set out to compete for the Hindenburg Trophy by flying from Berlin to Moscow. However, the flight turned out to be far more eventful. When he landed in Russia he was persuaded to visit the magnificent countryside near the Ural Mountains where he met the German Ambassador to Thailand. He accepted the Ambassador's invitation to visit Bangkok where he fell in love with a Thai princess. The Baron's friendship concerned members of the Royal Court and he had to make a hurried departure. He found a Persian kitten that the Princess hid in his aircraft as a parting gift and carried it with him from then on.

Singapore was his next stop and from there he shipped the tiny Klemm to Japan and across the Pacific to the United States.

His only accident was in a taxi on his way to the airport at El Paso, Texas. He was badly injured and spent three months in hospital. During this time, the famous Zeppelin dirigible was making its historic flight around the world and, when it flew over El Paso, the Baron was carried to the hospital roof to see it. The crew saluted him from overhead. Frederick Karl then continued his flight to New York before shipping the aircraft home to Bremen where he received a hero's welcome.

I was to meet Baron Koenig-Warthausen several times over the years and a warm friendship developed. I learned he was related to the Zeppelin family and was a third cousin of Queen Mary of England. I visited his castle, Schloss Sommershausen, in southern Germany on several occasions and, in 1970, had the pleasure of Frederick Karl coming to Australia to see us.

Because of my friendship with Elly Beinhorn, I have returned to Germany many times. When Elly began flying she tried to get sponsorship for long distance flights, but no one was interested. She gained her first job as a pilot by applying as E. Beinhorn, fearing that she would not get it if the company knew she was a woman. However, they just wanted someone who was cheap and Elly set off to join a scientific expedition in Portuguese Africa.

On the return journey Elly had a forced landing some miles out of Timbuctoo and was reported missing to the outside world for five days. Overcoming exhaustion, heat and other difficulties of this remote part of the world, she persuaded the natives to walk into Timbuctoo and there received help. (The expression 'You can go to Timbuctoo' means more to Elly than anyone I know.)

All at once Elly found the German Nation did care whether she was dead or alive. She had become news, and now the press really wanted her story.

Elly made bigger and better plans; this time she flew east to the Islands of Malaya and Java, and by sheer coincidence she ended up flying on to Australia. Here a tremendous welcome awaited her and after a triumphant tour of Sydney and Brisbane, Elly shipped her machine to Panama, and then flew all over the west coast of South America, Peru and Chile, and across the Andes. One year after her departure she returned to Berlin, a heroine indeed.

I remember map reading for her as we flew a Messerschmitt 108 to the 1938 Paris Air Show. I was extremely surprised when I found a place on the map called Charleville. As we flew over it, I wondered which nostalgic person had named an outback Australian town after this place.

I lost contact with Elly during and immediately after World War II and then in 1951 the Red Cross found her for me again. Elly had remarried and we found her with her two teenage children near the Black Forest. The thrill that her son Bernd experienced in driving our powerful modern car was the highlight of our visit.

I had no idea of the hardships and food shortages that Elly and her family had experienced during the war. Nor did Elly tell me, but I did learn she had cunningly saved herself from eviction and possibly rape during the occupation of Germany by French forces. Three drunken Algerian soldiers had banged on her door demanding entry. Elly courageously kept them waiting and then flung open the door, shouting at them in the same manner she had seen Arabian beggars treated in Cairo. The soldiers fell back in horror and she was never troubled again. Years later, I was in her kitchen and threw out a piece of stale bread. This earned me a severe reprimand. 'Since the war no German has ever thrown out a crust,' she said.

Before World War II, I was invited to visit Stuttgart to meet the father of gliding, Wolf Hirth, who was head of the Gliding Training School. I also met Hanna Rietsch who was considered to be one of the world's best glider pilots. Soon after Hanna began lessons, Wolf recognised her skill and personally supervised her progress. He employed her as an assistant in his workshop and then as an instructor. He became a close family friend and encouraged Hanna in her early long-distance soaring records.

Hanna was a fanatical aviatrix and could not bear a day to pass without flying. She was one of the world's champion glider pilots. In 1938, she became the first woman to be commissioned as a Flight Lieutenant in the German Air Force. She went on to become a test pilot of extraordinary courage.

Hanna's job was to test aircraft to the limit. One of the tests involved cutting off the propeller by flying into steel cables. Another was to fly alongside such cables, scraping the fuselage against them. Hanna defied death many times.

Hanna went on to fly virtually every type of aircraft which the Luftwaffe brought—or considered bringing—into service. Perhaps her greatest fame or notoriety was when she tested the world's first rocket, Germany's dreaded V1.

Believing that the war could be stopped by a demonstration of awesome proportions, Hanna and eight volunteers proposed to guide V1 rockets into major targets such as dams and power-houses. Such a mission would be on a par with Japan's Kamikaze squads—there would be no escape for the pilots. The Allies landed in France before this suicide mission got underway.

At the end of the war, Hanna knew more about rockets and guided missiles than most other people, and efforts were made to entice her to America. Her 'love of country' made her resist these approaches and so she was imprisoned for more than a year because it was feared that she would become a 'Nazi heroine'. She was released when the authorities apologised, telling her that they 'had made a mistake'.

Hanna had a tragic life. Her father, a doctor, put his grandchildren, wife and a daughter to sleep—and then took his own life—rather than face the terror of the advancing Russian army.

She was the only woman to be awarded the Iron Cross and Bar during World War II. That honour almost certainly contributed to the victimisation and suffering she endured in later years. This persecution included both Poland and Britain refusing her visas when she was selected as part of the German Gliding Team in 1957–58.

I first saw Hanna fly in 1938 at the world's largest aviation exhibition, the Paris Air Show. She gave a magnificent performance in a glider with slow rolls and loops at 'no feet nothing'. Later, I was invited by Professor Focke, the designer of the helicopter, to inspect a rotary wing aircraft that he had built. That machine was the forerunner of the helicopter. To demonstrate its performance, Hanna flew the machine inside an enclosed exhibition hall, the Deutschland Halle. I was thrilled to receive many photographs of this event, signed by the Professor. This helicopter was widely acclaimed as the world's first, although it had in fact been preceded by a Spanish machine. In 1923, Juan de la Cierya produced an auto gyro which contributed substantially to development of the helicopter.

Hanna's first love was gliding and she broke many world records. Her last success was just two years before her death. Because the Treaty of Versailles had prevented Germans from flying powered aircraft between 1919 and 1932, the country's keenest aviators turned to gliding.

Hanna died in 1979. I knew her as an intense, honourable and compassionate person, and as someone to whom the world's aviation industry owes a great debt.

CHAPTER 15

In November 1938, the American-German association gave a reception to honour Hanna Rietsch. At this reception I met a wonderful man, Stewart Herman, who was deeply involved with an American church in Berlin. I did not believe in love at first sight until it happened to me. Until then I had always thought of pastors as pious gentlemen, like those who had reported us for being inattentive during religious lessons at school. They seemed somewhat removed from everyday happenings and we feared rather than respected them. Stewart, however, had sailed on a world trip before the mast, which had been cut short when he was called to Berlin because of the illness of a pastor friend.

At the outbreak of war, Stewart not only liaised between the British and Germans, but refused to leave Berlin until he was shipped out on the *Gotenburg* exchange of internees. Later, he was the first civilian to return. He worked tirelessly for the displaced persons through both the military and Council of Churches, to obtain visas for people wanting to get to America and to collect orphans in Austria and place them in Swiss homes. The reports he wrote in 1938 and 1939 are now being published in Germany by the Council of Churches.

We saw a lot of each other in Germany, and when I returned to England in 1939, to my delight he visited me. Like many people, our paths were leading in different directions, and we went our separate ways. I have continued to meet him over the years, the last time in 1987. He looked remarkably well and although he had suffered a heart attack the previous year, was still as upright and articulate as ever. I feel a tremendous warmth, admiration and respect for this man.

I left Berlin in 1938 with a heavy heart and shed a few tears as I flew away. Breaking through the overcast Berlin sky that had existed for the previous month, I discovered, as always, the sun was still shining above the clouds. It was a shock to break into brilliant sunlight.

My destination was Sweden via Schipol in Holland where I waited on the ground for the snow and fog to lift. Not even KLM aeroplanes flew in such conditions in those days. Many of the passengers were Swedes who insisted that they spend Christmas with their families. They became panic-stricken when they thought they were not going to make it in time and set off by train. I had no alternative but to wait, as I was a guest of KLM. We waited three days for the fog to lift.

This trip was my first experience of complete Instrument Flight Rules (IFR) flying. To see those aeroplanes take off, then virtually disappear into the fog as their wheels left the ground, was quite amazing.

In Stockholm, the head of the Swedish Red Cross, Count Bernadotte, took charge of me. I was interested to see their Air Ambulance services. Every winter in Sweden, frozen lakes are used as airfields to get to remote and weather-bound places. It was arranged that I would fly to Aro with the distinguished Swedish pilot Kurt Bjorkvall and land on a frozen lake.

Kurt had attempted flying from New York to Stockholm in 1936 but had been forced down off the coast of Ireland where he was picked up by a French trawler. I learned more about this in Mary S. Lovell's book, *Straight on till Morning*. It reveals that the Baroness Eva von Blixen, of *Out of Africa* fame, had planned to fly with him, but he left without her at the last minute and she made some very scathing public comments about him. She was lucky, for she could have drowned in the Atlantic.

After landing on a frozen lake, your adventure is not over until you negotiate the path from the plane to the lake's edge. Wearing ordinary ski boots, you walk very cautiously on the ice, which makes ominous sounds as your weight is placed on it, and wonder if it is going to break. Karl Florman, head of ABA, had arranged for me to go by sled to the family winter cottage which Greta Garbo often used for her holidays. As the pony trotted through the snow I wondered if there were any wolves in this area and was told that sometimes they heard them!

Christmas in Sweden is certainly an experience for an Australian. Instead of temperatures of over 35°C, I was surrounded by people wearing fur coats, some made out of dog and wolf fur, attempting to keep out the bitter cold. Travelling alone, it was the worst time to try to see anybody! I did go skiing on the slopes where I met an English couple who had just come from Malaya and delighted in the fact that they could speak a language the multi-lingual Swedes could not understand.

In 1939 I flew to Russia with ABA; they were the only airline allowed to fly into Moscow and then only on alternate days. The Russians flew to Sweden on the other days of the week. Karl Florman and party were invited for the May Day celebrations and I was asked to join them.

As I was a guest of the Swedes, the Russians thought I was Swedish and were horrified to hear I was an Australian aviatrix. American Charles Lindbergh had recently been their guest and made some uncomplimentary comments about the Russians in Germany, so they were suspicious of flying people. The Swedes had to accept responsibility for me! Whatever criticisms of the Russian people I had observed in Moscow I kept to myself. I much admired the Soviet's magnificent underground railway, and enjoyed a feast of Russian music and ballet. I was suitably shocked at the way the Russians expect you to drink Vodka—straight down.

Fortunately for me, I was included in all the May Day celebrations including the Swedish Embassy parties. One of the young male secretaries at the Swedish Embassy paid me far too much attention and as I looked in the narrow stem of a glass of champagne, I said, 'Whenever I look into the hollow stem of a bubbling glass of champagne, I will remember you'—and I do. He became an Ambassador, but I never saw him again.

Russian women were already in the Air Force and assigned to combat duties. Among the heroes of Russia I met were Polina Osipenko and her two colleagues Marina Raskova and Valentia Grizadubova. In 1937 these three had created a long-distance record flying from Moscow to Vladivostok. Polina was made a Hero of the Soviet Union and one of the privileges was to be given her own car!

We were also guests at the Bolshoi Ballet for the Nutcracker Suite and I was completely transfixed by the music, the dances and the people in attendance. Many of the audience were dressed like peasants, and at each interval would rush down to the orchestra pit munching large bread sandwiches. Applauding the musicians with much enthusiasm, they seemed hungry for both bread and music which reminded me of how music-hungry I had been at Bourke.

After my brief visit, I flew to London direct from Moscow the same day to do a broadcast for the BBC. I understand I was the first person to make this commercial flight in one day and certainly the British thought so because the programme was broadcast in Australia and included this unique 'first'.

Back in England in 1939, the Cinderella-like quality of my trip continued. I was often the guest of airlines and oil companies, feted at fabulous restaurants and was even a guest at Buckingham Palace where I was presented at court. The day after my Palace appearance I was at a Lyons Corner House searching the menu for the cheapest meal which happened to be baked beans at fourpence a plate!

For my court presentation I was fortunate in being allowed to wear the pick of Molyneux's Paris collection. I also carried feathers and fan from his establishment. He was a leading designer who promoted his creations by giving them to people who appeared in public. 'Andrea' a famous social writer of that time, wanted a description of this stunning outfit to write up in her Australian column.

At Buckingham Palace, I remember hearing the names of several fellow Australians as they were called to be presented— Mrs Vincent Fairfax, Elizabeth Sharpe, Lesley Turner and the artist Russell Drysdale's mother. I should not have listened to the snobbish secretary at Australia House who advised me not to wear my Coronation Medal because it was not important enough. It would have been the only thing that distinguished me from the social set who were presented at the court. I distinctly remember the cold exclusiveness of the Empress Club where Florence Barwood of the Royal Aeronautical Society and I shared a chicken sandwich and a glass of champagne. Other Australians went on to parties at the Dorchester and Savoy. I would have been better off at my pension in Queenborough Terrace among those salt of the earth people where the atmosphere was full of warmth and enthusiasm. The way they had seen me off for my presentation at His Majesty's Court made me feel like Eliza Doolittle in *My Fair Lady*.

I expressed a wish to meet Lord Wakefield, patron of many long-distance flyers, so I went to visit him. He presented me with a book, *London Recalled*, in which he wrote, 'To Miss

Bird, with warmest wishes, Wakefield of Hyde.' Many aviators had wanted to meet Lord Wakefield, and he financed some, such as Amy Johnson and Jean Batten. Numerous others advertised his Castrol Oil on their planes.

Another highlight was my frequent visits to Hendon, the sportsmen pilots' mecca. There I met C. G. Grey, editor of *Aeroplane*, whose praise or criticism was of great consequence in the flying world. He made several scathing comments about the women pilots who wanted to fly during the war years. He was heard to say women who were anxious to serve their country should take on work more befitting their sex, instead of encroaching on a man's occupation.

All through my travels I was collecting material for an aircraft exhibition, which I planned to hold when I returned to Australia as a way of repaying the hospitality of the airlines. I wanted to call it *Wings the World Over*. As well as models, pictures and posters never before seen in Australia, I collected pamphlets, statistics on the performances of all the aircraft I had seen, the routes and the number of miles the airlines flew each year, and diagrams of the layouts of airport buildings.

Ground organisation and airline catering seemed the only thing a woman could do. Airlines were beginning to think of more interesting food for their passengers than merely a cup of tea and a biscuit. In fact, good hot meals were being served then by many of the European lines. Obviously, Australia would have to follow suit. In London I met with staff from Imperial Airways to learn something about catering. I even thought of taking a job with their newly formed catering department. However, I realised I could not live and pay rent on a salary of £3 a week, so I did not go ahead with those plans.

It was time to leave England. As I sailed away on the *Queen Mary* for the United States, the war clouds were gathering. Within a few months the Air Transport Auxiliary (ATA) was to be formed to help in the defence of Britain and her allies.

CHAPTER 16

I travelled tourist class although the Vacuum Oil Company's Australian representative, Fred Haigh, had asked a director, Frederick S. Fales, who was travelling on the ship 'to look after me' (he must have been quite important because they later named a tanker after him). Each evening he rescued me from the bowels of the ship to join him for dinner in the *Queen Mary* Grill Room. There I hobnobbed with the rich and famous. I especially remember actress Maureen O'Hara, who was then acclaimed as one of the world's best dressed woman. All I had to wear on these occasions was a little brocade frock made from a remnant costing 12 shillings and sixpence that I had bought in Manly. One night my host told me what a beautiful frock he thought it was, adding 'I know it is beautiful because I said so to one of the other women and she did not think much of it.' Youth was on my side!

On reaching New York, I found I had arrived before my letters so no-one was expecting me. The *Queen Mary* was faster than the post. Frederick Fales introduced me to his friend, Vladmir Steffansen, who had travelled in central Australia. I was delighted to meet this white-haired, famous explorer whose party, including Hubert Wilkins, had surveyed the Beaufort Sea in northern Canada during 1913. Vladmir was interested in the flying I had done and wanted to help me cross the States. I remember his words when I first met him, 'I have met many Australians who have been to Paris, but few who have been to Oodnadatta.'

When we sailed into New York harbour, I was spellbound by the sight of those skyscrapers and the magnificence of the city. In London I had been able to rent a room for £2 a week. Here it was going to cost me that much each day! The cost of America terrified me—how could I cross this vast land to board a boat home to Australia? Vladmir suggested the Greyhound bus as the cheapest way and arranged for me to break the journey at Cheyenne. These arrangements were never to be.

When organising my overseas trip, I had planned to return to Australia via America. Earlier, I had heard of the 'Ninety-Nines',* the national Women Pilots' Organisation of America, and had wanted to join. Bobbie Terry, the first woman in Australia to own her own aeroplane, nominated me to the organisation and I became a member in May 1938. Amelia Earhart was elected its first President and this has given rise to the incorrect impression that she was its founder. Marjorie Brown, Fay Gillis and Clair Studder were credited with forming the Association following the first women's Air Derby in July 1929. At the time there were 117 women pilots in the States. However, several declined to join a women's organisation.

Betty Gillies was the President at the time of my visit to America. Worried about my funds, I pondered as to whether I could afford the 25 cents to telephone and tell her I had arrived in the country. I finally took the plunge and it was the best 25 cents I have ever invested, for I made a life-long friend. I was immediately invited to stay with her at Syosset, Long Island, and through her met some wonderful and exciting people.

Betty had been born with a silver spoon in her mouth, but she spat it out during her teenage years. Finding the social life of New York unsatisfying, she decided to become a nurse, an unusual occupation for the granddaughter of the millionaire candy king, Huyler. During her training she met Brewster Alison Gillies (Bud), a young navy pilot, and fell in love.

Reading an article by Amelia Earhart in *Cosmopolitan* magazine entitled, 'You Too Can Fly', Betty thought she might get more attention from the young Navy pilot if she also flew. She signed up for lessons and soon qualified for a licence signed by Orville Wright. To build up her hours for a commercial licence Betty bought a de Havilland Cirrus Moth and took every opportunity to fly. Bud who had just left the navy was flying for dashing young bachelor Grover Loening, who was dating Amelia Earhart.

---

* The name 'Ninety-Nines' came about because at the inaugural meeting of the organisation the twenty-six attendees agreed that the association would bear the name of the number of charter members. There were ninety-nine.

The big sporting event in America, namely the Cleveland Air Races, was coming up and Amelia asked Bud to fly with her in a Curtiss Robin. Betty decided to go too, as did pilots from all over the world. There was to be a special event for women, but someone sabotaged both Betty and Amelia's aircrafts. Bud was working on Amelia's aircraft but had no time to fix Betty's. She was furious, so as soon as her aircraft was fixed, she flew off in a huff.

However, it did not take Bud long to recognise the remarkable qualities of this diminutive young woman, who by now had been snapped up by Curtiss aircraft as a demonstrator and sales expert of flying courses, and they were married in 1930. The young navy pilot proved to be a genius and became Vice President of the Grumann Aircraft Company, founder of various successful companies, aviator adviser and clever investor. Almost 60 years later, I would say it is the most successful marriage I have ever known! She is probably the most loved and respected woman in American aviation.

Betty feels her most worthwhile tribute to aviation was the nine years she spent as Chairman of the Powder Puff Derby. She lived the 'All Women's Transcontinental Air Race' night and day, proving that women could fly across the United States in a controlled, sensible way and encouraging many women to do so. This has had a tremendous influence on the acceptance of aviation as transport. Unfortunately it was poorly supported by those who had most to gain, the light aircraft industry, who only donated a miserable $200 each year. Women bought thousands of dollars worth of their aeroplanes, proving that even women could fly them. Betty and Bud flew the Atlantic in 1962 to visit their daughter in Italy, before private aircraft were being constantly flown across the oceans of the world.

Another love in Betty's life has been ham radio and her involvement has earned her several United States Naval decorations. With her 60-foot antenna, she worked the South Pole stations until the early hours of the morning for years on end: putting lonely men in communication with their families; and coping with emergencies, romances and tragedies.

When Nancy Love founded the Women's Auxiliary Ferrying Service in 1940, she immediately recruited Betty. This service began when Major Robert Love said in passing to General William Tunner 'I hope my wife has arrived at work alright this morning. She was flying herself to Baltimore.' General Tunner replied, 'Good Lord, I'm combing the woods for pilots and here's one right under my nose. Are there many more women like your wife?' 'Why don't you ask her,' was the Major's reply. A meeting was arranged and the WAFS were formed. Later, as the war progressed, this service became the Women Airforce Service Pilots (WASP). Why the change of name? I take an extract from Betty Gillies' speech given at Baltimore in 1985:

What is the difference between the WAFS and WASP? I am asked that question often! Well, the WAFS just got there first and so were the first women to be employed by the United States government as pilots to fly military aircraft. They were the right age at the right place, at the right time and with the required education and flying hours. The first three classes to graduate for the WFTC and be assigned to the Ferrying Division ATC were also WAFS. And WAFS they were until they woke up one morning and learned that someone had changed their name while they slept! All WAFS were now 'WASP'—Women Airforce Service Pilots. The Ferrying Division tried to retain the separate identity of their WAFS but to no avail.

Nancy Love headed the WAFS, and later was a WASP executive of the Air Transport Command's ferrying division. They became proficient in the fast fighter planes, flew every type of aircraft that was produced and delivered them to their bases. One woman delivered five pursuit planes in four days, each a distance of more than 2000 miles. Their other duties included aerial towing of targets under combat-like conditions, dive-bombing trials and camouflage photography. They did everything except go into combat. At one stage, to boost the morale of young pilots flying the Atlantic to England from the States, Nancy and Betty were detailed to fly the route. They arrived at Goose Bay and were on the runway ready to take off when they received an urgent telegram cancelling the flight. It also said 'there was to be no publicity, repeat no publicity concerning it'. General Arnold, the American chief of staff had been at a dinner party in London when he was advised of the flight. Apparently, he was furious and immmediately cancelled it. No reason was ever given.

The WASPs flew 16 million miles for the Army Air Forces. Twenty-five thousand women applied for pilot training and 1830 were accepted. One thousand and seventy-four graduated and 900 remained on duty at the time of demobilisation. The politically influential Jackie Cochran took control of the WASPs, and she trained women from scratch to be pilots (the WAFS only took those who had had previous experience). In 1944, however, because she was unable to establish a separate organisation of which she would be chief, Jackie disbanded the service. Ovita Culp Hobby was already Colonel-in-Chief of the Women's Army Corps (WAC) and Jackie would not serve under her. 'There were sixty-one aircraft waiting to be delivered on our field alone when we were told to go back to our kitchens', said pilot Barbara Erikson London, who was in charge of the California WASPs. 'We were furious!'

In disbanding the WASPs Cochran also had it written that no American woman could fly a military aircraft, and for more than 30 years that held. Her husband, one of the richest men in America, bought the Canadian Sabre factory, which enabled her to train as a jet pilot. The United States Air Force assigned Chuck Yaeger to her for six months, enabling her to establish women's world speed records, which were broken by Jacqueline Auriol of France, recaptured by Cochran and broken again by Auriol. This pattern went on for ten years.

In 1939, I accompanied Betty Gillies to a presentation of the Harmon trophy by Eleanor Roosevelt for Jacqueline Cochran. The following day, to my surprise, Eleanor Roosevelt wrote in her 'My Day' newspaper column of the Australian girl who had flown 'outback'.

We also went to Hicksville Country Club where Amelia Earhart was a frequent visitor. I met many aviators, including test pilot Jim Taylor who had given Amelia Earhart flying lessons. Jim invited me to fly with him in an amphibian. I was picked up at the Wall Street downtown airport and we took off alongside the *Queen Mary*, which had just been docked without tugs, due to a strike. We flew under two bridges, then around New York and 'Miss Liberty'. We landed at Roosevelt Field for lunch, then visited a country club after practising landings and take-offs on the water. From there it was on to Port Washington to see the Yankee Clipper land on her return from Bermuda.

It was through Betty Gillies that I met other test pilots including Barbara Jane Kibbee and Teddy Kenyon. Some years later, I recall travelling in a car with Teddy who at this time owned her own Lockheed Lightning. We happened to pass it and she longingly said, 'I love to fly it, but I can't afford to feed it.' This remark reminded me of the story of a woman who was flying into a major airfield one day. She twice called the tower, without success, when an irritated controller told her to get off the air because he was trying to land a B17 (Flying Fortress). The news that *she* was flying the B17 was greeted by a choked silence.

For nine years Betty was Chairman of the Powder Puff Derby, and for 59 years she owned her own aircraft and was still actively flying. During my visit in 1939, Betty was rewriting the Ninety-Nines' constitution. I made a few suggestions, one of which was that the association, instead of being national (they already had a couple of members in Australia), should become an international women pilots' organisation—and it did!

Some members were not keen to allow women pilots who were not actively flying to stay in the organisation. This restriction was not accepted, but you had to have 200 hours solo to retain membership. This restriction made inactive Daisy Kirkpatrick who had been the Ninety-Nines' fourth President. Although she flew a lot with her husband, she did not log her hours. Daisy was to become a very dear friend and her assistance from the minute we met was tremendous.

After being introduced to the VIPs of the airways, Daisy used all her influence to make sure I crossed America by air. I eventually went on United Airlines. To overcome the company's policy of no free flights I was sent to Kansas City and returned to the west coast as a prospective air hostess. When I arrived in Kansas City, I was met by Thomas Fortune Ryan, of the famous business magazine *Fortune*. He also turned up in Australia during the war years, as did many distinguished Americans.

Daisy introduced me to Cassius and Olive McCormack of Muncie, Indiana. Their home became a 'must stop' on my visits to America. Both flew for fun until well into their seventies and seldom missed a Sportsmen Pilots' meeting. They flew themselves on safaris in Australia, way up into the Gulf of Carpentaria and later in Africa where another adventurous safari was flown in formation with Ed and Viriginia Ball.

On several occasions I returned to visit Daisy, who considered herself my American 'Mom'. Interested in sailing, she and her husband followed Australia's first efforts to win the America's Cup. One day, at the Eastern Yacht Club, Harry Kirkpatrick said to me: 'Why do the Australians keep coming back? I'd like to see you win the Cup but you haven't got a chance. Financially, technically and in every other way, you have the whole weight of America against you.' Unfortunately, he did not live to see Australia win the Cup.

Daisy arranged for me to go on the maiden flight of the DC-4. The manufacturers, Donald Douglas, were having trouble selling this aircraft to airline companies because it was considered too big to be practical. Many people doubted if there would ever be landing grounds large enough for it. Others said an aircraft of such size would burst its tyres on landing. As a publicity stunt, to prove the aircraft was so safe that 'even a woman could fly it', Donald Douglas asked Jackie Cochran to pilot the DC-4 on its maiden flight from New York to Washington. I was lucky enough to sit in the right-hand seat for part of that flight. This prototype was finally sold to Japan, but it crashed in Okinawa during its delivery flight.

From the moment she started flying, Jackie Cochran wanted to be a star. Following her failure to complete the 1934 England–Australia Race and the Los Angeles–Cleveland Bendix race in 1935, Jackie flew a Beechcraft stagger wing to third place in the 1937 Bendix event. During the same year she flew a Seversky Executive non-stop from New York to Miami in 4 hours 12 minutes, breaking all existing records. In 1938, as the only woman entrant in the Bendix, and at the invitation of the Seversky's Russian manufacturer, she became the first pilot to fly the 1200 hp, P35 fighter plane. Jackie went on to win the Bendix race at Cleveland, then continued on to New York, achieving a new women's west-east transcontinental record. In the same year she won the Clifford Burke Harmon Trophy as the world's most oustanding female aviator. However, she never competed against another woman pilot.

During 1940 Jackie set many records, and in 1941 became the only woman to fly in a bomber delivery across the Atlantic.

The ferry pilots resented her intrusion and protested. The result was that Jackie flew in the bomber from Canada to Britain, but had to relinquish the controls to the pilot in command, Captain Grafton Carlisle, on take-off and landing. The British press made much of a woman delivering a bomber.

However, there was also another side to Jackie Cochran. When she visited Australia I was her aide-de-camp. She visited Melbourne first and under the wing of Lord Casey, she was given the VIP treatment she expected. However, on this trip nothing seemed to please her and her behaviour was, at times, extremely ungracious.

CHAPTER 17

When I arrived in Washington on the DC-4 trip, I was met by the Controller of Aviation, Oswald Ryan, and invited to the Mexican embassy to celebrate a non-stop record flight between Mexico City and Washington by Mexico's most famous pilot Francisco Sarabia. The very next day, he was killed in his Gee Bee racer. During the celebrations I sat next to Commander Towers, unaware that it was he who had navigated the navy aircraft across the Atlantic in 1919 with Commander Reid as captain. Originally three navy aircraft started out on that journey, but after landing in the Azores, only one got through. This was the first air crossing of the Atlantic.

I had met Captain Reid in 1933 when he had sailed into Sydney Harbour as the captain of the *Saratoga*. Because it had a couple of seaplanes on board which were lowered into the water, I had gone to see it and we had been introduced.

At that time, my most vivid memory of the visit was learning with shock that the sailors who showed me the aircraft on board wore mirrors on the toes of their shoes so they could see up the girls' skirts as they lifted us on to the wing of the aircraft!

Six years later in Los Angeles, as a guest of Pan Am Vice President Mark McKee and his lovely wife, I was invited to fly on the maiden flight of the Pan American Clipper into San Francisco. The World Fair was on and as we flew into the bay I saw the *Saratoga* at anchor. I was staying with a woman pilot, Ruth Wakeman. Taking up Captain Reid's invitation of 1933, with all the brashness of youth, I telephoned him. To my delight, both Ruth and I were invited to lunch—and piped on board as official guests. It was a memorable experience. Captain Reid later distinguished himself as an Admiral.

I was shown over the Douglas aircraft factory in California by Major Bertrandies who later became a General and visited Australia during World War II. On the same visit I was introduced to that genius of aviation Donald Douglas. I was intrigued to learn that he had an electric fence around his home to prevent his children from being kidnapped. His DC-3 was the work horse of the world. During World War II it was affectionately known as the *Dakota* and was used as a troop carrier, supply ship and anything else that was necessary. Only the 747 has earned that reputation since.

I left behind the extraordinary American hospitality that takes one with it like a tidal wave. I joined the Matson Line ship *Monterey* to return to Australia and found myself over the churning propellers in steerage class. By the time I reached Hawaii I decided I would like to move. I wired home for more money and through knowing the Purser's wife, whom I had met in Nevada, was able to change to the upper deck. If I had not made the change, I may never have met my future husband Charles Walton.

The Purser invited me to dine at his table and said, 'I'll put you between myself and this quiet Englishman to keep you in order. He'll control your exuberance.' Charles was returning to Australia and when told I was a famous aviatrix, he confessed he had never heard of me and had no interest in aviation whatsoever! With constant attention from this charming, attractive and gentle man the glorious days on the ocean ended each night dancing to the music of the American band . . . by the time the ship reached Australia we were deeply in love and became engaged. We kept the engagement secret because in the 1930s 'stars' had to be single.

Through Charles I widened my horizons to everything from archaeology to politics and horticulture. We have two children, Annemarie (Tweed) and John, plus four grandchildren. My shipboard romance has lasted fifty years!

Upon my return to Sydney in August 1939 I set to work unpacking the material for the *Wings the World Over* exhibition. Linda Littlejohn, an early Australian feminist, had convinced me I had organisational ability. I'm sure Linda would have pushed me into it anyway. Throughout Europe and America I had collected material showing what others were doing in aviation: the airlines that existed; pilots who flew with them;

150

airports; services and so on. It was an excellent collection, although the best exhibits were the magnificent models of the German aeroplanes and propaganda material that Lufthansa had so generously given. The war started in the week that the exhibition was to have commenced. As I opened the cases and saw the great black swastika, white circle and red flag of Germany on the tail of every aircraft, it was like a red rag to a bull. Obviously I could not include them in the display. I think some of the unpackers thought I was a Nazi spy! Germany was very advanced in aviation and wanted the world to know of its achievements.

One of these German models later ended up in New Guinea. Bobby Gibbes had imported a JU52 and he employed German engineers to work on it. I sent them a model of the aircraft, although in the meantime my little brother had painted over the swastikas. They were thrilled. It had been damaged but they repaired it with loving care.

The exhibition was a great success. Charles Lloyd Jones of David Jones Ltd offered to show it and help with the display. In addition he paid me £100, which seemed marvellous to me— I would have done it for nothing! Masses of people came to see it including an incredible number of schoolboys. For two weeks, Sydney Grammar School pupils seemed to call in on their way home each day.

Myer Emporium then asked me to take the display to Melbourne for two weeks. I thoroughly enjoyed talking to the flying enthusiasts and signing autographs. Here I met Maie Casey, who was an enthusiastic pilot. Maie and her husband Dick were due to leave for their ambassadorial post in America but the seeds of our lifelong friendship were sown at that time.

At the close of the exhibition, December 1939, Charles Walton and I were married in Sydney. I wanted this special day to be ours and had kept the date a secret to avoid journalists and well-wishers climbing over the pews. The Governor-General's secretary, Phyl Parkinson, had asked me if she could confidentially know the date of my marriage, with the result I received a telegram: 'To one of Australia's most valuable birds— Signed by Lord and Lady Gowrie.' The wedding ceremony was conducted by the same man who, a short time before, had begged me to give up flying and had taken such a fatherly interest in me—Flynn of the Inland, founder of the Inland Mission and Flying Doctor Service. His offsider was none other than Fred McKay, later Moderator General of the Presbyterian Church.

Before going overseas in May 1938, I had called a meeting at the Royal Aero Club in Mascot to discuss establishing a Women's Flying Club. Betty Mullins and Yvonne Worth called the next meeting and it was agreed to go ahead with the idea of providing training in aeronautics and to award scholarships to girls who wanted to fly but could not afford the fees. Fifty attended the first meeting; 200 the second and 300 from then on came to weekly meetings and bi-weekly lectures.

When war was declared in Britain, Pauline Gower became Commandant of the Women's section of the ATA. Prior to World War II, she and Dorothy Spicer had barnstormed around England, gaining engineering skills as well as good flying experience. With the outbreak of hostilities, Britain realised it had too few pilots to ferry aircraft. Pauline organised women pilots to assist in the war effort, although initially they were not trusted with anything larger than Tiger Moths. Rosamund Everard was also in the first enlistment. I had flown with her in Sir Lindsay Everard's Hornet Moth—51 years later I flew in the same beautifully restored aircraft to the de Havilland Moth Club Rally.

People think that the breakthrough of women on multi-engined aircraft and being 'taken on' by the airlines happened in the 1970s. But this was not so. The big break came in the war years when aircraft piled up outside factories and there were not enough pilots to deliver them to bases. The authorities had no choice but to use women. Eventually, women flew everything that came off the production line: even four-engined bombers.* However, contrary to popular belief, women, with the exception of American Jackie Cochran, who was listed as a co-pilot, did not ferry aircraft aross the Atlantic or the Pacific Oceans during

---

* Once I was listening to an Air Force officer, Jim Gering-Thomas, tell a group about how he had been grounded by weather at Cosford in the Midlands of England, 'when the roar of a bomber had us rushing to the windows,' and I said, 'what fool is flying in this weather?' The bomber circled and landed and out popped two petite young women. We were staggered because it took four of us to fly that thing.'

the war. Women pilots ferried thousands of aircraft around Britain and America from January 1940 to the end of hostilities. Incidentally, ATA announced that during the delivery of the first 3900 aeroplanes, only one had been written off and 14 slightly damaged. This prompted a comment from Pauline Gower that this record exploded the rumour, 'That the hand that rocked the cradle, wrecked the crate!'

Ratcliffe, the home of Sir Lindsay Everard, became No. 6 Ferry Pool and housed several of the American women pilots who had joined the ATA. Everyone at Ratcliffe dined with the family each night at a long refectory table hosted by Sir Lindsay and Lady Everard, and served by a butler. There are some fun stories of the girls hobnobbing with the English aristocracy. *Forgotten Pilots* by Lettice Curtis describes one such incident when Opal Pearl Anderson found herself sitting next to Lord Trenchard one night. In her broad American accent she said; 'You call me "Poil" and I'll call you "Lordie".'

Owing to the weather conditions in England, it is often not possible to fly by the horizon as Swoffer's technique had taught me. Great use is made of the turn and bank indicator when the horizon disappears in poor conditions. However, our maps were marvellous—every woodland and field was marked correctly by shape and location, so we arrived safely at Ratcliffe after seeking out almost every field and lane on our flight path. I was relieved to think that we did not have to rely on road maps, as there was a multiplicity of roads, crisscrossing the country. In Australia, I had been used to one road, and intercepting was imperative!

On my return to Australia in 1939, Sir Herbert Gepp, whose daughter Mardi was already in England, said to me, 'My daughter wants to learn to fly. Should I let her?' 'Certainly,' I replied enthusiastically. Mardi did, stayed in England and married Richard Gething an Air Force officer. Like the other girls, she joined ATA, ferried aircraft and flew more than 800 hours in Spitfires. She and her husband now live in Melbourne and have contributed substantially to the gliding and flying world.

Ferry pilots in England were in a war zone. They had to fly in radio silence, weave their way through balloon barrages and risk an enemy fighter in the sky. There was no concession to a civilian flying a military aircraft.

In the ATA, there were several foreign pilots including Polish, Chilean and Dutch. In Australia, Nancy Lyle of Melbourne was the only woman to fly for one of the armed services. Entirely on a voluntary basis, she used her Hornet Moth to give the Beaufort gunners range-finding practice and took photographers up over Melbourne, selecting possible targets to camouflage. She was one of the best women pilots in the field and like many of them, was self-effacing and did not seek out publicity and approbation. She was a gentle woman and a true achiever.

Jennie Broad, a former ATA pilot, began flying in 1936 and at 24, became Britain's first woman test pilot. At Hamworth, Midlands, Leicestershire, Jennie flew the second *Brawny*. Only two of these tiny sports aircraft were ever built and both killed their pilots. When the Broughton *Brawny* first went on the market, it was advertised as 'a well-built single-seater light aeroplane for 195 pounds sterling.' It had no rudder trim. While Jennie was flying, an oil pipe burst and she had to force land. The authorities later stopped further production.

After World War II, Jennie settled in Australia for a few years. In 1950 she went to South Africa where she sold aircraft in the Union and Rhodesia, mainly to farmers for cropdusting. She finally returned to Australia and has now retired to Norfolk Island.

Mary de Bunsen overcame polio and then flew in the ATA. In her book, *Mount up with Wings* she says '. . . flying people know the quintessence of living, in which death is the penalty of slackness . . .'. She also said they 'do not take life for granted and that is why they wear a look of perpetual youth . . . Youth at Heston was unconnected with the calendar, it was a quality of mind.' Mary, whose father had been a diplomat in Austria before the war, had sung in a Viennese Choir. Another of her phrases states, 'To sing in a big chorus, in a great work, is a liberation of the spirit, and so, in another sense, is flying an aeroplane alone . . .'

It is interesting to find that many flying people are artistic. Both Dolores Bonney and Jean Batten were pianists and many people, such as surgeons who have a dexterity of the hands, take up flying. Some say flying is also like riding—a horse responds to the touch of one's hands and so does an aeroplane. I tend to agree.

CHAPTER 18

Prior to the outbreak of war, the Australian women pilots' scene was beginning to unfold. Margaret Adams, already a pilot, was the first President of the Women's Flying Club and encouraged many of its early members. She became Margaret Kentley and remained a valuable member and historian of the Australian Women Pilots' Association until she died in 1988. (It is from her unpublished papers that I was able to confirm the formation of the AWFC and its successor, the WATC). Gwen Stark (Caldwell) was the next president, and with her invaluable experience in the Girl Guides, organised camps and training. Within a year, long before there was a Women's Auxiliary Australian Air Force (WAAAF) or any other Women's Service, the Club went on a war footing.

We were a step ahead when war was declared, already having girls trained in aircraft engine maintenance, navigation and meteorology. It was a small matter to extend their skills to work as drivers, suppliers, or learn signals. Mrs MacKenzie was our Signals Officer and, as an electrical engineer with her own shop, she took the girls there to teach them Morse code. Soon she broke away to form her own organisation and trained signallers for the Navy.

My admiration has never wavered for the girls who worked all day in shops and offices then spent their evenings equipping themselves to serve in the Air Force Women's Auxiliary. They would give up their weekends to go to camps and practise drill on bare grounds for hours on end. On their meagre wages, they paid all their own expenses including buying their uniforms. They worked at the recruiting centre, area finance office and drove Air Force personnel everywhere, often using their families' cars. With fuel rationing, these were not much use to civilians anyhow.

Deputy Matron of the Air Force, Muriel Dougherty, appealed to us for staff to service the RAAF hospital at Richmond. Pearl Cooper, Dorothy Wood and Margaret and Patricia Nutt volunteered to go, for which the Matron was exceedingly grateful as she had no domestic staff. While on the station they wore the Flying Club uniform and received two shillings and sixpence per day. The trade union woman rang me and said, 'Now that they need the women, see that they never work for less pay than a man,' to which I replied, 'Madam, for the war effort my girls would work for nothing,' as indeed they were doing! Matron Dougherty, in the immediate post war years, was sent by UNICEF to take over the Belsen concentration camp in Germany and turn it into a hospital. She died in 1988, unheralded and unsung.

The Women's Air Training Corps was formed in each state in 1940 and the Australian Women's Flying Club in New South Wales became the WATC for that state. The first head of it was Mrs J. H. (Paddy) Bell, a licensed pilot, of Melbourne. When she took over recruitment for the WAAAF, the Countess of Bective, whose husband was aide-de-camp to the South Australian Governor, became Commandant. I was the next Commandant, followed by Dame Mabel Brooks. Eugenie Craig was in charge in Western Australia, Yvonne McComb in Queensland and Mrs Campbell in Tasmania, so we had some fine leadership.

The WAAAF was authorised by the government in 1941. Most of the senior officers from the WATC and the Flying Club formed the nucleus of the new organisation. On 10 March 1941, pilot Gwen Stark, later 'Starkie', became the first servicewoman recruited by the WAAAF in New South Wales. However, recruiting stopped shortly afterwards when there was a change in government and Prime Minister Curtin announced that no more women would be taken into the services until every unemployed man in the country had been absorbed.

The first Director of the WAAAF was Clare Stevenson, a personnel officer with the Berlei Foundation Company. She was entertaining business guests at a Sydney restaurant when she was called to the telephone and told that she had been appointed. Even though Clare had emphasised she did not want this position, she reluctantly accepted. In *The WAAAF Book* Clare acknowledges that the WATC activities were largely responsible for the creation of the service.

As the war moved closer to Australia, recruiting for the WAAAF re-opened. After two months with the WAAAF in Sydney, Starkie was posted to Melbourne where she was responsible for billeting WAAAFs.

Athough the services had experienced little difficulty in billeting men, women were hesitant to take servicewomen into their homes.

To help overcome the shortage of accommodation, the exclusive Geelong Boys Grammar School was leased during the school holidays for an intake of 1000 girls who were enrolled for a four week rookies' course prior to being posted to RAAF establishments, mostly in Victoria.

The girls were kitted out with uniforms straight from RAAF stores. Their baggy overalls were either too big or too small and made for flat-chested men, complete with fly buttons. Although skirts had been made, the girls complained of having to be squeezed into men's jackets. Frequently the buttons flew off. One girl said that although she could fill the bust of a size 15 shirt, the shirt tail scraped the calves of her legs. It was hilarious!

However, Starkie's disciplinary training and sense of humour overcame many of the difficulties which faced young women making the transition to service life.

Starkie's next assignment was to take over the luxury hotel *Raneleagh* at Robertson, 2000 feet up in the southern tablelands of New South Wales. It was in a shocking state of repair. There was no water; the kitchen was vermin-infested and had to be completely pulled out; the floor boards had to be taken up and new stoves installed. The previously luxurious rooms were transformed into dormitories. Starkie's long experience in the Girl Guides was her saving grace. They cooked in the open, in fogs, mist and rain.

Thirty workmen from the Department of the Interior and air crews waiting for postings overseas were sent to Starkie's 'hotel' to carry out the alterations. Their presence worsened an already critical shortage of water.

Hearing that there was an army unit a few miles away, Starkie set off to see the officer in charge. She says that he was magnificent. With the army's enormous mobile water carts, they relieved the situation until the hotel's rusty leaking tanks had been replaced.

On her way back, Starkie saw a council worker grading the roads. The grader was just what she wanted to make a parade

157

ground. She contacted the shire and asked that the worker be allocated to her for two weeks. She even rang his wife seeking permission for him to stay at *Raneleagh* until the job was finished.

When girls got a posting to Robertson they often felt that this isolated mansion was the end of the earth—but it was not without its share of humour. Starkie recalls one incident when she went down to the station to meet an ACW (lowest rank). She greeted the girl at the station, and as she proceeded to her car, the ACW said 'You forgot my luggage!' Starkie apologised and picked up the luggage. Driving to the base, Starkie listened to a tirade as the girl told of the 'awful' things she had heard about the officer in charge at *Raneleagh*. She boasted that she wasn't going to take anything from her new boss. When they arrived at the base and started heading inside, the ACW called 'Just a minute, what about my luggage,' and again demanded that Starkie carry it. 'Half an hour later the girl had to report to me,' Starkie said. 'I can still remember the look on her face when she recognised me. I suggested to her that we had met before. Forty years later, I still get Christmas cards from her.'

Starkie's next posting was to North Eastern Area Headquarters, Townsville. The change of location coincided with the arrival in the area of the American 5th Air Force. She was in charge of a few hundred Air Force servicewomen who came from all walks of life and were surrounded by thousands of Army, Navy and Air Force men. It was indeed a frontier town.

Soon after her arrival, she returned to barracks quite late after inspecting Townsville, to be greeted by an American military policeman. 'You're late. You'll cop it,' he said. 'I'll be alright,' she said. 'Nope,' said the M.P., 'there's a new old dragon in charge. I'll show you a secret place in the bushes where there is no fence.'

As he escorted her to the spot, she asked him what the old dragon was like. 'Don't know,' he said, 'but I guess she's a grey-haired old dame with no sense of humour.' As he left she said, 'I'm awfully sorry, Corporal, but I'm that old dragon!' 'Goddam,' he said, 'count me for a sucker!'

Under the bushes, Starkie sat out the night greeting the girls who arrived late with 'See me in the morning!' From then on it was played her way. She trusted them and they trusted her.

On many occasions, Starkie vacated her flat so that honeymooners would have privacy, and she was frequently asked to give girls away when romances led to marriage, many of which—regrettably—were short-lived.

Starkie's greatest delight was flying a Tiger Moth that the American services allowed her to use. She chalked up considerable hours and in her words: 'The freedom of the sky was exhilarating! It was great relaxation and I loved flying.'

But there was a darker side to Townsville. Things in the town were pretty grim with 60 000-odd troops waiting to go into New Guinea to fight the Japanese.

On one occasion, a Japanese reconnaissance plane flew over in bright moonlight and a second one dropped a couple of bombs on the docks. Everyone was ordered to the trenches but there was no panic. In fact, the girls drowned out the awful sound of an air raid siren by singing.

Starkie earned the admiration of everyone for her dedication and tenacity during the war years. On the fortieth anniversary of the formation of the first women's service in Australia, she gave the Dawn Service address on Anzac Day in Sydney, the first woman to be so honoured.

Following the formation of the WATC in 1940, I believed we were doing useful work, though I admit there were times when it seemed to me that I was playing at being a soldier. We had to wear a uniform which was a burden to me because we were voluntary workers and it was not the King's uniform. I remember Nigel Love, head of the Air Training Corps, being horrified when I failed to return his salute at the yacht club, but as a civilian I was not supposed to salute.

As Commandant I would be required to travel interstate by train in two-berth sleepers. Often I found myself sharing with interesting women. Major Joyce Snelling of the Australian Women's Army Medical Corps, once found herself sharing with equal male ranking. Nothing so embarrassing happened to me!

During this time I conducted a survey among Australia's women pilots, logging details of their experience and their availability for overseas service. Pauline Gower and the women pilots of England were doing a magnificent job in Ferry

Command and we had women here who could swell their ranks. We had a hard battle ahead of us because the Australian Government had banned women leaving Australia—mainly to prevent wives joining their husbands in the Middle East, though some were doing a fine job there for the Red Cross. For the same reason I had to turn down Pauline's request for me to take up a position with the Air Transport Auxiliary in England. Because of the difficulties arising from the ban, by the time the register was completed the Battle of Britain was over and Australian girls were no longer needed by Air Transport Auxiliary.

Although we thought Mardi Gething was the only Australian ferry pilot in the ATA, Victoria Cholmondeley also became a First Officer. Another girl, Nancy Ellis, tried to leave for England by boat, but was 'manpowered' into a pickle factory!

Many of the servicewomen who were not subjected to great dangers or sent overseas, now find themselves looking back upon the comradeship of the services as the best years of their lives. This could not be said by the forgotten wives with young children, managing on a service pay and waiting at home feeling lonely and unimportant during those years. They had to struggle with rationing, one hundred-and-one ways of preparing mince meat, and the daily fear they might receive a telegram which read, 'We regret to inform you . . .' Many had husbands who were prisoners of war or listed as missing.

With the end of the war I took up a more personal life, devoting myself to domestic duties as a wife and mother. When wartime controls continued and the threat of bank nationalisation arose, I began taking an active interest in politics.

I joined the Australian Liberal Party, and in 1949 the Women's Movement Against Socialism, which had been founded by Millicent Preston Stanley Vaughan, the first woman to be elected a member of the New South Wales Parliament. We rallied women all over the state to work against bank nationalisation. The Liberals should have been grateful, but they were not.

Millicent had one failing, common to many politicians, namely she did not believe in training anyone who might become her successor. Years later I learnt that when the largest women's group (which was at Wagga) made requests for me, they were always told I was unavailable. However, Millicent did put through some worthwhile legislation in her time.

In 1951 I went to England and worked in Ernest Bevan's former electorate where Christopher Mayhew was standing, to gain political experience. I was amazed at how close together everything was and how much easier this made campaigning. While there I was welcomed to the House of Commons by Lady Maxwell-Fyfe, whom I later discovered was the sister of actor Rex Harrison.

In Australia, I was asked to accompany candidates on various political tours—one was with the then Premier, Vernon Treatt. He and I both spoke at a meeting which was held on the south coast. It attracted more people than usual. A woman speaker apparently attracted more ladies, and their husbands came to accompany them! However, I remember the vote of thanks when the old gentleman thanked Vernon Treatt, but said 'The little lady stole the show.' I was never asked by Treatt to share a platform with him again.

On another occasion I agreed to accompany a young candidate standing for the rural seat of Eden Monaro. It was to be a week's tour so I had to engage a nanny to look after my two children. I remember the anguish I felt at having to leave them and then telephoning home every evening to find out how they were. I fully understand why there are so few women in politics! Bill Keys was the candidate and he later became President of the Returned Servicemen's League (RSL) and was knighted. He addressed 19 meetings in those seven days and we were accompanied by his parents as chaperones. These days, however, Bill jokingly tells his audience if I am present, how we travelled together all those years ago.

Bill was one of the many excellent candidates who were lost to the Liberal Party in the 1950s. Invariably, people of this calibre were passed over by selection committees for party hacks and 'yes' men.

I later spoke at various meetings on behalf of Jack Beale, Jeff Bate and Bill McMahon. Bill always joked that his majority in the next election increased when I did not speak in support of his campaign. Finally I thought I would make my own bid for the Legislative Council. At the first attempt I was merely flying the flag, knowing it was not possible to win. On the second occasion, the Party told me it was necessary to put in a Newcastle resident because the seat was a Labor stronghold. At the last minute Eileen Furley, a Vice President of the Party, went in unopposed.

I had no illusions about what I might have contributed. I believe I would have been a reasonable politician. More women were needed in Parliament House, but it was not known how much their knowledge and votes counted. I had been dismayed by the use women were put to in the political parties and the attitude of the chauvinist males to even the most highly educated and articulate females. Time, however, is showing the value of women to our country.

With politics behind me, I was keen to continue devoting time to the community, and in the late 1950s was invited to head the women's section of the National Heart Appeal. In this era some of the great fund raisers of New South Wales were Margaret Fielding Jones, Nola Dekyvere and Joan Jones. I set up a committee and asked the Country Women's Association head, Thelma Kirkby, to take the chair. That was a mistake for she was a controversial figure in the CWA. She was too political for their liking and spent a lot of time living in the city. Some members felt this should have made her ineligible for the Presidency.

I went down to Melbourne to see Dame Merlin Myer who had raised one million dollars for the Heart Foundation in Victoria. How could I follow such a remarkable woman of such tremendous influence? Needing more speakers for our meetings, I approached the Penguin Club, a speakers' organisation which sent me several women. I found a star—Mickie Halliday. She later went on to be founder of the Asthma Foundation, married Judge Hardie and has been a tremendous success in everything to which she turned her hand.

Mickie Halliday had exceptional ability as did many Australian women, but in that generation few had the opportunity to break through the barriers of tradition and prejudice.

While having many other interests, I was also quietly moulding a women pilots' association. Throughout my early flying career I had found it difficult to make friends with other women aviators, with the exception of Peggy McKillop, of course. Most of them were very kind to me beause they saw me as doing a job that women had not previously tackled, but they were women of independent means and considerable social consequence such as Phyllis Arnott and Bobbie Terry.

In 1949 I called the women pilots together. We discussed what each had been doing in the war years, and in so doing, inspired an interest in one another. Believing it should not depend on one individual to get them together each year, the Australian Women Pilots' Association (AWPA) was formed the following year. I had seen how friendly and hospitable the women pilots were towards each other in America and I was confident that we Australians could benefit from such an organisation. Maie Casey, wife of the Minister for Foreign Affairs, consented to be our Patron.

Maie was important and influential in the worlds of politics and art, but as a pilot she also had an interest in the future of women pilots. She gave considerable help and encouragement to general aviation throughout the difficult years following the war. When she moved to Government House as wife of the Governor-General she gave functions and invited women pilots from all over Australia as her guests. Through her support, and because of her patronage, the AWPA gained widespread recognition and respect. Every year the Annual General Meeting was held in a different state, and whenever possible, Maie attended. She was always impressing on members to treat aviation as a serious means of transport, not just a pleasant pastime.

I often flew with her. Once, while on our way to an Annual General Meeting in Brisbane, we took Michael Taylor who later became the Marquis of Headford. He had founded an aviation business in England and ferried aircraft across the Atlantic to Africa after World War II. Another time, when Maie and I were flying from Melbourne to Adelaide, we had no idea where we were. Suddenly the voice on our radio asked us our position. Hurriedly we scanned the maps, looked out the window and there below us was the Glenelg River. With confidence we reported our position—and marvelled at our luck!

My friendship with Maie remains one of my most precious memories. Her understanding of those less privileged than herself influenced me profoundly. She loved going to art shows and some of her culture brushed off on me when I stayed with her in Melbourne. She was a true aristocrat who, in the words of Kipling, 'Could walk with kings and yet not lose the common touch'.

CHAPTER 19

The names of many of the early members of the AWPA appear in the Stockman's Hall of Fame, such as Margaret Gilruth whom I met in England in 1938. She was part of the last private flight in and out of Berlin in 1939 and was the first Australian woman to use her licence in the field of newspaper reporting. Margaret wanted to write an article on the exhilaration of parachute jumping and was even game enough to make the jump herself. Another was Beth Garrett who began flying in 1947. After three years with private airlines in the southern states, followed by 12 years instructing and charter flying, she joined the Flying Doctor Service in northern Queensland, serving remote areas in the west for 19 years. Many of the women in these outlying parts were delighted by her visits and she developed many friendships. Her daughter also became a commercial pilot.

After World War II, women pilots were able to creep into aviation by tackling the jobs male pilots did not want. One who made the breakthrough was Nancy Ellis Leebold. Her distinguished career began as an instructor teaching people to fly from their own homes in the country. Later, she found work as a co-pilot in a heavy freight carrier, the Lockheed Loadstar.

Australia's first woman crop-duster and aerial spraying pilot was Margaret Clarke. When she began this work, her employer rang the authorities in Adelaide to find out what she should be paid. Margaret was classified as an 'unskilled worker' and her wage was £10 per week, for the most dangerous form of flying. She subsequently earned more as a cleaner in Sydney. In 1949 she set the altitude record of 16 500 feet for a de Havilland Gipsy Moth. The first woman helicopter pilot was Rosemary Arnold, who actually held commercial licences to fly fixed and rotary wing aircraft. Rosemary was a beautiful blonde who dressed exotically. She once successfully applied for a job in Indonesia, but when the man's wife saw Rosemary, she was immediately sacked.

In 1963, Queenslander Wendy Lloyd Hare became the first woman to hold a senior commercial licence and the youngest person to become an A-grade flight instructor. She travelled throughout Queensland teaching property owners to fly. By 1979 she was working at Mascot, flying jet aircraft for Stillwell Aviation—the first woman ever to do so in Australia.

Gertrude McKenzie started a flying school in Moorabbin, Victoria, in 1953. One airline captain still expresses his gratitude to Gertrude. Earlier in his career he was going to take up crop-dusting in Tasmania as a way of increasing his flying time. She told him, 'You will kill yourself if you do that. Stay here with me and I will help you build up your hours.' He took her advice.

The following year, Hazel Roberts found her aircraft very useful and a great timer saver on her family's western Queensland properties. If a spare part was needed in the shearing shed, Hazel could fly to Richmond and be back in an hour. If she had to send an employee in a truck it would take a day. There were 13 gates between the property and Richmond and always a chance he would meet a few buddies!

In 1958 after carrying out aerial surveys for the CSIRO, Beryl Young was appointed official pilot to the Queensland government. She flew the Governor; the Premier, Sir Joh Bjelke-Petersen, and many ministers to meetings throughout Australia. She was also required to fly extensively overseas and logged up more than 10 000 hours in fast aircraft.

Since its inception, the Australian Women Pilots' Association has steadily increased its numbers. Today, there are more than 700 members. I was appointed Patron following Lady Casey's death in 1981.

Women pilots continued to be pioneers in their chosen aviation fields throughout the 1960s and 1970s. The person who made the greatest impact was Robin Miller. She was the daughter of Dame Mary Durack, well-known author, and Captain Horrie Miller, the co-founder of MacRobertson Miller Airlines. With top ratings in nursing, midwifery and flying she was Western Australia's best-loved woman pilot. During a polio epidemic, she persuaded the state government to let her fly into remote north-west regions to hand out sugar lumps containing Sabin oral vaccine. For two years from 1967 she flew 43 000 air miles. To the Aboriginal children in the north of the state, she became known as the 'Sugar Bird Lady'.

Between 1970 and 1975, she dedicated her skills to the Royal Flying Doctor Service in Western Australia and was ready for any emergency. On one occasion she had to fly a heavily pregnant woman to hospital. The baby decided it would not wait, so Robin calmly set her single-engine aircraft on automatic pilot and attended to her passenger. The air traffic controller was astonished when Robin reported she had gained another passenger during the flight and that there were now three on board!

Robin also ferried several aircraft to Australia from England and America and wrote two books on her flying career, *Flying Nurse* and *Sugar Bird Lady*. Her wonderful work earned her various nursing and aviation awards from Italy, Australia and Britain. Sadly, some of them were granted posthumously. In 1975, at the age of only 35, Robin died of cancer. Her death was a tragic loss.

Australia's first women air traffic controllers were both appointed in 1960: Olga Tarling a co-pilot with a Victorian airline became a controller at Brisbane Airport; and Shirley Anderson, after gaining the highest marks in the Canadian Air Force radar examinations, was appointed a controller at Sydney. Both held their positions for 25 years. Olga also became an instructor in air traffic control.

Distinguished aviatrix Senja Robey flew the world's shortest regular air service between Bankstown and Mascot in 1962. By 1988 Senja had been flying continuously for 39 years, earning many awards for outstanding performance. Besides charter flying, instructing and aerial photography she has delivered aircraft to various parts of Australia. Once she was flying as a co-pilot in a Powder Puff Derby when they were hit by a sudden storm approaching El Paso. Newspapers were flying past her as she prepared to land and Senja decided to open the throttle to climb out of the weather and turn right. The American pilot, Tommie Hayes, cried 'No, no, don't turn right, you will fly over Mexico!' To which Senja replied, 'To hell with Mexico' and continued her turn, waited on an airfield for the storm to pass and returned to El Paso.

Another notable pilot, Helen Blackburn, held both American and Australian licences. She lived in Darwin during the 1960s and her voluntary aerial work covered everything from collecting marine specimens from remote islands and beaches (where she would land and gather shells for universities and museums) to mercy flights and carrying mail, stores and people throughout the Northern Territory.

In 1963 America's Betty Miller was the first woman to fly the Pacific Ocean solo. Two years later Australian Rosalind Merrifield became the second to complete the dangerous flight. This flight has now been made many times by Australians, including Robin Miller, Aminta Hennessy and several American women pilots. The flight that we thought was so fantastic in 1928 is now becoming a regular journey!

After working as a nursing sister with Victoria's Air Ambulance Service in the mid-1960s, Barbara Stott is now Sister-in-Charge of the Aerial Medical Services in Darwin, providing health care and air transport for patients in some of Australia's most remote areas. Barbara was the second civilian to be accepted by the United States Aero Medical Training School, and in 1987, was awarded an Amelia Earhart Scholarship, which enabled her to further her aerial work.

Marcia Hremeviuc, an experienced charter pilot in Mount Isa, took up helicopter mustering in central Australia and became the most distinguished woman in this field. I loved her comment, 'Mustering is mostly done by inexperienced pilots. The experienced ones won't touch it!'

The AWPA brought many old hands back into flying. These women joined the Association after many years on the ground and then decided they had better do something about getting their licences back. As a matter of fact, I was one of them—I began to feel a little uncomfortable about the fact that I was a penguin president of a women's flying organisation.

I had let my licence expire during World War II because of the fuel rationing. At this time, the Aero Club sportsmen were allowed two hours flying a month. My brother Freddie, who had begun his apprenticeship as a mechanic at de Havilland's, was very keen on flying and was taking lessons when the restrictions were applied. Qantas approached him when it started using Catalina flying boats to cross the Indian Ocean. However, he only had six hours flying time and they required ten.

He was keen to take up the Qantas offer so he booked the Aero Club plane for his lunch hour at noon. Time and time again, as he eagerly kept an eye out for both the instructor and the Gipsy Moth in which he would get his hours, he would notice a socialite who had a regular eleven o'clock appointment. Because she talked to the instructors and other pilots, she would always be late taking off and then not get the plane back in time for his lesson. My brother never got the extra four hours he needed because nobody else at Mascot would make the hours available to an apprentice mechanic.

Unfortunately, I was not aware of this until many years later. As a member, I could have claimed two hours from the Aero Club and given them to him. Amost fifty years further on, my brother, who finally gained his licence in 1939, is still serving the aviation industry as a pilot and engineer. The socialites have long since given up flying.

An interesting offer came my way in 1950 when I was asked to go back to far western New South Wales. Strangely enough it was with the Far West Children's Health Scheme, but not to fly for them. Sid Coleman from Bourke had become Super-intendent of the Health Scheme and he invited me to join him and Dr Walter Wearn. I was to be dental nurse, clerical assistant, publicity officer and general help. Sid probably thought that because I knew the back country and would not mind mutton for breakfast, dinner and tea, or the primitive conditions, I would be better than someone with experience only in dental work.

In three weeks we saw 503 children, extracted 1113 teeth, filled 297 cavities and travelled 2500 miles. The Far West Children's Health Scheme is concerned with helping people where no other facilities exist, so we bypassed the towns that had dentists and made for the only road that led west. Sometimes they were just sandy tracks winding through the spinifex.

Years later, I was speaking at a National Party fund raising dinner where I met Kevin Lloyd who told me that he was one of the children whose head I had held while Dr Wearn extracted all his front teeth at Mt Hope in 1952. From then on his schoolfriends called him 'Fangs' and he never quite forgave me! I remember Mt Hope because it displayed the worst dental neglect we saw during our tour.

On a second trip I made a year later with the dental clinic it was wonderful to see the improvement in the children's general health. Unfortunately, on that trip, Sid Coleman collapsed at Ivanhoe. We put the car on the train and brought him back to Sydney but he never recovered. His dedication to the Far West Children's Health Scheme was such that he over-extended himself, eventually to his detriment.

I had been thinking for a long time that I should do a refresher course to renew my pilot's licence. However, I took out a student pilot's licence and was content to fly on that as co-pilot to Maie Casey on our various trips.

Maie was accompanying her husband to the Proclamation of Independence of Malaya in 1957, and by coincidence, I was on the same flight. I was going to Japan to meet my husband who was there on business. She immediately gathered me up and included me in many of the receptions for Merdeka. When the Caseys were leaving for Singapore, I found myself standing next to Prime Minister Tunku Abdul Rahman who said to me, 'Casey is a wonderful man and has done more to help me achieve this independence than anybody else.' I later learned that when the British withdrew from Malaya they left many gaps which Lord Casey had offered to fill with skilled personnel. It was an offer made to the Malayan Prime Minister on Australia's behalf.

Subsequently, many Australians did go to Malaya to help set up its financial and industrial base. After years of being treated as inferior by British bureaucrats, the Malays found the Australians a refreshing change. As one man said, 'Casey was colour-blind, he did not know the colour of a man's skin.'

As I continued my journey north I called at Alor Star. It had been a romantic name to me ever since the England–Australia pilots had to land there. It was also where Scotty Allan had crashed the aeroplane carrying the first Australia–England airmail, and where Charles Kingsford Smith had come to the rescue in the *Southern Star*. Later, Smithy disappeared somewhere off that coastline, so I joined a little boat going out to Langkawi Island, south of Aye, to see the place where it was thought he had disappeared.

I was concerned to find myself the only European woman on the boat and the island, but someone said there was a British rubber plantation owner a few miles inland. As there was nothing else to do, I took a taxi and went out to see him. Imagine his surprise to find an Australian visitor on his verandah, out in the middle of a foreign land. I had dinner with him and returned to the doorless, open-window bungalow that was the 'hotel'. I felt a little scared as the wind flapped the shutters throughout the night.

My next stop was Hong Kong where I again met Nancy Sung. I had first met her in Australia through my friend Val Salmon, and the women's social writer for the *Sydney Morning Herald*, Connie Robertson. Nancy had sent her daughters to school in Australia. Val had befriended them, and as a consequence, I had met them. I was amazed to discover that Nancy, who had started in a small way making shoes, later took over the exclusive shop in Hong Kong's prestigious Mandarin Hotel.

I also met Lady Grantham, the American wife of the British Governor. She sent me in the official car to see the New Territories and look across the border into China. There in the hills was a new camellia which had been recently cultivated and called 'Granthonia', in honour of the colony's Governor.

Years later, I invited Lady Grantham to afternoon tea at the Ritz Hotel in London, but she arrived on the wrong day. Coincidentally, the mother of my friend Yolande Sutton of Darling Point saw Lady Grantham waiting for me in the lounge, spoke to her and when I failed to arrive, Mrs Clarkson invited her to tea. She was delighted. Since her return to England she had experienced only social coldness and appreciated the warm Australian hospitality.

From Hong Kong I went to Tokyo where the Australian Ambassador had asked me to lunch the following day. My husband Charles arrived from Australia that evening and I told him of my luncheon appointment. 'Your diplomatic tour is over,' he said. He had arranged to leave for Osaka that day and I had to telephone an apology to the Ambassador. Later, an American friend said, 'We would not dream of doing that to our Ambassador.' It was only then that I realised that I had made a diplomatic faux pas!

In Japan I was very fortunate to meet one of that country's most remarkable women, Kusi Aso. Educated partly in France, Mrs Aso was the daughter and hostess for Japan's post war Prime Minister, Mr Yasuda. Some time earlier she had gained a pilot's licence and Maie Casey thought I should meet her. Years later I was invited to her daughter's wedding and thus learned of the family's importance. Their youngest daughter would marry the Emperor's grandnephew and become Princess Nabuko. Knowing the restrictions on freedom in the Japanese Royal family, one felt it was a great responsibility to impose on a young girl.

Later again, Mr Yasuda and Kusi visited Australia. Kusi claimed she had come to see Lady Casey and myself. Such flattery!

When her niece Yumi Iwamura came to Australia with her husband, who was working for Mitsubishi, she became part of my life. Never have I known a more charming or gracious woman. Two of her children were born in Australia, and the family was very happy to stay. However, after five years, they reluctantly left only to be transferred to New York for 18 years.

The beauty of Japan and its artistic quality convinced me it was probably the most artistic country in the world. My husband and I stayed with the parents of the Japanese Consul in Sydney. Our friend and neighbour Joyce Tebbutt was with us. We slept on the floor on Japanese beds and found the one lone flower that decorates most toilets funny. We joined Geisha parties where the momma san felt the texture of our clothing and was fascinated to have two Australian women at her table. Joyce had never been outside Australia before joining us on this trip. Dancing with a Japanese man one evening, she was introduced to language difficulties when her partner said, 'Sir, you are very beaut.' In shops off the beaten track a high school student was often called in to interpret our English. Many could read but few could speak our language, so with gesticulations and single words, we explored side streets and alleys, grateful to have Charles as an escort.

The same year I flew to New Guinea, which is more than 1500 miles north of Sydney, although the nearest Australian soil is only 400 miles. Here I planned to go into the highlands to visit a woman pilot, Pat Graham, who had married Colin Toole and was now living on a coffee plantation in the Whaghi Valley.

Before visiting Pat, I went to Port Moresby to see Don Cleland. In Perth he had stood for Parliament against John Curtin who later became Prime Minister. Though Don was not successful it started a whole new career for the young army officer and his efficient wife Rachael. After a sojourn in Sydney, Don was appointed Administrator of Papua New Guinea. I went to visit them in Port Moresby and was interested to learn how much

Rachael had involved herself with the beginnings of a museum and the welfare of the local inhabitants.

From Port Moresby I flew to war-devastated Rabaul where a missionary said it would have been a great help if the authorities had screened the people before sending them in. Many were go-getters anxious to make their fortune as quickly as possible and were exploiting the locals.

An amusing incident occurred as a result of my visit to Rabaul. On returning to Australia, I was in the queue at the local National Bank of Australia when a lady wanted to cash a New Guinea cheque. The teller advised her it would cost five cents, to which she replied, 'I simply do not have any Australian currency.' I piped up and said, 'I know New Guinea and will happily lend you five cents.' I asked her which part of the country she was from and she said 'Rabaul.' 'Oh,' I said, 'is that horrible man still in [such-and-such] hotel. He was so mean he would not even put a hook on the back of the bathroom door.' 'Yes,' she said. 'He's my husband.'

While in New Guinea, I flew into the highlands. I did not know where the Whaghi Valley was when I left Sydney, but on the assumption that people had to receive mail and stores no matter where they were, I felt certain there must be some means of getting to my destination.

Landing in Goroka, which had been established only eight years earlier, was like landing in America with Colombus. It was absolutely primitive. Although the Whaghi Valley had been discovered in 1933 it was not until after the war that Europeans began developing it. Gold had been discovered in New Guinea in rich strikes and the only practical way to get to those strikes at Bulolo was to fly. The alternative was a tough jungle crossing by foot through areas of malaria and hostile tribes. Out of necessity, New Guinea developed air transport long before many civilised countries used the aeroplane. At that time many world records for freight aircraft were set in New Guinea.

Mike Leagh, pioneer of New Guinea and one of the first white men to prospect in this country, went further afield, and from the top of a mountain range, saw clouds lifting into the sky. 'Those clouds are lifting off grasslands, not mountains, so somewhere up beyond the range there must be a plateau,' observed Mike. So they set to and built an airstrip, carried in enough fuel and arranged for pioneer airman Orm Denny (who later

172

became a Qantas captain) to fly out, refuel and then fly over the range to discover what lay beyond. Few men have known the exhilaration he must have felt when he crossed the Goroko mountain range and saw before him a plateau over 5000 feet up, stretching 80 miles and 18 miles wide. Orm did not land, however, and the first pilot to do so was Ian Grabowsky (the man who helped Amy Johnson in Australia). He had trouble getting out because the natives, having seen him descend from the sky in his white flying suit, thought he was an ancestor returning from the dead and wanted to keep him there!

Pat and Colin Toole's coffee plantation sat on this plateau in the Whaghi Valley. One of the little valleys off the Whaghi is the Shangri-la Valley, so called by an American, Margaret Rawlings, when she survived an air crash during the war and was stranded there for days in isolated country. While I was learning to fly I had heard much about flying in this treacherous country. Now I was seeing it for mself.

I had first met Pat Toole after World War II. She was a hairdresser on the north coast of New South Wales who decided to take up flying as a hobby. She went on to obtain her commercial licence, and in 1952 saw an advertisement for a pilot to work in New Guinea. She applied to Gibbes Sepik Airways. The owner was none other than Bobby Gibbes, the jackaroo on Burren station who in 1935 had said he wasn't interested in flying.

Bobby was having trouble with pilots who did not like flying single-engine aircraft without radio over rough, mountainous, uncontrolled territory where ridge tops were hidden by clouds and the tropical conditions were appalling. He gave Pat the job before he left for Germany to buy a Junkers 52, but did not tell his staff. His manager, Colin Toole and other staff members went to greet the new pilot and as Pat appeared in a trim white suit, one man said to Colin, 'My God, what are you going to do with her?'

One look at the tall blond girl brought his quick reply, 'Marry her,' and Colin Toole did just that. But not before Pat had flown many hours in what is considered one of the worst flying countries in the world. I admired the pilots who flew in New Guinea where every newspaper, can opener and car had to be flown in because there were no roads. I was especially proud of Pat. When I visited her she had already been married a few years and had a small child. She was supervising the building of a native reed house on their coffee plantation. I went with her to pay the native workers who 'dressed' in glamorous headdresses of Bird of Paradise feathers, lap laps and bunches of leaves on their buttocks and pig tusks through their noses.

We talked a lot about her flying days. She told me one story about leaving Wewak, becoming trapped in a valley and having to land in a remote creek. She waited to be rescued knowing that even if only half an hour overdue, the alert would be out. Feeling hot and dirty, she took off her clothes and washed them in the creek. As the search planes came over, Pat had to hide her naked body under the wing. Back at Goroka panic set in. They had found the plane, but there was no sign of the pilot. Had she survived? Had she been whipped off by head hunters? Her fiancé was panic-stricken. Bobby later said he was used to having distressed wives on his hands, but until then had never had a distraught man.

While in Goroka, Bobby invited me to fly all over the island with him in his newly acquired Junkers 52—the corrugated aluminium design with a massive wing span which the Germans had used as troop carriers for the invasion of Crete. Bobby felt their low landing speed made them ideal for the uphill/downhill short strips of New Guinea. Until he acquired the Junkers, he had used single-engined Norsemans which carried a much smaller load. I remember the amazement on the faces of the natives as we unloaded the Junkers; never had they seen so much come out of a 'Pigeon belonga Jesus'!

Bobby Gibbes also asked me to fly with him to Kegasugl at the base of Mount Wilhelm which is 12 000 feet above sea level. However, as I would have had to get out of bed before dawn, I decided not to go in the single-engined Norseman carrying a load of corrugated iron. I visualised an emergency landing at our destination and being decapitated by the roofing iron. The words that came to my mind then have often returned to my thoughts over the years—'No matter how foolish, it is not the things in life that you do, but the things that you do not do, that you regret . . .'

Here in New Guinea, I was again reminded of the fate of Amelia Earhart who, on the last stage of her fatal around the world record attempt, disappeared from Lae and was never seen again. Strange rumours have come from lonely islands from time to time about a white woman who was beheaded by the natives.

Another, that the Japanese brought her aircraft down, believing she was a spy checking up on their war preparations for the Pacific. But others feel that insufficient fuel and probably being slightly off course brought her to the same end as so many other ocean flyers including Hood and Moncrieff.

Soon after my visit, the natives began building a road by hand through incredibly mountainous country to Goroka. Their payment was in newspapers and salt which were more highly valued than money. They used to spend weeks going down to the sea to bring back bamboo poles full of salt water which was so essential to their diet. A sheet of newspaper was invaluable for making cigarettes.

Pat was the first Australian woman pilot to work in New Guinea and she was followed in 1953 by Betty Hay. Betty, who was a pilot, engineer and child welfare nurse, used her skills to help her husband with his flying missionary work. She was also instrumental in choosing locations for airfields throughout New Guinea's remote areas.

Another young woman who courageously coped with flying over the dangerous New Guinea terrain was Bronwyn Searle, who in 1965, took an office job with Crowley Airways in Lae so she could fly after hours. She became a full-time pilot and inspired Robyn Wells to successfully seek a flying job with Aerial Tours in Wewak in 1974. Later, Robyn returned to fly in the oil fields of Australia's arid centre. In the same adventurer category was Eileen Steensen who flew for Territory Airlines and Missionary Aviation from 1966 to 1970. Four years later, she wrote a book, *Flight Plan Papua New Guinea* detailing her experiences.

CHAPTER 20

In the 1930s, the world was awed by Germany's huge, twelve-engined Dornier flying boats. Years later, when visiting the German Star Fighter base at Memmingen, I found myself sitting next to its chief pilot, Wolfgang Von Gronau. The occasion was a reception which followed a ceremony marking the 40th anniversary of Herman Kohl's crossing of the Atlantic in 1928. With Fitzmaurice and Count Hughenfeld, Kohl had crash landed in Labrador at the end of their flight. The first completely successful crossing of the North Atlantic was by Australia's own Charles Kingsford Smith and his Dutch co-pilot, Van Dyke, in 1930. However, I did not mention that as we marched down the street to Herman Kohl's grave with a six-foot wreath, a Bavarian band and a contingent of Starfighter Base personnel.

Australians seem reluctant to celebrate history-making events. In 1978, the 50th anniversary of Kingsford Smith's feat was celebrated by a small number of people including his widow, only son and close family. The event was a tiny tribute compared with the honour the Germans paid their hero Herman Kohl.

Following the 1958 meeting of the Aero Club at Lake Constance, I was invited to fly around Switzerland with a Krupps' pilot in a stagger wing Beechcraft. As we skirted those mountain peaks in rising fog, I was grateful he knew the mountains like the back of his hand. It is a shock to see an aircraft land in a valley and seemingly disappear into a hillside. There were times when I longed for the wide, flat paddocks of Australia.

Several years earlier, I had met the President of the Swiss Aero Club, Eric Scotoni. He later became the World President of the prestigious Federation Aeronautique Internationale (FAI). On the 1958 visit, his wife, who was a member of the International Women Pilots' Association, invited me to stay with them at Chateau Mex, a beautiful old castle just out of Geneva.

I was also interested in Herman Geiger and his remarkable glacier flying. It started because he had been requested to fly in building materials for a refuge shelter that was to be built high in the mountains. With a Piper Cub fitted with skis, he took off from Scion. He was a very skilled pilot who found that by lightly touching the snow-covered glaciers at 12 000 feet and higher, he could determine if the surface was safe enough to land on. Coupled with the danger of an untried ski landing at the same time, he had to fly up the glacier, land, then quickly turn the craft sideways to prevent it sliding backwards. His first attempt was successful and the materials were unloaded within easy reach of the building site. So began a regular business which also blossomed into a sport, for a dedicated group of skilled enthusiasts.

I had hoped to fly with him, but the weather closed in and I wanted to keep an arrangement to join some friends, Deke and Louise Coleman, in Cannes. Something nagged at me 'go back, go back' and finally I did. Herman Geiger met me at Geneva airport. To fly in over those great glaciers, land in the deep snow and then take off over a cliff with 12 000 feet suddenly below me, was an unforgettable experience. Later, both Herman and his son were killed while glacier flying.

It was also in 1958 that I met the woman who is now, I think, the only woman General in the world. After meeting Valerie Andre in Paris, I wrote the following in my diary:

Tonight I have come home completely elated by a dinner with Commander Boris, a pilot of the 1921 vintage, and now a leading French helicopter man. He invited me to meet Madame Jacqueline Auriol, winner of the Harmony trophy, and one of the first two women to fly a jet aircraft, in which she broke the sound barrier. When we arrived at the restaurant however, Madame Auriol had telegraphed through a message to say she was held up in Morocco where she had been on flying duties as a full time test pilot in the French Air Force. Our other guest was Dr Valerie Andre and in her I met full value.

As I looked at her small sharp beautiful features across the table, I found it difficult to believe that this woman surgeon had parachuted into Indo China 121 times to attend the wounded and then became one of the very first helicopter pilots, so that she could use it in her medical work.

For three years she did outstanding work in the war-torn zones of French Indo China. In her Red Cross marked Hiller 360 she flew 120 helicopter missions, rescued 193 wounded and 38 pilots who had crashed. Many times she flew through enemy gunfire to collect the wounded and ferry them to hospital.

Valerie Andre crossed my path again in 1989, when I stayed with Jean Ross Howard Phelan, who in 1955 founded the 'Whirly-Girls', an association of women helicopter pilots. As Jean says, she was the 'lucky 13th' woman to receive a helicopter rating. She had joined the Women Airforce Service Pilots (WASP) and later became secretary to Jacqueline Cochran. She had considerable organising ability and an opportunity came for her to join the Red Cross.

Today Jean is still the executive director of 'Whirly-Girls' and affectionately called 'Den Mother' by its 675 members from 22 countries. Jean's extraordinary hospitality led her friends to dub her apartment the 'Howard Phelan Hilton'.

Jean had invited Valerie to 'Whirly-Birds'. It was only then that I learned Valerie had continued her aviation and medical skills in Algiers. She was appointed Chief Doctor of the Helicopter Wing and flew 356 peace keeping missions. Valerie spent 33 years on active duty before retiring in 1981 and today she is a member of the French Air Force Reserve.

Five feet tall with red well-groomed hair and the chic of a Parisian, only the strength of her hand clasp betrayed the character behind this feminine frame.

In 1968 when I was staying with Elly in Freiburg, the German women pilots decided to form their own association. They did not want to be just a branch of the American based international organisation, 'Ninety-Nines'. They wanted to run their own affairs and manage their own finances. Those who wished to join the Ninety-Nines as individuals could do so, or they could form a section in Germany just as we do here in Australia. As a long-time member of the American organisation, I thought it diplomatic not to attend the meeting because they may have thought I was barracking for the Ninety-Nines, so I missed out on being one of nine charter members. I am No. 10. I became their first international member and have been invited to many fly-ins and celebrations over the years.

After the war I visited the Zeppelin family at their castle in Biberach, through the invitation of Frederick Karl Koenig-Warthausen. Graf Zeppelin did not have any sons, and on his daughter's marriage, the family name became von Brandenstein. When I met the eldest son of this family, I could have been looking at a younger version of his grandfather. He became a hunting companion of my son John, but was killed in a car accident.

Among the many things my hosts showed me was their collection of the stamped envelopes which were carried on inaugural flights made by Zeppelin airships. The envelopes, addressed to people in many parts of the world, are undoubtedly valuable pieces of aviation history. I was surprised to learn that as well as the ocean crossings and the Hindenburg tragedy, there had been an enormous number of short journeys throughout Europe, about which Australians had not heard. Count von Brandenstein told me that the envelope collection had been made by an engineer whose daughter had exchanged it for a hunting lodge owned by the Count!

There had been great rivalry between the world's two major airship people during the late 1930s. In London, in 1938, I was given letters to each, with specific instructions not to let one know I was seeing the other. To my horror I discovered I had put the wrong letter in each envelope. I heard from one airship company and not the other.

I wonder how many people realise that it was an Australian convict, Dr Bland, who in 1852, designed the first airship! He was here as a 'guest of the government', pardoned by Governor Macquarie and became a doctor, inventor and politician. He designed an airship which was exhibited at the Crystal Palace in London and the Paris Aviation Exhibition. It was a steam-driven, hydrogen-filled balloon called an Atomic Ship. It never flew but may well have given Count Zeppelin the idea for his dirigible. The French President had wanted to buy it, but the French Treasurer would not let him. Even then, Australians were trying to bring the continent of Europe and Australia closer together.

In 1968, at Elly's suggestion, General Hannes Troutloft invited me to attend the Luftwaffe Ball. He was considered an air ace in the Spanish war. I was met at the train by two aides, included in the official party and partnered by Professor Messerschmitt, with whom I shared a bottle of red wine. I am sure he was expecting Elly! In the same group were Peter Townsend (previously a friend of Princess Margaret) and the Duke of Edinburgh's sister. When I thought it was time to go home about 1 am, I was amazed to find that everybody went downstairs to enjoy a meal of white sausages. Since then, I have been invited to several Club der Luftwaffe balls.

I was also invited to a reception at Baden Baden. It was being held by Senator Burda, owner of the high fashion *Burda* magazine. I was interested to hear he had his own formation of Piper Cub aircraft and gave displays throughout Germany. I visited this lovely part of Germany again on my way back from Nancy, the capital of Lorraine, after which I was named. Baron Koenig-Warthausen had taken me there to try to trace my grandmother's ancestors, who were Hugenots. I was unsuccessful but, on the way back, we had been invited to a party at the Hardenbergs' home at Baden Baden. Count Hardenberg was the German representative of the Bell Helicopter factory and the Countess was born Princess Furstenberg, a name almost as well known as the Danube. I was to meet them many times again at the Luftwaffe balls in Bonn and I deeply value their friendship.

Again through Elly, I met Blacky Fuchsberger who decided to visit Australia in 1984. Elly asked me to meet him, which I did, accompanied by Erik and Edith Glowatski, two most hospitable German Australians. What I did not know was that we were meeting one of the top personalities of Euro television with 90 big Saturday night shows to his credit. Blacky was also well-known as an actor, having featured in 80 films. I drove him around Sydney in my humble little Mazda station wagon, looking at apartments and houses which he thought he might like to buy.

CHAPTER 21

In 1958 I was to go to the United States and was also due to renew my student pilot's licence. I went to the Civil Aviation Department and Laurence Howell, the young man who came to the counter to look after me, said, 'Why don't you get your private licence back if you're going to the States? You are bound to be meeting a lot of private pilots and they do not understand student licences there.'

'I don't think I have time,' I said. 'And it's 20 years since I did any serious flying. I might be able to get the training in, but the three hours' solo would defeat me.'

'I think we might waive the solo in view of your previous experience,' he replied. 'Go out to Bankstown, do your training and we will see what we can do to help.'

I owe that young man a great deal. He made possible my return to flying. I had felt that I was pressed both for time and money and I could not afford to spend either on further training. However, he had confidence in me and I decided I would have a crack at it.

Believe me, it was quite an assignment. Getting an aircraft when you want it is a complicated game played between pupil and instructor, and since he is on the spot he has the upper hand. You leave a casserole cooking in the oven and drive to Bankstown to keep your appointment with him, only to find he is in the air already, or at a conference, or has gone to Melbourne. If none of that happens, flying has been banned because of unsuitable weather. It is not meant to be easy, I can tell you!

Eventually the day arrived when I was to do my test, and after making a two hour train journey, I was on the tarmac at the appointed time. I was to do my test in a Tiger Moth

181

so I dressed in slacks and a couple of sweaters to keep out the cold, which is part and parcel of an open cockpit aeroplane. All the Tiger Moths were lined up on the ground, but my instructor was aloft playing with a new toy, a Piper Tri-pacer. Then he radioed in that he had struck severe turbulence and all the Tiger Moths were forbidden to fly.

I wailed, 'No, you can't do this to me. I'm going to do that test today, turbulence or not!'

I was due to leave Australia in a week and knew I did not have another day free for flying. I was prepared to face anything, even turbulence, and no-one will ever know how I had grown to hate turbulence out in the west, where it was often so severe that I was physically ill. I gathered that the instructor disliked it just about as much as I did, but he was sympathetic and agreed to let me do the test in spite of the weather.

When I went back to the Civil Aviation Department, Laurence Howell smilingly handed me my licence. A lump came into my throat when I looked at it and saw that it was Number 1150—my old licence, originally issued in September 1933 and now renewed nearly 25 years later. My commercial licence, Number 494, lapsed in 1938.

With my licence renewed, America took on a new significance as Betty Gillies, chairman of the American All Women's Transcontinental Air Race Board, had written saying, 'We're looking forward so much to seeing you. Of course I'll be living Air Race night and day, but I know you'll fit in. If I hear of anybody who wants a co-pilot or navigator, I'll recommend you.'

Betty was referring to the famous Powder Puff Derby, an annual cross-country race for women sponsored by the Ninety-Nines. Suddenly I felt I wanted to be in that race more than anything else and I wrote back saying, 'I'll be navigator, co-pilot, paying passenger or just a willing pair of hands if I can go along.'

Then I began to think twice about it. Probably all the contestants had their teams already. How could I be sure of getting into the race? I went along to see Sir Hudson Fysh to ask if Qantas would sponsor me. He was enthusiastic but the Public Relations Department of that huge organisation was appalled. What? Qantas sponsor a single-engined aircraft on a United States transcontinental race? That was not what they considered safe flying.

Just before I boarded the plane for America, I rang Sir Hudson and asked him whether his organisation would help if I went to San Francisco to see them. Immediately he cabled his son John in San Francisco to arrange a press interview on my arrival, because he thought that might help me get a sponsor. When I arrived I telephoned Betty Gillies in San Diego to ask her whether she could get a co-pilot for me if I could find myself a sponsor.

'Don't worry,' Betty said. 'You find a sponsor and we'll get you a co-pilot without any trouble.'

There did not seem to be any sponsors offering in San Francisco, so I flew on to San Diego to stay with Betty and Bud. It was there that the real business of looking for a sponsor began. I wrote letters for hours at a time, to everyone I thought might have an interest in supporting an Australian entry. I tried Alfred Hitchcock and Art Linkletter because their television shows were beginning to appear in Australia; Cole of California, makers of swim-suits—I was almost prepared to wear a swim-suit from coast to coast if it meant a sponsorship; I even offered to chew Sunkist raisins from California to Carolina. And so it went on.

I telephoned Cessna at Wichita to ask if they would sponsor me, or else lend or hire me a machine. I knew they had a growing business in Australia selling light aircraft and that if I did well in the race they would get substantial publicity at no cost, regardless of sponsorship.

I then decided that I would enter and worry later about finding a sponsor. After all, what did I have to lose? The entrance fee was only $US30, so it was worth the gamble. But I found that to put in an entry I had to have a machine lined up and give details of it on my entry form. 'Blow them all,' I thought. 'Nothing's ever been achieved in aviation by thinking of business propositions.' I filled out the nomination form. I decided I would go it alone and my friends set to work to hire a machine. Bud Gillies found a Cessna 172 for me to hire and now I had to learn to fly it. I'd never flown a modern aircraft—one with flaps, a wheel instead of a joystick, a right-hand throttle, toe-brakes and radio. I knew the regulations obliged me to carry an American radio operator—because of the language difficulty! I thought of the lines from *My Fair Lady:* 'There even are places where English completely disappears—in America, they haven't used it for years.'

After the claypans of the outback, to have to fly off Lindbergh Field and Montgomery Field, San Diego, was a terrifying prospect. However, during practice runs in the Cessna 172 Bud nursed me patiently through the teething stages.

Betty was sympathetic, knowing what it must be like to make a come-back in an unfamiliar aircraft and with so much traffic about and a jet base only 3 miles away. 'If you find yourself getting tensed up, sing,' she said. 'That's what I used to do in the Air Force.' Then she told me about the first time she had flown a P47. She was CO of the women ferry pilots at Framingdale during the war and was the first woman to take up a P47. They had a 1000 hp single engine and a single cockpit, so once in the air no instruction was possible for the pilots who were flying them.

'What did it feel like when you opened the throttle?' I asked her. 'Oh gosh, I was way back on the tail somewhere. Then I had time to settle down and look around, but as I came in to land, gliding faster than I had ever had to before, I found myself so tensed up and holding the stick so tightly that the only thing I could do to ease the situation was to burst into song. So I eased that Thunderbolt down on to the runway singing the song "I'm cutting paper dollies I can call my own" at the top of my voice.'

I remembered Betty's advice the first time I left Bud on the ground and went off solo: I sang 'Sing a Song of Sixpence'— at the top of my voice!

Meanwhile, Betty had found a co-pilot for me—Iris Critchell, a former Olympic swimmer and a top-notch pilot who had been co-pilot in the winning machine in the 1957 race from San Mateo to Philadelphia. We were to fly a different route, from San Diego in California to Charleston in South Carolina—2170 miles across mountain and desert in the height of summer. I liked Iris immediately. I could see she was going to be good company and fun to have on board. During the war, she had flown fighters and bombers for the Women's Air Transport Command. I was lucky to have her flying with me. She understood weather and wind currents, where to fly to get the best out of the wind and what altitude to lean out the fuel mix for best performance. She had even been back through the records to find out what weather conditions had been like over the route in the July of previous years. Iris was always thorough.

Thirty years later, Iris and her husband visited Australia for the first time. They had taken a well-earned four week break from their aircraft charter and flying school. They engaged my son John in his Partenavia aircraft and flew to Kangaroo Island, Alice Springs, the Great Barrier Reef and remote places in between. For 19 years they had run their own flight academy in California and felt flying in a light aircraft was the only way to see the country. I had boasted about our clear visibility; however, I doubt if they even saw the horizon. The dead heart of Australia had its annual rainfall of four inches all in one day! They were constantly circumnavigating thunderstorms.

I spent the days between my arrival and the beginning of the air race swotting up United States Air Navigation rules and visiting flying friends. Before leaving San Diego I had to get an international licence and a national aeronautics licence. To do this I had to pass an American Air Legislation examination. I swotted for hours, learning the correct legislation so that if asked a question I could write the reply. To my mind, the Americans have a much better system of examinations than we have. Here, they give you a statement and ask 'true or false?' I have always been lucky with my choice of answers!

I think the use made of private aircraft in America impressed me as much as anything. The owning and operating of private machines in the outback of Australia had increased enormously since the days when I was flying in the west. I guess that to some extent I blazed part of the trail and perhaps stimulated some fresh interest in aviation on the part of many of the outback aircraft owners. However, compared with the Americans, we do not have a proportionate number of private flyers. These get-togethers of private flyers in the states are family affairs—probably mum and dad both fly an aircraft and they bring the whole family along to the festivities. Many of them, admittedly, are people who work in aviation, electronics, radio or some other business that warrants the use of a small machine and allows them to write off a good deal of the expense as a business necessity. It is exciting to go to one of these gatherings and see little aeroplanes winging in from every state, piloted by people who use their aircraft for business and pleasure just the way the average motorist uses a car.

The All Women's Transcontinental Air Race, or the Powder Puff Derby as it is affectionately called, is entirely organised, run and flown by women pilots. My entry was the first overseas entry ever made and I had a kangaroo emblem stencilled on the side of the aircraft. For Americans the kangaroo is synonymous with Australia and anyway it seemed appropriate because our effective range was short, only about three-and-a-half hours. This meant that we were going to be hopping from state to state across the continent!

Since 1958 several Australians have entered the race. In 1973, Robin Miller—who was then a pilot with the Royal Flying Doctor Service—and Rosemary de Pierres—who was mustering cattle on her husband's property at Wyalkatchem, Western Australia—entered to help raise funds for the Royal Flying Doctor Service. Both were members of the Zonta Club of Perth which organised their sponsorship. When Robin and Rose were going to America, I telephoned my friends Mr and Mrs Jack Blanton of Houston, Texas, advising that the girls would be in Houston on a certain date. Laura Lee Blanton telephoned every motel in the area to find out where they were and invited them to stay, saying she felt they would be more comfortable in her home than in a motel. Also, the Blantons had a King Air and a pilot who was able to help the girls tremendously with the aviation shopping that they had to do in Houston.

The wonderful thing about the Blantons is their extraordinary hospitality to Australian people; they are an inspiration to everyone. Jack, at present, is the Chairman of the Texas University system with four large teaching hospitals and eight universities under his chairmanship. He calls himself a joiner—and he certainly is a doer!

Their daughter married the grandson of the World War I pilot, John F. Staub, who, in 1918, became the first American flying in England to drop a bomb on a German submarine. In his words: 'I was flying along the coast and saw this sub beneath me, so I just let the bomb go. It was a direct hit and, to my surprise, I was decorated for it.' His architectural work graces many of Houston's most beautiful homes and his grandson now lives in the home John built for his bride.

Australians Margaret Kentley and Marie Richardson have also entered the Powder Puff Derby and learnt to use the winds. Years later, in 1976, they entered the New South Wales Air Race and while Air Force personnel and commercial pilots swotted over their maps and computers, the eventual winners were these two grandmothers.

I was fortunate to take part in three Powder Puff Derbys.

186

As mine were Australian entries, I had to be Pilot-in-Command in 1958 and 1961, but my American co-pilots were both highly experienced ex-wartime ferry pilots. Again, in 1976, on the thirtieth anniversary of the Race, I was a passenger. The final derby was sponsored by the Smithsonian Institution.

The Derby is a handicap race, so the first plane in is not necessarily the winner. A 'par speed' handicap in miles per hour is established for each model of aircraft before the race begins. The winning aircraft is the one that averages the highest ground speed in relation to its par speed. Times in the log books are calculated down to the fifth decimal point.

On our first attempt, Iris Critchell and I came fifth. We had taken 16 hours and 39 minutes to fly the journey and won $200, a large map of the United States and a magnificent trophy. I think the greatest thrill of all for me was that I was the first outsider ever to compete in the race.

It was also a thrill to take one of the five major trophies out of the country with me. I felt very proud of my little Australian flags and of the kangaroo emblem on the side of the fuselage. I had felt timid and nervous at my decision to enter the race and the best way to strengthen myself, I discovered, was to go out and do what I was scared of doing.

In 1961 I was sponsored in the race by an Australian stockbroker, Roland Walton. A financier, and a patriotic Australian, he was enthusiastic about his country and about overseas investment in Australia. Here was a new way to foster good relations between our two countries from someone with enough foresight to recognise the opportunity.

Each night I rang to tell Roland Walton how we were getting on, but usually left a message, 'Mrs Walton phoned'. His wife said, 'People began to wonder who I was!'

At that time I was deeply involved in a voluntary job of raising funds for the National Heart Campaign and the thought came to me that Roland Walton's sponsorship should be on behalf of the Campaign: anything that I might win or gain from the race, together with any publicity before the race, would benefit the Campaign. I had very little time to wind up my part of the Heart Campaign affairs and get to know a new type of aircraft. From five machines offered to me I chose a 250 hp Piper Comanche, which flew at twice the speed I had ever been used to and had more than twice the horsepower. I had made less

187

than a dozen landings and take-offs in it when I boarded a mighty Pan Am 707 to cross the Pacific to California.

My co-pilot on this occasion was Lauretta Foy Savory. Barbara London, a distinguished aviatrix and wartime ferry pilot, who does so much work in organising the air race, put me in touch with this delightful American woman. Lauretta had an interesting background. She was at college when the Water Follies of the 1930s went to Hollywood to make a film with Eddie Cantor. On the set it was suddenly discovered that the stars and glamour girls who were to appear in the film could not swim. In panic the producer rang up the college and asked them to send over their best swimmers. Lauretta was included. She was also a dancer and it was not long before Warner Brothers offered her a ten year contract. She became a stand-in for such famous stars as Loretta Young, Irene Dunne, Claudette Colbert and Barbara Stanwyck. One weekend a flying friend took Lauretta to the airport and she became so interested in flying that she began having lessons. She then quickly gained an instructor rating. Later she became a demonstrator and then a test pilot for Piper Aircraft. During the war, Lauretta joined the Women Airforce Service Pilots (WASP), a ferry command similar to Britain's Air Transport Auxiliary, and flew everything from light aircraft to heavy bombers.

In 1954, Lauretta's husband was killed in an air crash and this changed the course of her life. She invested her small savings and was so enthusiastic about trading in stocks and shares that she became a practising stockbroker with a California company. She maintained a strong involvement in aviation and was one of the first three helicopter pilots allowed to land on the rooftops in Los Angeles. At one stage, when she was training men to be helicopter pilots for Vietnam, she probably had more helicopter flying hours than any woman in the world.

There were a record number of entries in the 1961 Annual Powder Puff Derby. One hundred and one aircraft and 196 women pilots were accepted. Six girls chose to fly solo. There was a cross-section of American womanhood, with ages ranging from 17 to an admitted seventy.

From the beginning, we were dogged by bad weather. At the end of the first day we landed at Tucson, Arizona, and 24 hours later we were still there waiting for the promised westerly tailwind. Because this is a handicap race, it sometimes pays to sit on the ground for a day and get more favourable winds than to rush straight through. You must try to outwit other competitors in navigation and weather—and it might work, providing you make the finish by the deadline. As I looked round, many of the top pilots were playing the same game. It must be right.

Next morning, Lauretta went aloft for an hour flying a pattern to locate a tailwind. Sure enough, she found it at 13 000 feet, so we climbed into the sky, crossed the continental divide without seeing it beneath the clouds and were on our way to Dallas, Texas. Before take-off we had been specifically briefed on the need to make radio contact with the military before crossing the Big Springs jet area. But call them as we might, we could get no reply. Light aircraft are not permitted to fly in this area above 12 000 feet and there were clouds at that height so we had to get down quickly to the base at 2000 feet. After the smooth, beautiful world of the cloud-tops suddenly we had descended into severe turbulence. Yes, it was rough and somehow the door came open. 'Hang on to it!' yelled Lauretta. 'But if it starts to go, let it go or it may pull you out.' I gave my seat belt an extra tug as we headed for an emergency landing at Abilene, Texas. Again our radio was not receiving the tower, so we circled the field and landed on the signal of a green light. We had estimated we could just make Dallas, Texas, but we would have no fuel to spare. Was it fate that necessitated an emergency landing during which we picked up more fuel?

A rule of the race is that both departure and destination points must have Visual Flight Rules (VFR) conditions. Another rule is that if one aircraft of 130 hp or less has not crossed the finishing line, the race can be extended until one of that type does finish the course. There were only two such aircraft in the race that year and both were weather-bound at Jackson near the Mississippi. How we prayed that Jackson would be the last place to open, and it was. However, our part in the race that year ended when we hit a storm just 70 miles short of our last overnight stop.

I was at the controls and I headed westward to try to get around, but when the storms and hills began to meet, we were forced to turn back. There seemed no hope of getting through and daylight was fading. On our left a large town appeared in a small break in a thunderstorm, and because of its size we felt

189

sure that there would be an aerodrome. Sure enough, there was a magnificent airfield whose black runways looked like velvet to us. We circled and circled. It seemed to be deserted: no control tower, not even a windsock. We took the wind direction from a smoke-stack nearby and landed. The concrete was awash as we taxied along the runway towards the fuel pumps. 'What's the name of this town?' we asked the attendant. 'Gainsville, Georgia,' he said. No wonder the airfield was such a size: Gainsville had been a naval air station in the war and Ground Control Approach techniques had been perfected there. Even the church spire had been removed because it was in line with one of the runways. The aerodrome was no longer in regular use.

Georgia is also the chicken capital of the world and we had a laugh about us being too 'chicken' to fly on in the bad weather.

Eighteen of us were eliminated for staying overnight at undesignated stops. The race was won by Frances Bera for the sixth time in 11 years! With 9000 hours flying and every possible rating, as well as having qualified as one of the first women chosen for space flight, Fran Bera was indeed one of the world's most outstanding racing women pilots. She was placed in 17 out of 20 Powder Puff derbies.

CHAPTER 22

During this time, I delighted in meeting many interesting people—pilots and non-pilots, men and women, some were well-known and others less so. I was deeply impressed by the professionalism, education and elegance of the American women. I looked and listened.

Danny Kaye was an enthusiastic pilot who flew himself everywhere. I met him at Van Nuys airport in California. Lauretta Foy and I had been practising approaches and landings at Lancaster in the Mojave Desert in a Piper Comanche. After landing we taxied up and I parked the aircraft beside the one ahead of me. I thought the pilot's face was a bit familiar and out stepped Danny Kaye. We talked of flying and Australia and I asked if I could have a photo taken with him.

As I listened to the women pilots each night, I heard many names mentioned. Betty Gillies said, 'I admire Marion Rice Hart,' so I asked who she was. I was amazed to hear that Marion had first flown the Atlantic from Newfoundland to Ireland in 1958 at the age of sixty-six. She flew the course again in 1962, and when she landed at Shannon airfield this time, the Irish refused to allow her to hire a car saying that at age 70 they thought she was too old to drive. Marion again made this flight when she was eighty-two. On the first Altantic crossing, Marion had Louise Sacchi as navigator. Louise then continued flying this and other routes 333 times! Not a bad record for someone who was turned down for the WAFS because she wore glasses.

Louise had completed a navigation course and in 1942 was sent to the British RAF Navigation School in Texas as an instructor. She had gained considerable flying experience by volunteering to relieve a pilot who flew ten-hour shifts at 10 000 feet up and down the east coast for General Electric. Once she found herself running short of fuel while crossing the Pacific from California to Melbourne in a single-engine Beech so she landed at Auckland, New Zealand. As the fuel man poured in the petrol he said, 'Where did you come from, lady?' 'California,' she said. 'Where are you going?' 'Melbourne,' was the reply. A 1200-mile water hop. On her arrival at Melbourne, customs would not believe her and demanded to see the pilot.

I took Louise to a Qantas lunch at Captain St Leon's home where she heard one woman telling of the 'nut' her husband had spoken to who had flown a single-engine aircraft across the Pacific. Louise quietly said, 'I think you are talking about me.'

In 1971 Louise established a record flying New York to London in a light aircraft and during 1974–75 she delivered 75 single and twin aircraft to the Spanish Air Force. They decorated her with the highest aviation award they can give a civilian, the 'Cruz de Aeronautica Blanca', making her the first foreigner and woman to receive it.

Louise wrote about her experiences in *Ocean Flying* and reading it is a must for anyone who wants to fly the oceans.

The first so-called Powder Puff Derby, from Santa Monica to Cleveland, was held in 1929, and won by 23-year-old Louise Thaden. Louise won the Bendix Race against all starters and at the time she already held the women's altitude, speed and endurance records. While setting an endurance record in 1930 she and Frances Martalus refuelled in mid-air 78 times, staying aloft for 196 hours! In 1936 Louise won the Powder Puff Derby again with Blanche Noyes. Blanche became the champion of air marking and was responsible for 13 000 airfields being marked.

Elinor Smith was another early competitor. She flew solo at the age of fifteen. Twelve months later she became the youngest licensed pilot in the United States. Orville Wright was the man who signed her flying licence. Elinor went on to set altitude, endurance and refuelling records which culminated in her winning the 1930 'Best Woman Pilot' award. She attracted national attention when she flew under four bridges in New York City, a stunt which resulted in the temporary suspension of her licence.

I did not meet her until 1987 when, among other things, I learnt she had read my first book *Born to Fly* many years before. I found her book *Aviatrix* an exciting account of many of the early American aviators and their experiences.

Before the 1958 Air Race, I stayed with Jimmie Kolp of Dallas who was one of the most charming American women I have met. She had flown her own aircraft for more than 30 years and called herself a 'hat and glove' pilot. We visited her neighbours on the Waggoner Ranch, home of the quarter horses, long before they were introduced to Australia. On several occasions I stayed with Barbara Evans and her husband Ed. Their names were often mentioned amongst the women pilots because of their hospitality to dozens of overseas and local visitors. Even in retirement, they built a home with two guest rooms to enable their many visitors to stay with them. Barbara was on the Powder Puff Derby Board for 19 years.

In 1963, Betty Miller of Santa Monica became the first woman to fly the Pacific solo when she delivered a Piper Apache from Oakland, California, to Brisbane. At the time, Betty had more than 5000 flying hours, she had a Flight Instructor's rating, an Instrument Rating for both single and multi-engine aeroplanes and a helicopter rating. With stops at Honolulu, New Caledonia and Fiji, Betty landed at night in Brisbane. It was the first night landing of a light aircraft that I had seen and it shocked the air traffic controllers!

Kay Brick was chairman of the Powder Puff Derby for ten years. She already had a Master's degree in Psychology, before she gained her pilot's licence in 1941. Soon afterwards, at Jackie Cochran's request, she joined the WASP training programme. Kay was one of the first 15 girls selected to train for Radio Control Missions. As the medium was so new, no manuals existed, and they relied on their lecture notes. She had many achievements to her credit including the laying of smoke screens, anti-aircraft strafing and target towing. She said: 'We'd fly in from the sun, very low to surprise the ground crew. They'd be kneeling with guns at their shoulders. Sometimes they would even throw rocks at us. I pulled up in a hurry and decided that my survival depended on dating anti-aircraft men instead of pilots. They might say, "Hey, careful, that might be my girl up there." '

Kay was also involved in the first test to confuse radar. Four aircraft would fly a pattern dropping chaff of aluminium chips so that the radio people could record the consequences and train radar guys.

Among the contestants in the 1958 Powder Puff Derby, I met Jerry Cobb. She already held long distance and altitude records and had planned a pole-to-pole flight, but it was vetoed by the authorities. Jerry tried to get a job in aviation flying her Aero Commander aircraft in which she had created her records. Tom Harris, the Chairman of Aero Commander said, 'You would be a luxury. First of all we don't need another pilot and second this is a man's industry. With the exception of Olive Ann Beech, who took over her husband's company when he died, aircraft manufacturers' front offices are womanless and I'm afraid it is going to continue that way.'

Jerry was the first woman to be chosen for space flight. In 1959 she underwent the Mercury astronaut tests at Lovelace Foundation, Albuquerque, New Mexico. Her pass proved that women could undergo the same psychological and physical stress tests as men and were just as physically and mentally capable of carrying out space missions. Jerry was included among the women chosen for astronaut testing. Others were Jean Hixon, Myrtle Cagle, Earner Robins, Jerry Sloan, Sara Gorlick, Gene Nora Jessen, Jan Dietrich, Marion Dietrich, Mary Fink, Rhea Hurrle, Beatrice Trimble, Irene Leverton and Jane Hart. NASA (National Aeronautics and Space Administration) required 'jet test pilots'. Some of the women had three times the amount of flying as the men, but no jet time, because women had not been taken into the Air Force, which had the only jets. The jet simulator was also not available to them for training.

Jerry said: 'I find it a little ridiculous when I read in the newspapers that there is a place called Chimp College in Mexico where they are training fifty chimpanzees for space flight, one a female named Glenda. I think it would be at least as important to let the women undergo training for space flight.' When asked if she was willing to undergo the training, she said 'Yes, even if I have to substitute for a female chimpanzee.'

Jerry decided if she could not be an astronaut she would go to the Amazon to a remote area where communications were extremely bad. She felt she could use her flying skills and aeroplane to help people. For 25 years she flew doctors and patients in and out of this area. Jerry formed a foundation in the United States to raise funds to help these poor, primitive people. She bought seeds and showed them how to grow crops. Among her successes was the introduction of the wing bean, a plant of which every portion can be used for food. Only when guerilla war became dangerous was Jerry forced to move on and then went to Guyana to continue her contribution to humanity.

I thought of this woman in the heat and primitive conditions, continuing her magnanimous work. Her contribution to space flight would never have been of such importance and satisfaction. Nor would so many lives have been so directly touched by her dedication.

I met another of these female astronauts in 1983. Medico Rhea Seddon was the guest at an AWPA meeting held at Airlie Beach, Queensland. Rhea was in the current intake, yet it was still a few years before her turn came. It was not until 1984, that the first woman was launched into space. Her name was Sally Ride and I was fortunate to meet her in America during that year, at the Amelia Earhart 'Forest of Friendship' in Atchison, Kansas. She actually went into space twice and is now a Professor at San Diego University.

When speaking with her, she said: 'There's no way of preparing us in simulation for what we will feel at lift off. There's a lot of thrust that is not in the simulation. They can't simulate the joy of weightlessness, or the emotional impact of seeing earth from space. It's beautiful. My words don't do it justice.'

I had a rewarding though somewhat sad involvement with the NASA space programme when I flew to Bundaberg in Queensland in May, 1987. I was accompanying Dr June Scobee, widow of Commander Scobee, captain of the ill-fated *Challenger* flight. June was returning a piece of spar from Bert Hinkler's original glider that had been built in 1912. The spar had been placed on board as part of Australia's involvement in the flight, and had the flight been successful, it was to have been returned to its Queensland home at the Hinkler memorial exhibition. The spar had been carried on the *Challenger* by her late husband in his personal bag and had been found among the wreckage floating in the Atlantic Ocean.

June, a Doctor of Education, has an interest in a children's educational programme relating to space travel and exploration. Because of this interest and the work her husband had been dedicated to, she was chosen to return it to Queensland during the Hinkler Memorial Lecture week.

Pauline Glasson of Corpus Christi, Texas, who was always in the Powder Puff Derby, now has more flying hours than any woman in the world. Indeed, few men have logged her staggering 40 000 hours. Gini Richardson who runs her own airline in Alaska follows her with 35 000 hours and several American women are in the 30 000 range. As aircraft become faster, however, such times will become impossible.

Australia's first subsidised air service was the Adelaide/Sydney flight in 1924. It took two hours longer than the train, which gave passengers a half day stopover in Melbourne. One newspaper reported: 'No one in their right mind would subject himself to such a journey by air.' The flight had to carry an engineer in case of forced landings, which were quite frequent. The engineer for Larkin, who operated the service, was Arthur Butler. He had not been able to afford to go to Melbourne for the job interview, when in the mail he received a cash prize from the Technical College, for an article he had written on Lawrence Hargrave. It paid his fair and was a godsend.

Arthur Butler taught himself to fly by taxiing back and forth across the landing ground at Hay. He made his first solo flight by accident when, in his haste to get back to work on time, he opened the throttle too wide and the aeroplane took off. He managed to return to earth unharmed. After much saving he had bought a crashed aircraft and rebuilt it. Later, he established himself as an aircraft operator in New South Wales. He also flew the Charleville/Cootamundra section of the first England–Australia Air Mail service.

Arthur Butler gave a lot to Australian aviation. His years of barnstorming and the breaking of the England–Australia record in the smallest aeroplane ever, the Comper Swift, showed determination, skill and tenacity, which should earn him a place in history books. He was a man of remarkable quality whose contributions and self sacrifices to the industry can only be grasped by reading between the lines of his, as yet unpublished, autobiography.

Arthur Butler was a major force in the formation of the New South Wales Air Ambulance service and in 1961 he asked me to help.

The campaigns of World War II, Korea and early Vietnam had taught us that the number of deaths could be greatly reduced if casualties received quick medical attention. Incredibly, the Ambulance Road Service was still the only means of getting country patients to specialist centres in the 1960s. In New South Wales alone, there were many cases of sick or injured people taking 16 hours to reach specialised treatment. Sadly, I remember a nightmare trip through dust, bogging rain, fog and finally, traffic jams. After being in transit for 20 hours, the patient died just one hour after reaching hospital. It seemed logical to attach an air wing to the New South Wales Road Ambulance Service but, as always, there was little government funding available. It was to cost £250,000 and Jack Renshaw, the State Treasurer, persuaded the government to give £10,000 towards the project. It was a pittance, so the Ambulance Board employed a professional fund-raising organisation to raise the rest of the money by public subscription.

Surprisingly, we struck opposition to the establishment of the service from three areas. First, charter pilots objected because they felt we would be taking the bread and butter out of their mouths. They had done excellent work whenever emergencies arose, but poor communication and their relatively unsophisticated planes couldn't do the job as well as all-weather medically-equipped ambulance aircraft. If it was necessary to have someone care for the patient in flight, a Sister from the understaffed local hospital would be called. But often she was untrained for evacuations and would be sick or terrified throughout the trip. Frequently these gallant pilots were also defeated by bad weather and several lost their lives trying to push through in adverse conditions.

Secondly, the airlines objected because they were able to convert two seats to fit a stretcher, so selling two seats instead of one. Patients were put aboard regular scheduled flights, but air hostesses had neither the time nor the training to cope with them. The shortcomings of this arrangement climaxed when the moans of a badly burnt patient distressed passengers, including a Member of Parliament. As the flight continued, the stench of the poor man's burnt flesh turned the journey into a horror flight. Although the airlines welcomed us using their services for humanitarian purposes, the practice could not continue.

Finally, many doctors at large base hospitals in the country were concerned that they would be overflown, if patients were taken to the major teaching hospitals in the city. They had seen this happen when the RAAF aircraft flew emergency cases to Sydney and Canberra. The Air Force has always done a marvellous job on these flights but it did not consider being a civilian air ambulance one of its roles. The doctors' fears were later seen to be unfounded, as the profession maintained its freedom of choice as to where patients could be sent for treatment.

Mainly through the efforts of Arthur Butler we went to the people of New South Wales and finally raised £116,000. It was a great effort with towns such as tiny Brewarrina, with a population of 1000, having oversubscribed their target total fourfold. However, we were competing with the Churchill Fund and the Freedom From Hunger Campaign and we were far short of our £250,000 goal. Arthur was dispirited and considered returning the money to those who had given it, but I begged him to get into the air with something—any aircraft—to give it a try. I felt that New South Wales could not do without an aerial ambulance service any longer.

The things we did to raise money! Joan Jones, a very dignified social lady, and I actually collected from workers as they stumbled out of the Pymble Hotel. I felt like one of those Salvation Army girls who brave the bars for their cause.

Fortunately, the Ambulance Board, under the authority of Harry Jago, the then Liberal Minister for Health, was subsequently allowed to borrow money, and the service came into existence in 1967. I arranged for Kay Brick, Chairman of the Powder Puff Derby Board and a former United States wartime ferry pilot, to co-pilot the service's first aircraft (VH-AMB) across the Pacific. I often felt sorry for Laurie Buckland the controller, for if the aircraft became unserviceable, there were still patients awaiting transport all over the state. Doctors and ambulance drivers complained bitterly, but the service proved an unparalleled success. VH-AMB became Queen of the fleet and did more flying than any Beech Queenair in the world—a massive 24 000 hours— and carried thousands of patients before resting in the Sydney Powerhouse Museum.

The service is now operated by the New South Wales Government and flies three pressurised Beech Kingairs and three Queenairs. Since 1967 it has carried more than 100 000 patients.

CHAPTER 23

In the early 1970s I decided to have a radio cassette installed in my car so that I could learn German as I drove about the city. I had heard there was an enthusiastic radio buff operating a sales outlet at St Leonards in Sydney. I sought his advice, bought a radio cassette player but failed miserably in my attempt to learn German. Sometime later I was invited to a function at Kendall, a town only 2 kilometres from where I was born, where Lady Gallagher of the Red Cross was guest of honour. I arrived early and was met by old friends Herb and Joan Smith. Herb had been Sales Manager at Angus & Robertson, the publishers, when *Born to Fly* was released in 1961. His wife Joan was a talented artist and was the daughter of one of my husband's closest friends, Harold Cazneaux, one of Australia's greatest photographers.

Naturally, our conversation got around to our interests and I asked if I could see some of her work. She replied, 'My son has a painting that he does not think much of—why not call in and see it at St Leonards?' I took up her invitation and that is how I again met the radio buff, Dick Smith.

At that time he had obtained a private pilot's licence and we talked a little of flying. Unexpectedly, he was on the telephone a little later, 'How would you like to fly in the Perth to Sydney Air Race?' I was flabbergasted!

'I'm much too rusty and out of date,' I protested.

'I want you to come as co-pilot,' he said. 'I'm putting my twin Comanche in the Race.'

'But I have never flown a twin-engined aircraft,' I responded.

'Then you can have a loan of mine to get an endorsement,' he replied.

Deeply aware of my inadequate qualifications, I agreed to have a shot at it. Jim Hazelton was my patient and considerate instructor. Full of understanding for an old timer, he nursed me through engine failures and all the things you have to learn when you have two engines instead of one. It was a new world to me.

Though I did have some Australian Air Race experience, Dick had certainly not invited me on his aircraft to make use of that! Times and aircraft had changed considerably since 1936 when I had participated in the South Australian Brisbane–Adelaide Air Race.

In 1966 I flew the Ansett Air Race, which was a re-enactment of the one held in 1936, making me the only pilot to have participated in both Air Races. Garry Richardson had become one of the championship team at the New South Wales Aero Club and I asked if his company, Victa, would lend me an aircraft for the race. I also asked if he would choose a co-pilot and he selected a member of the team, Bob White, who was a very competent pilot. We finished fiftieth in the race, which brought the comment from a fellow woman competitor, that I was a passenger, to which I replied, 'Margaret, I flew that aircraft. The result would have been much better if I hadn't!'

The Victa was a joy to fly. It was almost like wrapping a cloak around one's shoulders and becoming part of the aeroplane. It had extremely sensitive lateral control and seemed to respond almost to one's thoughts. Australia was later to sell the design rights to New Zealand and then import the machines back into the country. How often have we failed to recognise the value of Australian design and workmanship?

Dick also invited Ian Smith, an ex-employee, because he wanted the plane taken ahead to Perth where he would join us a couple of days before the event. Dick had encouraged and helped Ian to learn to fly. At that time Ian was with Qantas.

We left Sydney on a rainy, cloud-covered day and sailed through big cloud formations until 400 miles (644 km) out. After a glimpse of the ground we flew back into whiteout. Adelaide came up through the lights on the instrument approach like a golden sun beckoning us in. Then we saw the runway, straight ahead. Ian had made a perfect instrument flight . . . the first I had experienced in a light aircraft. Blind flying had hardly been invented when I learnt to fly and certainly was not necessary out in the Australian bush where visibility is usually as far as the eye can see.

On the few occasions that I encountered poor visibility in the inland, I went right down almost to the road, or the telegraph line or even the river, twisting and turning, intent on following their direction.

Seventeen aircraft had taken part in the first Transcontinental Air Race and here we were 47 years later about to do it again. Only one person, veteran Horrie Miller, now in the official aircraft, had been in that 1929 race. He was up in the morning before most of us and stole the show with his address to the banquet that night.

A few were in the race to win but most for the fun of it. They flew everything from Lear jets to vintage aircraft. One hundred and fifty two planes were lined up. Edmund and Virginia Ball were among those who came from the United States to take part in 'The Great Australian Air Race'. Ed, the quiet gentle giant of the aerospace industry, whose company 'tiles' graced the first space ship, is a member of the famous Explorers Club and has flown his own aeroplane for some 40-odd years. Now in his eighties, he delights in activities such as scuba diving and flying himself to all corners of the earth. He is extremely fit and puts most of us to shame.

The 2272-nautical-mile race was to be under visual flight conditions, all IFR instruments having been blacked out and sealed. Ed wrote of the race in the *Saturday Evening Post* and says he soon learnt the meaning of the words like 'whinger', 'crook' and 'schamozzle'. He also observed that Australians are pretty critical of the organisers no matter how hard working, patient and courteous they may be. Ed gave them full marks for their ability and organisation and their patience with tired, angry and often hungry competitors.

Flying with Dick Smith and Ian Smith in a twin Comanche, we were flagged off by Sir Douglas Bader, who acquired the nickname 'tin legs' when the Germans took away his artificial legs to prevent him escaping from a prisoner-of-war camp for the second time. Our first 'must stop' was Norseman, a tiny gold mining town with a large natural white claypan as its aerodrome. The local ladies had erected a stand at one side where they were refreshing crews with tea and sandwiches. We were allowed an hour on the ground. Dick Smith immediately went into action. A local lad volunteered a car and not a minute was wasted. Short of going down a mine, we saw everything in Norseman. I wondered if we would miss out on the race or be disqualified for exceeding our time on the ground.

The real 'schamozzle', however, began at Forrest, a town in the middle of the Nullarbor Plain. It was a flight of 622 nautical miles over a desolate desert with few landmarks. Forrest itself is no more than a 4500-foot runway with a few railway workers' huts to service the longest straight railway in the world. Years ago the flight to Perth from the east coast used to overnight there, and a guest house had been built to accommodate about 12 people. Now, 500 descended. Contestants had been told they would have to sleep in their aircraft and to bring a sleeping bag. Some even had nylon tents, but as Forrest is usually hot, no-one was prepared for the biting southerly wind coming straight up from the Antarctic. It was freezing.

The frozen chicken for the barbecue had been left behind and an aircraft had been dispatched to retrieve it. Starving crews waited in long queues while it was being defrosted and cooked. I grabbed one of the first bits and took it over to Ed Ball who was about to retire, still hungry, to his aircraft. He accepted it in an ice cream container (which I had taken for my ration of water for washing). He considered himself fortunate to get anything.

The next morning the organisers couldn't give away loads of cheese and biscuits that some fool had failed to produce when the starving multitudes were queueing for hours for the chicken to thaw.

But the real fun started when the caretaker refused to let the large room in the rest house be used for shelter for some of the women pilots and the few women VIPs. He said there might be some 'goings on'! Nothing was further from the thoughts of exhausted crews. Not until a big shot threatened to telephone the Minister for Air, Sid Oakey, and raise a rumpus in the Press, did the caretaker hand over the keys. We rolled out our sleeping bags on the floor and slept like peas in a pod, frightened to turn for fear of waking the person next to us. Just as we were about to fall asleep a woman rushed in, snatched up her sleeping bag and muttered how much she hated men because her husband insisted she sleep in the aircraft with him!

Our subsequent briefing in Adelaide was at 6 am, so everyone left their motels in the dewy dawn without breakfast. Pilot Kath Sutherland, head of the Domestic Science School, had offered to feed everyone at the airport, but was told it was not necessary. However, weather delayed out departure, and when everything edible had been emptied from the tiny Club shop, we started on our emergency rations. I handed out lots of raisins and some suggested that maybe I was hoping these would force some contestants to land en route. Nevertheless, someone must have appreciated it because when we got to Melbourne I received a grubby bit of paper on which was written, 'Air Race 46 wishes to meet Air Race 52 (me) view Mat.' Unfortunately, I never had time to find out who 46 was!

The race was won by the Army helicopter, which was not allowed to take the cash prize. Being a handicap race, the slower aircraft had a great advantage and the first seven places went to Cessna and Piper aircraft with speeds of 125 miles per hour.

The final landing in Sydney was also a 'schamozzle' because the officials made the aircraft park as far away as possible from the crowds who had come to see them.

Perhaps Kay Baillieu, the TV commentator who accompanied the race as a passenger-observer, best summed up the reflective feelings of all the participants. 'It was a real schamozzle, but I can't wait now to learn to fly, to get married and have grandchildren so I can tell them all about the Great Australian Air Race of 1976.' (From Edmund Ball's article in *Saturday Evening Post*.)

In spite of everything, it was a tremendous undertaking, which I am sure did a great deal for Australia's general aviation. It was an experience long to be remembered, but not soon to be repeated.

We too finished well down the list. I nagged the two men all the way to keep the aircraft on the step. Kindly, they said I was like a mother to them—but I have a suspicion that they meant a mother-in-law!

Many Australians have played key roles in the development of aviation throughout the years. In the 1920s and 1930s, Charles Kingsford Smith was a name on many people's lips. In the 1980s, Dick Smith (no relation) established himself as a world record breaker.

From his humble beginnings, the man who describes himself as being not very bright, came from repairing radios 20 years ago, to being one of Australia's most successful businessmen. He is, in every sense, a maverick among millionaires, and one guesses this is a deliberate ploy. He is also a contradiction. He loves what wealth brings him—the freedom to circle the globe in a helicopter or zoom through the desert in a solar car—but he hates being called a millionaire. He prefers bushwalking clothes to three-piece suits, and cut lunches to three-course restaurant meals. He admits he would rather be out in the bush than studying a balance sheet.

Often described as a man with many faces, Dick insists he is just a normal, very simple man. 'What you see is what you get. I am very predictable.' He is proud of his achievements and honest about his failings.

He recalls: 'When I was at school, my parents used to say to their friends—not to me, thank heavens—"Whatever will happen to Dick?" They were worried because I was so bad at school. I tried hard but I found it difficult learning from a book. I just loved going into the bush and climbing trees. I had a terrible inferiority complex because all my friends were going to university and I failed at technical college. I thought I was doomed to sit on a bench in the back of a factory.'

Dick began work in a factory, fitting valve sockets to two-way radios with a pop-rivet gun. He then moved up to fixing radios. Then he sold two-way radios and eventually set up his own business with his savings and $10 given to him by his lovely fiancée Pip.

The rest is history. After 21 years, Dick and Pip have two daughters and Dick Smith Electronics has been sold to Woolworths. Dick also tried his hand at publishing. His publication the *Australian Geographic* was meant to be a labour of love. He anticipated that after five years he would be selling 25 000 copies a year and still just covering his operating costs. But his intentions did not go according to plan. His first issue sold 100 000 copies and his aim now is to increase subscriptions to two hundred thousand.

'The idea was, if we did make any money, we would put it back into something important,' Dick says. His family has given generously to Ted Noff's Life Education Movement and to a wide range of areas, including scientific research and to people undertaking adventures and explorations.

Early in his career, Dick became interested in flying fixed-wing aircraft and then learned to fly helicopters. In 1982, he took delivery of a Jet Ranger and left from Fort Worth, Texas, to circumnavigate the world. Fourteen days later he arrived in London after successfully completing the first solo helicopter flight across the Atlantic. On landing he discovered that the craft had a bullet hole in the fuselage just above the fuel tank. He assumed the shot had been fired by hunters, but luckily had not damaged the controls. The second stage of his flight began from the Farnborough Air Show, and concluded at Sydney's Darling Harbour Heliport.

Dick left Sydney on the final leg to Fort Worth in June 1983. Because clearance for a refuelling stop on Soviet territory between Kushiko, Japan, and Shemya in the Aleutian Islands, was not forthcoming, a mid-ocean rendezvous with Ms *Hoegh Marlin* was made and he landed on the ship's deck to refuel. Dick had his own radio operator on board the ship. As the appointed time approached, the ship disappeared in a fog bank and it seemed that he had no alternative but to divert to a landing inside Russia. Canberra was alerted, but miraculously the ship emerged from the fog bank and Dick found the speck in the China Sea. Quickly refuelling, he was soon back in the air, narrowly missing disaster when the ship lurched as the helicopter was taking off.

On arriving in Alaska, after 1450 nautical miles over water in one day, the United States Air Force staff asked, 'Where is your chase plane?' Dick replied, 'I do not have one.' 'What about your mechanic?' Dick pointed to a black tool box and said, 'That is my mechanic.' Dick completed his fantastic flight over the massive mountain peaks of Canada then down to Texas. He filmed this trip with cameras strapped to the aircraft.

Dick followed up these flights with three attempts to be the first person to fly a helicopter to the North Pole. On the first occasion his instruments froze and he turned back just 90 miles short of his destination. On his third trip he was successful.

In November 1988 Dick Smith and his co-pilot Giles Kershaw successfully completed the first direct flight from Australia to Australian Antarctic Territory. After a 14 hour, 1833-nautical-mile flight they landed their de Havilland Twin Otter on an ice plateau just east of Casey Station, thus demonstrating the feasibility of a direct air link.

Dick bought the Twin Otter, registration VH-GHW, to honour the great Australian explorer and aviator Sir Hubert Wilkins, and to use in documentary film production. When he learned that the Australian National Antarctic Research Expeditions (ANARE) was interested in using a Twin Otter for exploration and scientific research in Antarctica (but could not raise the necessary finance), Dick offered to make his aircraft available.

As well as flying from station to station, Dick and Giles made ice reconnaissance flights for the Antarctic Division supply ship *Icebird*. Ice conditions off Davis Station kept *Icebird* from anchoring within 140 miles (250 km) so the men were flown by helicopter to an ice floe. The Twin Otter then ferried mail, passengers and freight between the station and the ice floe allowing the station changeover to proceed without delay.

Dick's most important objective was to fly-in Antarctic Division scientists to measure ice thickness on the Amery Ice Shelf and the Lambert Glacier, the largest in the world. To do this, a special transmitter in the plane sent signals down from a height of 300 metres and special antennas, fitted on the wings, picked up two reflected echoes, one from the glacier's surface and one from bedrock. This information helps determine if the ice sheet is melting and at what rate, and is thus vital to our understanding of the 'Greenhouse' effect—the heating of the atmosphere from the use of fossil fuels.

On this journey, the Twin Otter made a special landing on the sea ice off Davis Station to commemorate the 60th Anniversary of Sir Hubert Wilkins making the first ever flight in Antarctica.

Dick has acquired a great interest in the history of Australian aviators and his achievements will ensure his own place with these heroes.

Among the awards he has received are several Federation Aeronautique Internationale world records; the Guild of Air Pilots and Air Navigators Sword of Honour; and the Royal Federation of Aero Clubs of Australia Oswald Watt Gold Medal for 'the most notable contribution to aviation by an Australian'. Other awards include the Helicopter Association Internationals' 1984 Helicopter Pilot of the Year and the United States Institute of Navigation Superior Achievement Award. He was named Australian of the Year in 1987.

CHAPTER 24

The story of Australia's and possibly the world's, greatest air race has been told many times. It was held in 1919 and a £10 000 prize was donated by the Australian government for an all-Australian crew to make the inaugural flight from England to Australia. The race was from Hounslow to Darwin and was to be completed within 30 days.

Eventually, only two aircraft completed the course. R. J. Parer and J. C. McIntosh left England after the race had been won and arrived months beyond the deadline, but they were the first to fly a single-engined aircraft over the route. Theirs was a remarkable feat because they flew a DH9 selected from a disposal dump. The young airmen completed the course in eight months. They replaced five propellers, extinguished two engine fires, holed the radiator, crumpled their petrol and oil tanks, gashed the fuselage and, among other damage, wiped off the undercarriage. They survived attacks by Arabs; and paid for repairs by stunting and roaring up the main streets of Calcutta tossing out pamphlets for tea, oil and other products. They even escaped the offer of $30 000 dowries made by a Chinese millionaire for them to marry two of his rather comely daughters! Finally, they landed in Darwin and, as they were taxiing towards the welcoming crowd, their engine cut out. The tank was bone dry! The pair received a £1000 consolation prize from an admiring country in recognition of their inspiring feat.

They had been backed by a Scottish whisky baron and carried with them a bottle of whisky for the Prime Minister. They still had it after their hazardous flight!

The winning crew flew a Vickers Vimy. This craft had been developed by Vickers for long-range bombing missions over Germany. It had a cruising range of 2405 miles and was fitted with two 360 hp Rolls-Royce Eagle machines, which gave the giant bi-plane a maximum speed of 103 miles per hour. The 11 060-mile flight took an air time of 135 hours and 55 minutes over 27 days and 20 hours. Aircraft letterings were a recent innovation and the Vimy was allocated 'G-EAOU', which was immediately amplified by the crew to 'God—'elp all of us!'

As with most successful flights, this win was due to wise forward planning and meticulous organisation of equipment and schedules.

Captain Ross Smith was favoured to win because, together with Brigadier Borton, he had already pioneered an air route to India and then went to the East Indies where the Dutch Governor-General had agreed to lay out an airfield at Koepang to halve the last 1750-mile hop of the proposed route to Australia. Originally, Brigadier Borton was to be part of the four man crew but he was excluded because he was not Australian. Ross Smith's brother, Keith, replaced him in the crew just weeks before the flight.

All four men were very experienced and had served with the Australian Flying Corps except for Keith, who had unsuccessfully applied to enlist in the AIF. He paid his own fare to England, and was accepted by the RFC in 1917. They all distinguished themselves, but both Ross Smith and James Bennett were tragically killed in 1922 when they were accepting the handover of a Vickers amphibian in which they had intended to fly around the world.

Ross had piloted Lawrence of Arabia on secret missions, was highly decorated and considered the most outstanding pilot in the Middle East.

Keith was born in Aelaide two years earlier than his brother and was a lieutenant in the Royal Flying Corps. My first meeting with Sir Keith was at the Aero Club in Mascot when he arrived for lunch dressed in his distinctive black, English-style coat and Homburg hat. Sir Keith later became the Commonwealth Representative for Vickers Armstrong in Australia and was appointed Vice Chairman of British Commonwealth Pacific Airlines, Director of Tasman Airways and Director of Qantas. He died in 1955.

Both brothers were each awarded a KBE in 1919 for their Great Air Race exploits.

James Bennett joined the AIF as a mechanic. He attained the rank of sergeant and received the Meritorious Service Award.

He was the flight mechanic in 1919. Both he and Walter Shiers, the aircraftsman on that flight, were given commissions in recognition of their efforts. Walter Shiers, like Bennett, joined the Australian Flying Corps. He was an electrical engineer and became chief engineer at Airlines of Australia before dying in 1968.

I met Wally Shiers when he was working at Mascot and I was learning to fly. He was a very friendly person and I often talked with him. What a shame I did not know his history as I do now.

It was 50 years later that I learnt the story of Reg Williams, the last surviving competitor of the Great Air Race. I had been a guest of his daughter, the Hon Beryl Evans of Dabee, Rylstone, and asked if I could talk with him about his experiences. Though he was both elderly and ill, his memory was as clear as a bell.

He gained his licence through the New South Wales State School of Aviation in 1915 after seven hours' flying, going solo in 3¾ hours. Showing great aptitude after six hours solo, he was appointed as an instructor! That was an incredible feat. By today's standards it would cost at least $20 000 to gain the experience and hours to qualify for an instructor's rating!

Williams ferried new aircraft from England to Europe until the war's end. During World War II his appointments included Deputy Director of Training at Air Force Headquarters, Melbourne. He then returned to civilian life and his family motorcycle business until he retired.

He was to fly a Blackburn Kangaroo in the 1919 Race with Hubert Wilkins as his navigator, Garnsey Potts as his mechanic and Valdemar Rendle as the other pilot. Engine failure caused them to crashland in Crete.

I read Reg's handwritten notes on this experience only recently and he said. 'We had left Estres near Marseilles when we had engine trouble and made a forced landing on a seaboard strip. On examination we found the outer magneto which was exposed to view, had been filled with dirt (some well wishers had taken off the end and filled it with dirt and replaced the cap).'

They then flew on to Crete and landed in a boggy field. Heavily overloaded with fuel, they staggered off the field. With a strong tail wind of 40–50 knots to help them on their way, they were already making the best of time.

Reg continued his story:

Looking back for the last glimpse of Crete I noticed one side of the tail covered with black. It could only be oil. We turned back as already valves were sticking and many noises were coming from the engine. The tail wind was now a head wind. As we reached the land, the engine locked with such suddenness, bits flew everywhere and I thought the sudden stop was going to cause the propeller to wrench the engine out altogether. . . . However, we got down on the swampy ground, splashing water like a wounded bird. . . . If I had not noticed the black tail plane, we would have drowned half way across the Mediterranean.

I rang Governor James Rowland's secretary and told him that Reg Williams was the last surviving competitor of the air race. As Reg was very elderly, I suggested it would be wonderful if the Governor could ring him. He did and this kind gesture was most appreciated by Reg, particularly as at the time he was entertaining a visitor who was equally impressed!

In talking with Reg, I could not help admiring his qualities and his achievements over the years.

The 1919 Air Race was flown by all male crews, but times have changed and women are now an accepted part of aviation. Some of these women are actively involved in the Australian industry today.

The highest aviation appointment bestowed upon a woman was the Examiner of Airmen status awarded in 1987 to Mary O'Brien. As a pilot and instructor, Mary has considerable flying experience in Australia and overseas, particularly in South-East Asia and America.

Australia's first woman captain of a passenger airline was champion skier, Christine Davy who, in 1974, became a Senior Captain with a First Class Air Transport Licence. She flew Fokker Friendships between Alice Springs and Ayres Rock regularly. Between 1981 and 1983, Christine flew the same area in helicopters on mineral exploration and medical evacuations flights. Eddy Connellan said the first thing he had to teach the gentle, cultured Christine was command. Her soft voice and good manners were misunderstood. Often it is necessary to learn how to be the commander of a crew.

One 747 pilot told me that her captain was an older man who said, 'I am old and I am tough, but if you see anything I don't, tell me!' A much younger captain looked at her and jokingly said, 'Another empty kitchen.'

In 1979, after a 15-month court battle against discrimination, Deborah Lawrie, who had ten years flying experience, became Ansett Airlines' first woman pilot. She flew Fokker Friendships, Douglas DC9s and Boeing 737s and 727s. Qantas now have 16 women training to be pilots.

Over in the vast state of Western Australia, where many women take up flying because of the great distances, the Royal Aero Club of Western Australia (Australia's largest) appointed Shirley Adkins as its first woman President. Involved with aviation since 1946 and a holder of many awards, she became a Vice-President of the Royal Federation of Aero Clubs in 1982 and a Life Member of the Western Australian Club in 1987.

Many girls have made genuine sacrifices to become pilots, often giving up a comfortable, secure background. Aminta Hennessy, an English girl from an aristocratic background, came to Australia to follow her love of flying by working in ski lodges, catering for people's parties, and as a barmaid in a rough outback hotel, to pay for flying lessons. As she climbed higher into the skies she became an instructor, commercial pilot and then with a senior commercial licence, took a job as a lone pilot flying the de Havilland Dove carrying 11 passengers to the Pacific Island of Lord Howe 400 miles off the Australian coast on to a very dicey airstrip, subject to severe crosswinds.

In 1977 she ferried a single-engine aircraft from Texas to Australia via Greenland, England and India in time for a Ninety-Nines convention in Canberra. It was a long way round to a meeting, 18 000 miles, but more recently she has taken to delivering single-engined aircraft across the Pacific, at the rate of one a month. In between times she runs a flying school and charter operation.

Aminta also instigated the Fear of Flying clinics in Australia, which are run by women pilots in conjunction with Qantas. She supports the women pilots' organisation and encourages women to upgrade their flying skills.

There are many more women like her who have made similar sacrifices. Trudi White, for example, also operates her own flying schools and before she was tragically murdered in New Guinea, Heather Mitchell was one of the pilots who pioneered cattle mustering in helicopters throughout northern Australia.

In 1988, Deborah Hicks and Robyn Williams became the first two women to be accepted as pilots with the Royal Australian Air Force.

Throughout Australia there are many women who simply fly for fun. Only recently, Mitzi Farr from Western Australia celebrated her 80th birthday flying a Tiger Moth! Many have been recorded in the 'Browsing Book' at the Stockman's Hall of Fame, but it is impossible to mention all the women and their wonderful achievements since World War II.

It has been my privilege to speak to many organisations over the years. Naturally, many of these talks have related to aviation and its exciting history. Australians have been at the forefront in pioneering long-distance flights and it has been a joy to me to develop my knowledge of the events and the people involved. Little anecdotes are constantly being handed to me that have been stored away for several generations. Sadly though, much of our verbal and written history has disappeared.

Before I went to England in 1986 I contacted Marge McGrath, Kingsford Smith's secretary. We discussed writing a book to record her wonderful experiences with one of the most daring and competent men in aviation history. Returning from England six months later, I telephoned her to discuss the proposed book, but there was something wrong. I could hear what seemed to be choked breathing. I was too far away to help, so I called an ambulance. Marge had suffered a massive stroke.

She always had a story to recount, most of them will never be told again. I recall her telling me of the incident of the young woman who wanted Smithy to take her baby back to King George V, as she was sure it was his; and the man who escaped from a mental asylum and swam Cooks River, which is beside the Mascot aerodrome. He came into the office dripping wet, grabbed a paper knife and demanded to be flown to England in the model aeroplane sitting on the table! Marge managed to escape by telling him she was going out to the hangar to make sure they had enough fuel for the plane.

This is why I have taken the time to record some of the highlights of our glorious achievements, together with some of the failures, too!

In 1966 I received from Her Majesty the Queen at Buckingham Palace, the Order of the British Empire for services to the community. I was humbled when I was awarded the degree of Master of Engineering (honoris causa) by the Sydney University, which was presented to me in 1987. In 1990 I received the Order of Australia, which makes me think of the quotation, 'some are born great, some acquire greatness and some have greatness thrust upon them . . .'

Following the formation of the AWPA, attitudes have changed to the acceptance of women in flying associations. My experience in the United States of America had shown me that women pilots can help each other if only by offering a friendly hand. By sharing an aircraft to a 'fly-in' or offering hospitality on overnight stops, friendships can be developed all over the world.

Looking back, I realise that I was a very naive young woman when I took an aeroplane into the Australian outback and successfully flew it for three years. Completely isolated from the aeronautical world, I was on the very fringe of the enormous development that was to take place in aviation from then on. Ironically, I sold my aeroplane because I could see no future in aviation for women pilots.

Today, women have become airline captains, trained as Air Force pilots and have even gone into space.

It would seem the sky is no longer the limit.

POSTSCRIPT

Fifty-four years after Charles Russell gave me the title to my book a Sydney businessman Michael Lee hired a light aircraft in Brisbane to take him and a colleague into the country.

As they approached the aircraft, Michael's colleague grabbed his arm and said, 'My God, I'm not going to fly in that. The pilot's a woman!'

BIBLIOGRAPHY

Batten, Jean *Alone in the Sky*, The Airlife Publishing Company, England, 1979.

Baumbach, Werner *Broken Swastika—The Defeat of the Luftwaffe* St Edmundsbury Press Limited, England, 1960.

Bird, Nancy *Born to Fly*, Angus & Robertson, Sydney, 1961.

Boase, Wendy *The Sky's the Limit—Women Pioneers in Aviation*, Osprey Publishing Limited, London, 1979.

Briggs, F. S. & S. H. Harris *Joysticks and Fiddlesticks*, Hutchinson & Co. Ltd., London.

Butler, Arthur C. *Flying Start*, Edwards & Shaw, Australia, 1971.

Cochran, Jacqueline & Maryann Bucknum Brinley *Jackie Cochran—An Autobiography*, Bantam Books, USA, 1987.

Coote, Errol *Hell's Airport*, Peterman Press, Australia, 1934.

Coupar, Anne Robertson *The Smirnoff Story*, Jarrolds Publishers, London Ltd. 1960.

Curtis, Lettice *The Forgotten Pilots—A story of the Air Transport Auxiliary 1935-1945*, E. L. Curtis, England, 1971.

De Bunsen, Mary *Mount up with Wings*, Hutchinson & Co. Publishers Ltd., London, 1960.

Docker, Edward Wyberg *Clear the Runway*, George Allen & Unwin, Australia Pty. Ltd., 1984.

Eustis, Nelson *Australia's Greatest Air Race—England to Australia 1919*, Rigby Australia, 1969.

Fenton, Clyde *Flying Doctor*, Georgian House, Melbourne, 1947.

Gwynn-Jones, Terry *Aviation's Magnificent Gamblers*, Lansdowne Press, Australia, 1981.

Gwynn-Jones, Terry *Pioneer Airwoman*, Rigby Limited, Adelaide, 1979.

Henshaw, Alex *Sigh for a Merlin*, John Murray Publishers Ltd., London.

Henshaw, Alex *The Flight of the Mew Gull*, John Murray Publishers Ltd., London, 1980.

Hughes, Robert *The Fatal Shore*, Collins Harvill, London, 1987.

Joy, William *The Aviators*, Golden Press Pty. Ltd., Australia, 1983.

Lomox, Judy *Women of the Air*, John Murray Publishers Ltd., London, 1986.

Lovell, Mary S. *Straight on till Morning*, St. Martin's Press, New York, 1987.

Lyle, Nancy *Simple Flying for Simple People*, Angus & Robertson Limited, Australia, 1937.

MacKenzie, Roy *Solo—The Bert Hinkler Story*, Ure Smith, Sydney, 1979.

McNally, Ward *The Man on the Twenty Dollar Bill—Sir Charles Kingsford Smith*, A. H. and W. A. Reed, Sydney, 1976.

Markham, Beryl *West with the Night*, Virago Press Limited, London, 1984.

Miller, Robin *Flying Nurse*, Rigby Limited, Australia, 1971.

Miller, Robin *Sugar Bird Lady*, Rigby Limited, Australia, 1979.

Moolman, Valerie and the Editors of Time-Life Books *Women Aloft*, Time-Life, Illinois, USA, 1981.

Palmer, Joan *Goggles and God Help You*, The Dominion Press, Hedges & Bell, 1986.

Powell, Neville Trevor Boughton *Flypast—A Record of Aviation in Australia*, Australian Government Publishing Service, Canberra, 1988.

Purvis, Harry with Joan Priest *Outback Airman*, Rigby Ltd., Australia, 1979.

Quill, Jeffery *Spitfire—A Test Pilot's Story*, John Murray, London, 1983.

Sacchi, Louise *Ocean Flying*, McGraw-Hill Inc., USA, 1979.

Schaeder *Australian Ace*, Rigby Australia, 1979.

Scharr, Adela Riek *Sisters in the Sky*, The Patrice Press, USA, 1986.

Shields, Beau and S. Simpson, *Caesar of the Skies*, Cassell Publishers, London, 1937.

Smith, Elinor *Aviatrix*, Harcourt Brace Jovanovich, Inc., New York, 1981.

Steenson, Eileen *Flight Plan PNG*, Robert Hale, 1974.

Swoffer, Frank *Learning to Fly*, Sir Isaac Pitman & Sons, London, 1936.

Trevor-Roper, Hugh *The Last Ten Days of Hitler*, Macmillan, England, 1978, 5th edition.

Van Wagenen Kell, Sally *Those Wonderful Women in their Flying Machines*, Rawson, Wade Publishers, Inc., New York, 1979.

White, T. W. *Guests of the Unspeakable*, Halstead Printing Company, Sydney, 1935.

Wixted, Edward P. *The North-West Aerial Frontier 1919–1934*, Boolarong Publications, Brisbane, 1985.